NON SANZ DROICT.

THE
CRONICLE

Hiſtory of Henry the fift,

With his battell fought at *Agin Court* in
France. Togither with *Auntient*
Piſtoll.

As it hath bene ſundry times playd by the Right honorable
the Lord Chamberlaine his ſeruants.

LONDON

Printed by *Thomas Creede,* for Tho. Milling-
ton, and Iohn Busby. And are to be
ſold at his houſe in Carter Lane, next
the Powle head. 1600.

The earliest printed version (1600) of *Henry V* is a "bad" quarto, an
abridged text apparently pieced together by some actors for a touring
company. Not until 1623 was an authoritative text published.

William Shakespeare

The Life of
Henry V

With New and Updated
Critical Essays
and a Revised Bibliography

Edited by John Russell Brown

THE SIGNET CLASSIC SHAKESPEARE
General Editor: Sylvan Barnet

A SIGNET CLASSIC

SIGNET CLASSIC
Published by New American Library, a division of
Penguin Group (USA) Inc., 375 Hudson Street,
New York, New York 10014, USA
Penguin Group (Canada), 10 Alcorn Avenue, Toronto,
Ontario M4V 3B2, Canada (a division of Pearson Penguin Canada Inc.)
Penguin Books Ltd., 80 Strand, London WC2R 0RL, England
Penguin Ireland, 25 St. Stephen's Green, Dublin 2,
Ireland (a division of Penguin Books Ltd.)
Penguin Group (Australia), 250 Camberwell Road, Camberwell, Victoria 3124,
Australia (a division of Pearson Australia Group Pty. Ltd.)
Penguin Books India Pvt. Ltd., 11 Community Centre, Panchsheel Park,
New Delhi - 110 017, India
Penguin Group (NZ), cnr Airborne and Rosedale Roads, Albany,
Auckland 1310, New Zealand (a division of Pearson New Zealand Ltd.)
Penguin Books (South Africa) (Pty.) Ltd., 24 Sturdee Avenue,
Rosebank, Johannesburg 2196, South Africa

Penguin Books Ltd., Registered Offices:
80 Strand, London WC2R 0RL, England

Published by Signet Classic, an imprint of New American Library, a division of
Penguin Group (USA) Inc. The Signet Classic edition of *The Life of Henry V*
was first published in 1965, and an updated edition was published in 1988.

First Signet Classic Printing (Second Revised Edition), August 1998
20 19 18 17

Ⓒ REGISTERED TRADEMARK—MARCA REGISTRADA

Library of Congress Catalog Card Number: 97-62229

Printed in the United States of America

Contents

122201

Shakespeare: An Overview

Biographical Sketch

Between the record of his baptism in Stratford on 26 April 1564 and the record of his burial in Stratford on 25 April 1616, some forty official documents name Shakespeare, and many others name his parents, his children, and his grandchildren. Further, there are at least fifty literary references to him in the works of his contemporaries. More facts are known about William Shakespeare than about any other playwright of the period except Ben Jonson. The facts should, however, be distinguished from the legends. The latter, inevitably more engaging and better known, tell us that the Stratford boy killed a calf in high style, poached deer and rabbits, and was forced to flee to London, where he held horses outside a playhouse. These traditions are only traditions; they may be true, but no evidence supports them, and it is well to stick to the facts.

Mary Arden, the dramatist's mother, was the daughter of a substantial landowner; about 1557 she married John Shakespeare, a tanner, glove-maker, and trader in wool, grain, and other farm commodities. In 1557 John Shakespeare was a member of the council (the governing body of Stratford), in 1558 a constable of the borough, in 1561 one of the two town chamberlains, in 1565 an alderman (entitling him to the appellation of "Mr."), in 1568 high bailiff—the town's highest political office, equivalent to mayor. After 1577, for an unknown reason he drops out of local politics. What *is* known is that he had to mortgage his wife's property, and that he was involved in serious litigation.

The birthday of William Shakespeare, the third child and the eldest son of this locally prominent man, is unrecorded, but the Stratford parish register records that the infant was baptized on 26 April 1564. (It is quite possible that he was born on 23 April, but this date has probably been assigned by tradition because it is the date on which, fifty-two years later, he died, and perhaps because it is the feast day of St. George, patron saint of England.) The attendance records of the Stratford grammar school of the period are not extant, but it is reasonable to assume that the son of a prominent local official attended the free school—it had been established for the purpose of educating males precisely of his class—and received substantial training in Latin. The masters of the school from Shakespeare's seventh to fifteenth years held Oxford degrees; the Elizabethan curriculum excluded mathematics and the natural sciences but taught a good deal of Latin rhetoric, logic, and literature, including plays by Plautus, Terence, and Seneca.

On 27 November 1582 a marriage license was issued for the marriage of Shakespeare and Anne Hathaway, eight years his senior. The couple had a daughter, Susanna, in May 1583. Perhaps the marriage was necessary, but perhaps the couple had earlier engaged, in the presence of witnesses, in a formal "troth plight" which would render their children legitimate even if no further ceremony were performed. In February 1585, Anne Hathaway bore Shakespeare twins, Hamnet and Judith.

That Shakespeare was born is excellent; that he married and had children is pleasant; but that we know nothing about his departure from Stratford to London or about the beginning of his theatrical career is lamentable and must be admitted. We would gladly sacrifice details about his children's baptism for details about his earliest days in the theater. Perhaps the poaching episode is true (but it is first reported almost a century after Shakespeare's death), or perhaps he left Stratford to be a schoolmaster, as another tradition holds; perhaps he was moved (like Petruchio in *The Taming of the Shrew*) by

> Such wind as scatters young men through the world,
> To seek their fortunes farther than at home
> Where small experience grows.
>
> (1.2.49–51)

In 1592, thanks to the cantankerousness of Robert Greene, we have our first reference, a snarling one, to Shakespeare as an actor and playwright. Greene, a graduate of St. John's College, Cambridge, had become a playwright and a pamphleteer in London, and in one of his pamphlets he warns three university-educated playwrights against an actor who has presumed to turn playwright:

> There is an upstart crow, beautified with our feathers, that with his *tiger's heart wrapped in a player's hide* supposes he is as well able to bombast out a blank verse as the best of you, and being an absolute Johannes-factotum [i.e., jack-of-all-trades] is in his own conceit the only Shake-scene in a country.

The reference to the player, as well as the allusion to Aesop's crow (who strutted in borrowed plumage, as an actor struts in fine words not his own), makes it clear that by this date Shakespeare had both acted and written. That Shakespeare is meant is indicated not only by *Shake-scene* but also by the parody of a line from one of Shakespeare's plays, *3 Henry VI*: "O, tiger's heart wrapped in a woman's hide" (1.4.137). If in 1592 Shakespeare was prominent enough to be attacked by an envious dramatist, he probably had served an apprenticeship in the theater for at least a few years.

In any case, although there are no extant references to Shakespeare between the record of the baptism of his twins in 1585 and Greene's hostile comment about "Shake-scene" in 1592, it is evident that during some of these "dark years" or "lost years" Shakespeare had acted and written. There are a number of subsequent references to him as an actor. Documents indicate that in 1598 he is a "principal comedian," in 1603 a "principal tragedian," in 1608 he is one of the "men players." (We do not have, however, any solid information about which roles he may have played; later traditions say he played Adam in *As You Like It* and the ghost in *Hamlet*, but nothing supports the assertions. Probably his role as dramatist came to supersede his role as actor.) The profession of actor was not for a gentleman, and it occasionally drew the scorn of university men like Greene who resented writing speeches for persons less educated than themselves, but it was respectable enough; players, if prosperous, were in effect members of the bourgeoisie, and there is nothing to suggest that Stratford considered William Shakespeare less than a solid citizen. When, in 1596, the Shakespeares were granted a coat of arms—i.e., the right to be considered gentlemen—the grant was made to Shakespeare's father, but probably William Shakespeare had arranged the matter on his own behalf. In subsequent transactions he is occasionally styled a gentleman.

Although in 1593 and 1594 Shakespeare published two narrative poems dedicated to the Earl of Southampton, *Venus and Adonis* and *The Rape of Lucrece*, and may well have written most or all of his sonnets in the middle nineties, Shakespeare's literary activity seems to have been almost entirely devoted to the theater. (It may be significant that the two narrative poems were written in years when the plague closed the theaters for several months.) In 1594 he was a charter member of a theatrical company called the Chamberlain's Men, which in 1603 became the royal company, the King's Men, making Shakespeare the king's playwright. Until he retired to Stratford (about 1611, apparently), he was with this remarkably stable company. From 1599 the company acted primarily at the Globe theater, in which Shakespeare held a one-tenth interest. Other Elizabethan dramatists are known to have acted, but no other is known also to have been entitled to a share of the profits.

Shakespeare's first eight published plays did not have his name on them, but this is not remarkable; the most popular play of the period, Thomas Kyd's *The Spanish Tragedy*, went through many editions without naming Kyd, and Kyd's authorship is known only because a book on the profession of acting happens to quote (and attribute to Kyd) some lines on the interest of Roman emperors in the drama. What is remarkable is that after 1598 Shakespeare's name commonly appears on printed plays—some of which are not his. Presumably his name was a drawing card, and publishers used it to attract potential buyers. Another indication of his popularity comes from Francis Meres, author of *Palladis Tamia: Wit's Treasury* (1598). In this anthology of snippets accompanied by an essay on literature, many playwrights are mentioned, but Shakespeare's name occurs more often than any other, and Shakespeare is the only playwright whose plays are listed.

From his acting, his play writing, and his share in a playhouse, Shakespeare seems to have made considerable money. He put it to work, making substantial investments in Stratford real estate. As early as 1597 he bought New Place, the second-largest house in Stratford. His family moved in soon afterward, and the house remained in the family until a granddaughter died in 1670. When Shakespeare made his will in 1616, less than a month before he died, he sought to leave his property intact to his descendants. Of small bequests to relatives and to friends (including three actors, Richard Burbage, John Heminges, and Henry Condell), that to his wife of the second-best bed has provoked the most comment. It has sometimes been taken as a sign of an unhappy marriage (other supposed signs are the apparently hasty marriage, his wife's seniority of eight years, and his residence in London without his family). Perhaps the second-best bed was the bed the couple had slept in, the best bed being reserved for visitors. In any case, had Shakespeare not excepted it, the bed would have gone (with the rest of his household possessions) to his daughter and her husband.

On 25 April 1616 Shakespeare was buried within the chancel of the church at Stratford. An unattractive monument to his memory, placed on a wall near the grave, says that he died on 23 April. Over the grave itself are the lines, perhaps by Shakespeare, that (more than his literary fame) have kept his bones undisturbed in the crowded burial ground where old bones were often dislodged to make way for new:

> Good friend, for Jesus' sake forbear
> To dig the dust enclosed here.
> Blessed be the man that spares these stones
> And cursed be he that moves my bones.

A Note on the Anti-Stratfordians, Especially Baconians and Oxfordians

Not until 1769—more than a hundred and fifty years after Shakespeare's death—is there any record of anyone expressing doubt about Shakespeare's authorship of the plays and poems. In 1769, however, Herbert Lawrence nominated Francis Bacon (1561–1626) in *The Life and Adventures of Common Sense*. Since then, at least two dozen other nominees have been offered, including Christopher Marlowe, Sir Walter Raleigh, Queen Elizabeth I, and Edward de Vere, 17th earl of Oxford. The impulse behind all anti-Stratfordian movements is the scarcely concealed snobbish opinion that "the man from Stratford" simply could not have written the plays because he was a country fellow without a university education and without access to high society. Anyone, the argument goes, who used so many legal terms, medical terms, nautical terms, and so forth, and who showed some familiarity with classical writing, must have attended a university, and anyone who knew so much about courtly elegance and courtly deceit must himself have moved among courtiers. The plays do indeed reveal an author whose interests were exceptionally broad, but specialists in any given field—law, medicine, arms and armor, and so on—soon find that the plays do not reveal deep knowledge in specialized matters; indeed, the playwright often gets technical details wrong.

The claim on behalf of Bacon, forgotten almost as soon as it was put forth in 1769, was independently reasserted by Joseph C. Hart in 1848. In 1856 it was reaffirmed by W. H. Smith in a book, and also by Delia Bacon in an article; in 1857 Delia Bacon published a book, arguing that Francis Bacon had directed a group of intellectuals who wrote the plays.

Francis Bacon's claim has largely faded, perhaps because it was advanced with such evident craziness by Ignatius Donnelly, who in *The Great Cryptogram* (1888) claimed to break a code in the plays that proved Bacon had written not only the plays attributed to Shakespeare but also other Renaissance works, for instance the plays of Christopher Marlowe and the essays of Montaigne.

Consider the last two lines of the Epilogue in *The Tempest*:

As you from crimes would pardoned be,
Let your indulgence set me free.

What was Shakespeare—sorry, Francis Bacon, Baron Verulam—*really* saying in these two lines? According to Baconians, the lines are an anagram reading, "Tempest of Francis Bacon, Lord Verulam; do ye ne'er divulge me, ye words." Ingenious, and it is a pity that in the quotation the letter *a* appears only twice in the cryptogram, whereas in the deciphered message it appears three times. Oh, no problem; just alter "Verulam" to "Verul'm" and it works out very nicely.

Most people understand that with sufficient ingenuity one can torture any text and find in it what one wishes. For instance: Did Shakespeare have a hand in the King James Version of the Bible? It was nearing completion in 1610, when Shakespeare was forty-six years old. If you look at the 46th Psalm and count forward for forty-six words, you will find the word *shake*. Now if you go to the end of the psalm and count backward forty-six words, you will find the word *spear*. Clear evidence, according to some, that Shakespeare slyly left his mark in the book.

Bacon's candidacy has largely been replaced in the twentieth century by the candidacy of Edward de Vere (1550–1604), 17th earl of Oxford. The basic ideas behind the Oxford theory, advanced at greatest length by Dorothy and Charlton Ogburn in *This Star of England* (1952, rev. 1955), a book of 1297 pages, and by Charlton Ogburn in *The Mysterious William Shakespeare* (1984), a book of 892 pages, are these: (1) The man from Stratford could not possibly have had the mental equipment and the experience to have written the plays—only a courtier could have written them; (2) Oxford had the requisite background (social position, education, years at Queen Elizabeth's court); (3) Oxford did not wish his authorship to be known for two basic reasons: writing for the public theater was a vulgar pursuit, and the plays show so much courtly and royal disreputable behavior that they would have compromised Oxford's position at court. Oxfordians offer countless details to support the claim. For example, Hamlet's phrase "that ever I was born to set it right" (1.5.89) barely conceals "E. Ver, I was born to set it right," an unambiguous announcement of de Vere's authorship, according to *This Star of England* (p. 654). A second example: Consider Ben

Jonson's poem entitled "To the, Memory of My Beloved Master William Shakespeare," prefixed to the first collected edition of Shakespeare's plays in 1623. According to Oxfordians, when Jonson in this poem speaks of the author of the plays as the "swan of Avon," he is alluding not to William Shakespeare, who was born and died in Stratford-on-Avon and who throughout his adult life owned property there; rather, he is alluding to Oxford, who, the Ogburns say, used "William Shakespeare" as his pen name, and whose manor at Bilton was on the Avon River. Oxfordians do not offer any evidence that Oxford took a pen name, and they do not mention that Oxford had sold the manor in 1581, forty-two years before Jonson wrote his poem. Surely a reference to the Shakespeare who was born in Stratford, who had returned to Stratford, and who had died there only seven years before Jonson wrote the poem is more plausible. And exactly why Jonson, who elsewhere also spoke of Shakespeare as a playwright, and why Heminges and Condell, who had acted with Shakespeare for about twenty years, should speak of Shakespeare as the author in their dedication in the 1623 volume of collected plays is never adequately explained by Oxfordians. Either Jonson, Heminges and Condell, and numerous others were in on the conspiracy, or they were all duped—equally unlikely alternatives. Another difficulty in the Oxford theory is that Oxford died in 1604, and some of the plays are clearly indebted to works and events later than 1604. Among the Oxfordian responses are: At his death Oxford left some plays, and in later years these were touched up by hacks, who added the material that points to later dates. *The Tempest*, almost universally regarded as one of Shakespeare's greatest plays and pretty clearly dated to 1611, does indeed date from a period after the death of Oxford, but it is a crude piece of work that should not be included in the canon of works by Oxford.

The anti-Stratfordians, in addition to assuming that the author must have been a man of rank and a university man, usually assume two conspiracies: (1) a conspiracy in Elizabethan and Jacobean times, in which a surprisingly large number of persons connected with the theater knew that the actor Shakespeare did not write the plays attributed to him but for some reason or other pretended that he did; (2) a conspiracy of today's Stratfordians, the professors who teach Shakespeare in the colleges and universities, who are said to have a vested interest in preserving Shakespeare as the author of the plays they teach. In fact, (1) it is inconceivable that the secret of Shakespeare's non-authorship could have been preserved by all of the people who supposedly were in on the conspiracy, and (2) academic fame awaits any scholar today who can disprove Shakespeare's authorship.

The Stratfordian case is convincing not only because hundreds or even thousands of anti-Stratford arguments—of the sort that say "ever I was born" has the secret double meaning "E. Ver, I was born"—add up to nothing at all but also because irrefutable evidence connects the man from Stratford with the London theater and with the authorship of particular plays. The anti-Stratfordians do not seem to understand that it is not enough to dismiss the Stratford case by saying that a fellow from the provinces simply couldn't have written the plays. Nor do they understand that it is not enough to dismiss all of the evidence connecting Shakespeare with the plays by asserting that it is perjured.

The Shakespeare Canon

We return to William Shakespeare. Thirty-seven plays as well as some nondramatic poems are generally held to constitute the Shakespeare canon, the body of authentic works. The exact dates of composition of most of the works are highly uncertain, but evidence of a starting point and/or of a final limiting point often provides a framework for informed guessing. For example, *Richard II* cannot be earlier than 1595, the publication date of some material to which it is indebted; *The Merchant of Venice* cannot be later than 1598, the year Francis Meres mentioned it. Sometimes arguments for a date hang on an alleged topical allusion, such as the lines about the unseasonable weather in *A Midsummer Night's Dream*, 2.1.81–117, but such an allusion, if indeed it is an allusion to an event in the real world, can be variously interpreted, and in any case there is always the possibility that a topical allusion was inserted years later, to bring the play up to date. (The issue of alterations in a text between the

time that Shakespeare drafted it and the time that it was
printed—alterations due to censorship or playhouse practice
or Shakespeare's own second thoughts—will be discussed
in "The Play Text as a Collaboration" later in this over-
view.) Dates are often attributed on the basis of style, and
although conjectures about style usually rest on other
conjectures (such as Shakespeare's development as a playwright, or the appropriateness of lines to character), sooner
or later one must rely on one's literary sense. There is no
documentary proof, for example, that *Othello* is not as early
as *Romeo and Juliet*, but one feels that *Othello* is a later,
more mature work, and because the first record of its performance is 1604, one is glad enough to set its composition at
that date and not push it back into Shakespeare's early years.
(*Romeo and Juliet* was first published in 1597, but evidence
suggests that it was written a little earlier.) The following
chronology, then, is indebted not only to facts but also to
informed guesswork and sensitivity. The dates, necessarily
imprecise for some works, indicate something like a scholarly consensus concerning the time of original composition.
Some plays show evidence of later revision.

Plays. The first collected edition of Shakespeare, published
in 1623, included thirty-six plays. These are all accepted as
Shakespeare's, though for one of them, *Henry VIII*, he is
thought to have had a collaborator. A thirty-seventh play,
Pericles, published in 1609 and attributed to Shakespeare on
the title page, is also widely accepted as being partly by
Shakespeare even though it is not included in the 1623
volume. Still another play not in the 1623 volume, *The Two
Noble Kinsmen*, was first published in 1634, with a title page
attributing it to John Fletcher and Shakespeare. Probably
most students of the subject now believe that Shakespeare
did indeed have a hand in it. Of the remaining plays
attributed at one time or another to Shakespeare, only
one, *Edward III*, anonymously published in 1596, is now
regarded by some scholars as a serious candidate. The
prevailing opinion, however, is that this rather simple-
minded play is not Shakespeare's; at most he may have
revised some passages, chiefly scenes with the Countess of

Salisbury. We include *The Two Noble Kinsmen* but do not include *Edward III* in the following list.

1588–94	*The Comedy of Errors*
1588–94	*Love's Labor's Lost*
1589–91	*2 Henry VI*
1590–91	*3 Henry VI*
1589–92	*1 Henry VI*
1592–93	*Richard III*
1589–94	*Titus Andronicus*
1593–94	*The Taming of the Shrew*
1592–94	*The Two Gentlemen of Verona*
1594–96	*Romeo and Juliet*
1595	*Richard II*
1595–96	*A Midsummer Night's Dream*
1596–97	*King John*
1594–96	*The Merchant of Venice*
1596–97	*1 Henry IV*
1597	*The Merry Wives of Windsor*
1597–98	*2 Henry IV*
1598–99	*Much Ado About Nothing*
1598–99	*Henry V*
1599	*Julius Caesar*
1599–1600	*As You Like It*
1599–1600	*Twelfth Night*
1600–1601	*Hamlet*
1601–1602	*Troilus and Cressida*
1602–1604	*All's Well That Ends Well*
1603–1604	*Othello*
1604	*Measure for Measure*
1605–1606	*King Lear*
1605–1606	*Macbeth*
1606–1607	*Antony and Cleopatra*
1605–1608	*Timon of Athens*
1607–1608	*Coriolanus*
1607–1608	*Pericles*
1609–10	*Cymbeline*
1610–11	*The Winter's Tale*
1611	*The Tempest*

| 1612–13 | *Henry VIII* |
| 1613 | *The Two Noble Kinsmen* |

Poems. In 1989 Donald W. Foster published a book in which he argued that "A Funeral Elegy for Master William Peter," published in 1612, ascribed only to the initials W.S., *may* be by Shakespeare. Foster later published an article in a scholarly journal, *PMLA* 111 (1996), in which he asserted the claim more positively. The evidence begins with the initials, and includes the fact that the publisher and the printer of the elegy had published Shakespeare's *Sonnets* in 1609. But such facts add up to rather little, especially because no one has found any connection between Shakespeare and William Peter (an Oxford graduate about whom little is known, who was murdered at the age of twenty-nine). The argument is based chiefly on statistical examinations of word patterns, which are said to correlate with Shakespeare's known work. Despite such correlations, however, many readers feel that the poem does not sound like Shakespeare. True, Shakespeare has a great range of styles, but his work is consistently imaginative and interesting. Many readers find neither of these qualities in "A Funeral Elegy."

1592–93	*Venus and Adonis*
1593–94	*The Rape of Lucrece*
1593–1600	*Sonnets*
1600–1601	*The Phoenix and the Turtle*

Shakespeare's English

1. Spelling and Pronunciation. From the philologist's point of view, Shakespeare's English is modern English. It requires footnotes, but the inexperienced reader can comprehend substantial passages with very little help, whereas for the same reader Chaucer's Middle English is a foreign language. By the beginning of the fifteenth century the chief grammatical changes in English had taken place, and the final unaccented *-e* of Middle English had been lost (though it survives even today in spelling, as in *name*); during the fifteenth century the dialect of London, the commercial and political center, gradually displaced the provincial dialects, at least in writing; by the end of the century, printing had helped to regularize and stabilize the language, especially spelling. Elizabethan spelling may seem erratic to us (there were dozens of spellings of *Shakespeare*, and a simple word like *been* was also spelled *beene* and *bin*), but it had much in common with our spelling. Elizabethan spelling was conservative in that for the most part it reflected an older pronunciation (Middle English) rather than the sound of the language as it was then spoken, just as our spelling continues to reflect medieval pronunciation—most obviously in the now silent but formerly pronounced letters in a word such as *knight*. Elizabethan pronunciation, though not identical with ours, was much closer to ours than to that of the Middle Ages. Incidentally, though no one can be certain about what Elizabethan English sounded like, specialists tend to believe it was rather like the speech of a modern stage Irishman (*time* apparently was pronounced *toime*, *old* pronounced *awld*, *day* pronounced *die*, and *join* pronounced *jine*) and not at all like the Oxford speech that most of us think it was.

An awareness of the difference between our pronunciation and Shakespeare's is crucial in three areas—in accent, or number of syllables (many metrically regular lines may look irregular to us); in rhymes (which may not look like rhymes); and in puns (which may not look like puns). Examples will be useful. Some words that were at least on occasion stressed differently from today are *aspèct*, *còmplete*, *fòrlorn*, *revènue*, and *sepùlcher*. Words that sometimes had an additional syllable are *emp[e]ress*, *Hen[e]ry*, *mon[e]th*, and *villain* (three syllables, *vil-lay-in*). An additional syllable is often found in possessives, like *moon*'s (pronounced *moones*) and in words ending in *-tion* or *-sion*. Words that had one less syllable than they now have are *needle* (pronounced *neel*) and *violet* (pronounced *vilet*). Among rhymes now lost are *one* with *loan*, *love* with *prove*, *beast* with *jest*, *eat* with *great*. (In reading, trust your sense of metrics and your ear, more than your eye.) An example of a pun that has become obliterated by a change in pronunciation is Falstaff's reply to Prince Hal's "Come, tell us your reason" in *1 Henry IV*: "Give you a reason on compulsion? If reasons were as plentiful as blackberries, I would give no man a reason upon compulsion, I" (2.4.237–40). The *ea* in *reason* was pronounced rather like a long *a,* like the *ai* in *raisin,* hence the comparison with blackberries.

Puns are not merely attempts to be funny; like metaphors they often involve bringing into a meaningful relationship areas of experience normally seen as remote. In *2 Henry IV,* when Feeble is conscripted, he stoically says, "I care not. A man can die but once. We owe God a death" (3.2.242–43), punning on *debt,* which was the way *death* was pronounced. Here an enormously significant fact of life is put into simple commercial imagery, suggesting its commonplace quality. Shakespeare used the same pun earlier in *1 Henry IV,* when Prince Hal says to Falstaff, "Why, thou owest God a death," and Falstaff replies, " 'Tis not due yet: I would be loath to pay him before his day. What need I be so forward with him that calls not on me?" (5.1.126–29).

Sometimes the puns reveal a delightful playfulness; sometimes they reveal aggressiveness, as when, replying to Claudius's "But now, my cousin Hamlet, and my son," Hamlet says, "A little more than kin, and less than kind!" (1.2.64–65). These are Hamlet's first words in the play, and we already hear him warring verbally against Claudius. Hamlet's "less than kind" probably means (1) Hamlet is not of Claudius's family or nature, *kind* having the sense it still has in our word *mankind*; (2) Hamlet is not kindly (affectionately) disposed toward Claudius; (3) Claudius is not naturally (but rather unnaturally, in a legal sense incestuously) Hamlet's father. The puns evidently were not put in as sops to the groundlings; they are an important way of communicating a complex meaning.

2. Vocabulary. A conspicuous difficulty in reading Shakespeare is rooted in the fact that some of his words are no longer in common use—for example, words concerned with armor, astrology, clothing, coinage, hawking, horsemanship, law, medicine, sailing, and war. Shakespeare had a large vocabulary—something near thirty thousand words—but it was not so much a vocabulary of big words as a vocabulary drawn from a wide range of life, and it is partly his ability to call upon a great body of concrete language that gives his plays the sense of being in close contact with life. When the right word did not already exist, he made it up. Among words thought to be his coinages are *accommodation, all-knowing, amazement, bare-faced, countless, dexterously, dislocate, dwindle, fancy-free, frugal, indistinguishable, lackluster, laughable, overawe, premeditated, sea change, star-crossed*. Among those that have not survived are the verb *convive,* meaning to feast together, and *smilet,* a little smile.

Less overtly troublesome than the technical words but more treacherous are the words that seem readily intelligible to us but whose Elizabethan meanings differ from their modern ones. When Horatio describes the Ghost as an "erring spirit," he is saying not that the ghost has sinned or made an error but that it is wandering. Here is a short list of some of the most common words in Shakespeare's plays that often (but not always) have a meaning other than their most usual modern meaning:

'a	he
abuse	deceive
accident	occurrence
advertise	inform
an, and	if
annoy	harm
appeal	accuse
artificial	skillful
brave	fine, splendid
censure	opinion
cheer	(1) face (2) frame of mind
chorus	a single person who comments on the events
closet	small private room
competitor	partner
conceit	idea, imagination
cousin	kinsman
cunning	skillful
disaster	evil astrological influence
doom	judgment
entertain	receive into service

envy	malice
event	outcome
excrement	outgrowth (of hair)
fact	evil deed
fancy	(1) love (2) imagination
fell	cruel
fellow	(1) companion (2) low person (often an insulting term if addressed to someone of approximately equal rank)
fond	foolish
free	(1) innocent (2) generous
glass	mirror
hap, haply	chance, by chance
head	army
humor	(1) mood (2) bodily fluid thought to control one's psychology
imp	child
intelligence	news
kind	natural, acting according to nature
let	hinder
lewd	base
mere(ly)	utter(ly)
modern	commonplace
natural	a fool, an idiot
naughty	(1) wicked (2) worthless
next	nearest
nice	(1) trivial (2) fussy
noise	music
policy	(1) prudence (2) stratagem
presently	immediately
prevent	anticipate
proper	handsome
prove	test
quick	alive
sad	serious
saw	proverb
secure	without care, incautious
silly	innocent

sensible	capable of being perceived by the senses
shrewd	sharp
so	provided that
starve	die
still	always
success	that which follows
tall	brave
tell	count
tonight	last night
wanton	playful, careless
watch	keep awake
will	lust
wink	close both eyes
wit	mind, intelligence

All glosses, of course, are mere approximations; sometimes one of Shakespeare's words may hover between an older meaning and a modern one, and as we have seen, his words often have multiple meanings.

3. Grammar. A few matters of grammar may be surveyed, though it should be noted at the outset that Shakespeare sometimes made up his own grammar. As E.A. Abbott says in *A Shakespearian Grammar,* "Almost any part of speech can be used as any other part of speech": a noun as a verb ("he childed as I fathered"); a verb as a noun ("She hath made compare"); or an adverb as an adjective ("a seldom pleasure"). There are hundreds, perhaps thousands, of such instances in the plays, many of which at first glance would not seem at all irregular and would trouble only a pedant. Here are a few broad matters.

Nouns: The Elizabethans thought the *-s* genitive ending for nouns (as in *man's*) derived from *his*; thus the line " 'gainst the count his galleys I did some service," for "the count's galleys."

Adjectives: By Shakespeare's time adjectives had lost the endings that once indicated gender, number, and case. About the only difference between Shakespeare's adjectives and ours is the use of the now redundant *more* or *most* with the comparative ("some more fitter place") or superlative

("This was the most unkindest cut of all"). Like double comparatives and double superlatives, double negatives were acceptable; Mercutio "will not budge for no man's pleasure."

Pronouns: The greatest change was in pronouns. In Middle English *thou, thy,* and *thee* were used among familiars and in speaking to children and inferiors; *ye, your,* and *you* were used in speaking to superiors (servants to masters, nobles to the king) or to equals with whom the speaker was not familiar. Increasingly the "polite" forms were used in all direct address, regardless of rank, and the accusative *you* displaced the nominative *ye.* Shakespeare sometimes uses *ye* instead of *you,* but even in Shakespeare's day *ye* was archaic, and it occurs mostly in rhetorical appeals.

Thou, thy, and *thee* were not completely displaced, however, and Shakespeare occasionally makes significant use of them, sometimes to connote familiarity or intimacy and sometimes to connote contempt. In *Twelfth Night* Sir Toby advises Sir Andrew to insult Cesario by addressing him as *thou:* "If thou thou'st him some thrice, it shall not be amiss" (3.2.46–47). In *Othello* when Brabantio is addressing an unidentified voice in the dark he says, "What are you?" (1.1.91), but when the voice identifies itself as the foolish suitor Roderigo, Brabantio uses the contemptuous form, saying, "I have charged thee not to haunt about my doors" (93). He uses this form for a while, but later in the scene, when he comes to regard Roderigo as an ally, he shifts back to the polite *you,* beginning in line 163, "What said she to you?" and on to the end of the scene. For reasons not yet satisfactorily explained, Elizabethans used *thou* in addresses to God—"O God, thy arm was here," the king says in *Henry V* (4.8.108)—and to supernatural characters such as ghosts and witches. A subtle variation occurs in *Hamlet.* When Hamlet first talks with the Ghost in 1.5, he uses *thou,* but when he sees the Ghost in his mother's room, in 3.4, he uses *you,* presumably because he is now convinced that the Ghost is not a counterfeit but is his father.

Perhaps the most unusual use of pronouns, from our point of view, is the neuter singular. In place of our *its, his* was often used, as in "How far that little candle throws *his* beams." But the use of a masculine pronoun for a neuter noun came to seem unnatural, and so *it* was used for the possessive as well as the nominative: "The hedge-sparrow fed the cuckoo so long / That it had it head bit off by it young." In the late sixteenth century the possessive form *its* developed, apparently by analogy with the *-s* ending used to indicate a genitive noun, as in *book*'s, but *its* was not yet common usage in Shakespeare's day. He seems to have used *its* only ten times, mostly in his later plays. Other usages, such as "you have seen Cassio and she together" or the substitution of *who* for *whom,* cause little problem even when noticed.

Verbs, Adverbs, and Prepositions: Verbs cause almost no difficulty: The third person singular present form commonly ends in *-s,* as in modern English (e.g., "He blesses"), but sometimes in *-eth* (Portia explains to Shylock that mercy "blesseth him that gives and him that takes"). Broadly speaking, the *-eth* ending was old-fashioned or dignified or "literary" rather than colloquial, except for the words *doth, hath,* and *saith.* The *-eth* ending (regularly used in the King James Bible, 1611) is very rare in Shakespeare's dramatic prose, though not surprisingly it occurs twice in the rather formal prose summary of the narrative poem *Lucrece.* Sometimes a plural subject, especially if it has collective force, takes a verb ending in *-s,* as in "My old bones aches." Some of our strong or irregular preterites (such as *broke*) have a different form in Shakespeare (*brake*); some verbs that now have a weak or regular preterite (such as *helped*) in Shakespeare have a strong or irregular preterite (*holp*). Some adverbs that today end in *-ly* were not inflected: "grievous sick," "wondrous strange." Finally, prepositions often are not the ones we expect: "We are such stuff as dreams are made on," "I have a king here to my flatterer."

Again, none of the differences (except meanings that have substantially changed or been lost) will cause much difficulty. But it must be confessed that for some elliptical passages there is no widespread agreement on meaning. Wise editors resist saying more than they know, and when they are uncertain they add a question mark to their gloss.

Shakespeare's Theater

In Shakespeare's infancy, Elizabethan actors performed wherever they could—in great halls, at court, in the courtyards of inns. These venues implied not only different audiences but also different playing conditions. The innyards must have made rather unsatisfactory theaters: on some days they were unavailable because carters bringing goods to London used them as depots; when available, they had to be rented from the innkeeper. In 1567, presumably to avoid such difficulties, and also to avoid regulation by the Common Council of London, which was not well disposed toward theatricals, one John Brayne, brother-in-law of the carpenter turned actor James Burbage, built the Red Lion in an eastern suburb of London. We know nothing about its shape or its capacity; we can say only that it may have been the first building in Europe constructed for the purpose of giving plays since the end of antiquity, a thousand years earlier. Even after the building of the Red Lion theatrical activity continued in London in makeshift circumstances, in marketplaces and inns, and always uneasily. In 1574 the Common Council required that plays and playing places in London be licensed because

> sundry great disorders and inconveniences have been found to ensue to this city by the inordinate haunting of great multitudes of people, specially youth, to plays, interludes, and shows, namely occasion of frays and quarrels, evil practices of incontinency in great inns having chambers and secret places adjoining to their open stages and galleries.

The Common Council ordered that innkeepers who wished licenses to hold performance put up a bond and make contributions to the poor.

The requirement that plays and innyard theaters be licensed, along with the other drawbacks of playing at inns and presumably along with the success of the Red Lion, led James Burbage to rent a plot of land northeast of the city walls, on property outside the jurisdiction of the city. Here he built England's second playhouse, called simply the Theatre. About all that is known of its construction is that it was wood. It soon had imitators, the most famous being the Globe (1599), essentially an amphitheater built across the Thames (again outside the city's jurisdiction), constructed with timbers of the Theatre, which had been dismantled when Burbage's lease ran out.

Admission to the theater was one penny, which allowed spectators to stand at the sides and front of the stage that jutted into the yard. An additional penny bought a seat in a covered part of the theater, and a third penny bought a more comfortable seat and a better location. It is notoriously difficult to translate prices into today's money, since some things that are inexpensive today would have been expensive in the past and vice versa—a pipeful of tobacco (imported, of course) cost a lot of money, about three pennies, and an orange (also imported) cost two or three times what a chicken cost—but perhaps we can get some idea of the low cost of the penny admission when we realize that a penny could also buy a pot of ale. An unskilled laborer made about five or sixpence a day, an artisan about twelve pence a day, and the hired actors (as opposed to the sharers in the company, such as Shakespeare) made about ten pence a performance. A printed play cost five or sixpence. Of course a visit to the theater (like a visit to a baseball game today) usually cost more than the admission since the spectator probably would also buy food and drink. Still, the low entrance fee meant that the theater was available to all except the very poorest people, rather as movies and most athletic events are today. Evidence indicates that the audience ranged from apprentices who somehow managed to scrape together the minimum entrance fee and to escape from their masters for a few hours, to prosperous members of the middle class and aristocrats who paid the additional fee for admission to the galleries. The exact proportion of men to women cannot be determined, but women of all classes certainly were present. Theaters were open every afternoon but Sundays for much of the year, except in times of plague, when they were closed because of fear of infection. By the way, no evidence suggests the presence of toilet facilities. Presumably the patrons relieved themselves by making a quick trip to the fields surrounding the playhouses.

There are four important sources of information about the

structure of Elizabethan public playhouses—drawings, a
contract, recent excavations, and stage directions in the
plays. Of drawings, only the so-called de Witt drawing (c.
1596) of the Swan—really his friend Aernout van Buchell's
copy of Johannes de Witt's drawing—is of much signifi-
cance. The drawing, the only extant representation of the
interior of an Elizabethan theater, shows an amphitheater of
three tiers, with a stage jutting from a wall into the yard or

Johannes de Witt, a Continental visitor to London, made a drawing
of the Swan theater in about the year 1596. The original drawing is
lost; this is Aernout van Buchell's copy of it.

center of the building. The tiers are roofed, and part of the stage is covered by a roof that projects from the rear and is supported at its front on two posts, but the groundlings, who paid a penny to stand in front of the stage or at its sides, were exposed to the sky. (Performances in such a playhouse were held only in the daytime; artificial illumination was not used.) At the rear of the stage are two massive doors; above the stage is a gallery.

The second major source of information, the contract for the Fortune (built in 1600), specifies that although the Globe (built in 1599) is to be the model, the Fortune is to be square, eighty feet outside and fifty-five inside. The stage is to be forty-three feet broad, and is to extend into the middle of the yard, i.e., it is twenty-seven and a half feet deep.

The third source of information, the 1989 excavations of the Rose (built in 1587), indicate that the Rose was fourteen-sided, about seventy-two feet in diameter with an inner yard almost fifty feet in diameter. The stage at the Rose was about sixteen feet deep, thirty-seven feet wide at the rear, and twenty-seven feet wide downstage. The relatively small dimensions and the tapering stage, in contrast to the rectangular stage in the Swan drawing, surprised theater historians and have made them more cautious in generalizing about the Elizabethan theater. Excavations at the Globe have not yielded much information, though some historians believe that the fragmentary evidence suggests a larger theater, perhaps one hundred feet in diameter.

From the fourth chief source, stage directions in the plays, one learns that entrance to the stage was by the doors at the rear (*"Enter one citizen at one door, and another at the other"*). A curtain hanging across the doorway—or a curtain hanging between the two doorways—could provide a place where a character could conceal himself, as Polonius does, when he wishes to overhear the conversation between Hamlet and Gertrude. Similarly, withdrawing a curtain from the doorway could "discover" (reveal) a character or two. Such discovery scenes are very rare in Elizabethan drama, but a good example occurs in *The Tempest* (5.1.171), where a stage direction tells us, *"Here Prospero discovers Ferdinand and Miranda playing at chess."* There was also some sort of playing space "aloft" or "above" to represent, for instance, the top of a city's walls or a room above the street. Doubtless each theater had its own peculiarities, but perhaps we can talk about a "typical" Elizabethan theater if we realize that no theater need exactly fit the description, just as no mother is the average mother with 2.7 children.

This hypothetical theater is wooden, round, or polygonal (in *Henry V* Shakespeare calls it a "wooden O") capable of holding some eight hundred spectators who stood in the yard around the projecting elevated stage—these spectators were the "groundlings"—and some fifteen hundred additional spectators who sat in the three roofed galleries. The stage, protected by a "shadow" or "heavens" or roof, is entered from two doors; behind the doors is the "tiring house" (attiring house, i.e., dressing room), and above the stage is some sort of gallery that may sometimes hold spectators but can be used (for example) as the bedroom from which Romeo—according to a stage direction in one text—"goeth down." Some evidence suggests that a throne can be lowered onto the platform stage, perhaps from the "shadow"; certainly characters can descend from the stage through a trap or traps into the cellar or "hell." Sometimes this space beneath the stage accommodates a sound-effects man or musician (in *Antony and Cleopatra* "*music of the hautboys* [oboes] *is under the stage*") or an actor (in *Hamlet* the "*Ghost cries under the stage*"). Most characters simply walk on and off through the doors, but because there is no curtain in front of the platform, corpses will have to be carried off (Hamlet obligingly clears the stage of Polonius's corpse, when he says, "I'll lug the guts into the neighbor room"). Other characters may have fallen at the rear, where a curtain on a doorway could be drawn to conceal them.

Such may have been the "public theater," so called because its inexpensive admission made it available to a wide range of the populace. Another kind of theater has been called the "private theater" because its much greater admission charge (sixpence versus the penny for general admission at the public theater) limited its audience to the wealthy or the prodigal. The private theater was basically a large room, entirely roofed and therefore artificially illuminated, with a stage at one end. The theaters thus were distinct in two ways: One was essentially an amphitheater that catered to the general public; the other was a hall that catered to the wealthy. In 1576 a hall theater was established in Blackfriars, a Dominican priory in London that had been suppressed in 1538 and confiscated by the Crown and thus was not under the city's jurisdiction. All the actors in this Blackfriars theater were boys about eight to thirteen years old (in the public theaters similar boys played female parts; a boy Lady Macbeth played to a man Macbeth). Near the end of this section on Shakespeare's theater we will talk at some length about possible implications in this convention of using boys to play female roles, but for the moment we should say that it doubtless accounts for the relative lack of female roles in Elizabethan drama. Thus, in *A Midsummer Night's Dream*, out of twenty-one named roles, only four are female; in *Hamlet*, out of twenty-four, only two (Gertrude and Ophelia) are female. Many of Shakespeare's characters have fathers but no mothers—for instance, King Lear's daughters. We need not bring in Freud to explain the disparity; a dramatic company had only a few boys in it.

To return to the private theaters, in some of which all of the performers were children—the "eyrie of . . . little eyases" (nest of unfledged hawks—2.2.347–48) which Rosencrantz mentions when he and Guildenstern talk with Hamlet. The theater in Blackfriars had a precarious existence, and ceased operations in 1584. In 1596 James Burbage, who had already made theatrical history by building the Theatre, began to construct a second Blackfriars theater. He died in 1597, and for several years this second Blackfriars theater was used by a troupe of boys, but in 1608 two of Burbage's sons and five other actors (including Shakespeare) became joint operators of the theater, using it in the winter when the open-air Globe was unsuitable. Perhaps such a smaller theater, roofed, artificially illuminated, and with a tradition of a wealthy audience, exerted an influence in Shakespeare's late plays.

Performances in the private theaters may well have had intermissions during which music was played, but in the public theaters the action was probably uninterrupted, flowing from scene to scene almost without a break. Actors would enter, speak, exit, and others would immediately enter and establish (if necessary) the new locale by a few properties and by words and gestures. To indicate that the scene took place at night, a player or two would carry a torch. Here are some samples of Shakespeare establishing the scene:

This is Illyria, lady.   (*Twelfth Night*, 1.2.2)

Well, this is the Forest of Arden.   (*As You Like It*, 2.4.14)

This castle has a pleasant seat; the air
Nimbly and sweetly recommends itself
Unto our gentle senses.   (*Macbeth*, 1.6.1–3)

The west yet glimmers with some streaks of day.
                                          (*Macbeth*, 3.3.5)

Sometimes a speech will go far beyond evoking the minimal setting of place and time, and will, so to speak, evoke the social world in which the characters move. For instance, early in the first scene of *The Merchant of Venice* Salerio suggests an explanation for Antonio's melancholy. (In the following passage, *pageants* are decorated wagons, floats, and *cursy* is the verb "to curtsy," or "to bow.")

Your mind is tossing on the ocean,
There where your argosies with portly sail—
Like signiors and rich burghers on the flood,
Or as it were the pageants of the sea—
Do overpeer the petty traffickers
That cursy to them, do them reverence,
As they fly by them with their woven wings.   (1.1.8–14)

Late in the nineteenth century, when Henry Irving produced the play with elaborate illusionistic sets, the first scene showed a ship moored in the harbor, with fruit vendors and dock laborers, in an effort to evoke the bustling and exotic life of Venice. But Shakespeare's words give us this exotic, rich world of commerce in his highly descriptive language when Salerio speaks of "argosies with portly sail" that fly with "woven wings"; equally important, through Salerio Shakespeare conveys a sense of the orderly, hierarchical society in which the lesser ships, "the petty traffickers," curtsy and thereby "do . . . reverence" to their superiors, the merchant prince's ships, which are "Like signiors and rich burghers."

On the other hand, it is a mistake to think that except for verbal pictures the Elizabethan stage was bare. Although Shakespeare's Chorus in *Henry V* calls the stage an "unworthy scaffold" (Prologue 1.10) and urges the spectators to "eke out our performance with your mind" (Prologue 3.35), there was considerable spectacle. The last act of *Macbeth*, for instance, has five stage directions calling for *"drum and colors,"* and another sort of appeal to the eye is indicated by the stage direction *"Enter Macduff, with Macbeth's head."* Some scenery and properties may have been substantial; doubtless a throne was used, but the pillars supporting the roof would have served for the trees on which Orlando pins his poems in *As You Like It*.

Having talked about the public theater—"this wooden *O*"—at some length, we should mention again that Shakespeare's plays were performed also in other locales. Alvin Kernan, in *Shakespeare, the King's Playwright: Theater in the Stuart Court 1603–1613* (1995) points out that "several of [Shakespeare's] plays contain brief theatrical performances, set always in a court or some noble house. When Shakespeare portrayed a theater, he did not, except for the choruses in *Henry V*, imagine a public theater" (p. 195). (Examples include episodes in *The Taming of the Shrew*, *A Midsummer Night's Dream*, *Hamlet*, and *The Tempest*.)

A Note on the Use of Boy Actors in Female Roles

Until fairly recently, scholars were content to mention that the convention existed; they sometimes also mentioned that it continued the medieval practice of using males in female roles, and that other theaters, notably in ancient Greece and in China and Japan, also used males in female roles. (In classical Noh drama in Japan, males still play the female roles.) Prudery may have been at the root of the academic failure to talk much about the use of boy actors, or maybe there really is not much more to say than that it was a convention of a male-centered culture (Stephen Greenblatt's view, in *Shakespearean Negotiations* [1988]). Further, the very nature of a convention is that it is not thought about: Hamlet is a Dane and Julius Caesar is a Roman, but in Shakespeare's plays they speak English, and we in the audience never give this odd fact a thought. Similarly, a character may speak in the presence of others and we understand, again without thinking about it, that he or she is not heard by the figures on the stage (the aside); a character alone on the stage may speak (the soliloquy), and we do not take the character to be unhinged; in a realistic (box) set, the fourth wall, which allows us to see what is going on, is miraculously missing. The no-nonsense view, then, is that the boy actor was an accepted convention, accepted unthinkingly—just as today we know that Kenneth Branagh is not Hamlet, Al Pacino is not Richard III, and Denzel Washington is not the Prince of Aragon. In this view, the audience takes the performer for the role, and that is that; such is the argument we now make for race-free casting, in which African-Americans and Asians can play roles of persons who lived in medieval Denmark and ancient Rome. But gender perhaps is different, at least today. It is a matter of abundant academic study: The Elizabethan theater is now sometimes called a transvestite theater, and we hear much about cross-dressing.

Shakespeare himself in a very few passages calls attention to the use of boys in female roles. At the end of *As You Like It* the boy who played Rosalind addresses the audience, and says, "O men, . . . if I were a woman, I would kiss as many of you as had beards that pleased me." But this is in the Epilogue; the plot is over, and the actor is stepping out of the play and into the audience's everyday world. A second reference to the practice of boys playing female roles occurs in *Antony and Cleopatra*, when Cleopatra imagines that she and Antony will be the subject of crude plays, her role being performed by a boy:

> The quick comedians
> Extemporally will stage us, and present
> Our Alexandrian revels: Antony
> Shall be brought drunken forth, and I shall see
> Some squeaking Cleopatra boy my greatness.   (5.2.216–20)

In a few other passages, Shakespeare is more indirect. For instance, in *Twelfth Night* Viola, played of course by a boy, disguises herself as a young man and seeks service in the house of a lord. She enlists the help of a Captain, and (by way of explaining away her voice and her beardlessness) says,

> I'll serve this duke
> Thou shalt present me as an eunuch to him.   (1.2.55–56)

In *Hamlet*, when the players arrive in 2.2, Hamlet jokes with the boy who plays a female role. The boy has grown since Hamlet last saw him: "By'r Lady, your ladyship is nearer to heaven than when I saw you last by the altitude of a chopine" (a lady's thick-soled shoe). He goes on: "Pray God your voice . . . be not cracked" (434–38).

Exactly how sexual, how erotic, this material was and is, is now much disputed. Again, the use of boys may have been unnoticed, or rather not thought about—an unexamined convention—by most or all spectators most of the time, perhaps *all* of the time, except when Shakespeare calls the convention to the attention of the audience, as in the passages just quoted. Still, an occasional bit seems to invite erotic thoughts. The clearest example is the name that Rosalind takes in *As You Like It*, Ganymede—the beautiful youth whom Zeus abducted. Did boys dressed to play female roles carry homoerotic appeal for straight men (Lisa Jardine's view, in *Still Harping on Daughters* [1983]), or for gay men, or for some or all women in the audience? Further, when the boy actor played a woman who (for the purposes of the plot) disguised herself as a male, as Rosalind, Viola, and Portia do—so we get a boy playing a woman playing a man—what sort of appeal was generated, and for what sort of spectator?

Some scholars have argued that the convention empowered women by letting female characters display a freedom unavailable in Renaissance patriarchal society; the convention, it is said, undermined rigid gender distinctions. In this view, the convention (along with plots in which female characters for a while disguised themselves as young men) allowed Shakespeare to say what some modern gender

critics say: Gender is a constructed role rather than a bio-
logical given, something we make, rather than a fixed binary
opposition of male and female (see Juliet Dusinberre, in
Shakespeare and the Nature of Women [1975]). On the other
hand, some scholars have maintained that the male disguise
assumed by some female characters serves only to reaffirm
traditional social distinctions since female characters who
don male garb (notably Portia in *The Merchant of Venice*
and Rosalind in *As You Like It*) return to their female garb
and at least implicitly (these critics say) reaffirm the status
quo. (For this last view, see Clara Claiborne Park, in an
essay in *The Woman's Part*, ed. Carolyn Ruth Swift Lenz et
al. [1980].) Perhaps no one answer is right for all plays; in
As You Like It cross-dressing empowers Rosalind, but in
Twelfth Night cross-dressing comically traps Viola.

Shakespeare's Dramatic Language: Costumes, Gestures and Silences; Prose and Poetry

Because Shakespeare was a dramatist, not merely a poet,
he worked not only with language but also with costume,
sound effects, gestures, and even silences. We have already
discussed some kinds of spectacle in the preceding section,
and now we will begin with other aspects of visual language;
a theater, after all, is literally a "place for seeing." Consider
the opening stage direction in *The Tempest*, the first play in
the first published collection of Shakespeare's plays: *"A
tempestuous noise of thunder and Lightning heard: Enter a
Ship-master, and a Boteswain."*

Costumes: What did that shipmaster and that boatswain
wear? Doubtless they wore something that identified them
as men of the sea. Not much is known about the costumes
that Elizabethan actors wore, but at least three points are
clear: (1) many of the costumes were splendid versions of
contemporary Elizabethan dress; (2) some attempts were
made to approximate the dress of certain occupations and of
antique or exotic characters such as Romans, Turks, and
Jews; (3) some costumes indicated that the wearer was

supernatural. Evidence for elaborate Elizabethan clothing can be found in the plays themselves and in contemporary comments about the "sumptuous" players who wore the discarded clothing of noblemen, as well as in account books that itemize such things as "a scarlet cloak with two broad gold laces, with gold buttons down the sides."

The attempts at approximation of the dress of certain occupations and nationalities also can be documented from the plays themselves, and it derives additional confirmation from a drawing of the first scene of Shakespeare's *Titus Andronicus*—the only extant Elizabethan picture of an identifiable episode in a play. (See pp. xxxviii–xxxix.) The drawing, probably done in 1594 or 1595, shows Queen Tamora pleading for mercy. She wears a somewhat medieval-looking robe and a crown; Titus wears a toga and a wreath, but two soldiers behind him wear costumes fairly close to Elizabethan dress. We do not know, however, if the drawing represents an actual stage production in the public theater, or perhaps a private production, or maybe only a reader's visualization of an episode. Further, there is some conflicting evidence: In *Julius Caesar* a reference is made to Caesar's doublet (a close-fitting jacket), which, if taken literally, suggests that even the protagonist did not wear Roman clothing; and certainly the lesser characters, who are said to wear hats, did not wear Roman garb.

It should be mentioned, too, that even ordinary clothing can be symbolic: Hamlet's "inky cloak," for example, sets him apart from the brightly dressed members of Claudius's court and symbolizes his mourning; the fresh clothes that are put on King Lear partly symbolize his return to sanity. Consider, too, the removal of disguises near the end of some plays. For instance, Rosalind in *As You Like It* and Portia and Nerissa in *The Merchant of Venice* remove their male attire, thus again becoming fully themselves.

Gestures and Silences: Gestures are an important part of a dramatist's language. King Lear kneels before his daughter Cordelia for a benediction (4.7.57–59), an act of humility that contrasts with his earlier speeches banishing her and that contrasts also with a comparable gesture, his ironic

kneeling before Regan (2.4.153–55). Northumberland's failure to kneel before King Richard II (3.3.71–72) speaks volumes. As for silences, consider a moment in *Coriolanus*: Before the protagonist yields to his mother's entreaties (5.3.182), there is this stage direction: *"Holds her by the hand, silent."* Another example of "speech in dumbness" occurs in *Macbeth*, when Macduff learns that his wife and children have been murdered. He is silent at first, as Malcolm's speech indicates: "What, man! Ne'er pull your hat upon your brows. Give sorrow words" (4.3.208–09). (For a discussion of such moments, see Philip C. McGuire's *Speechless Dialect: Shakespeare's Open Silences* [1985].)

Of course when we think of Shakespeare's work, we think primarily of his language, both the poetry and the prose.

Prose: Although two of his plays (*Richard II* and *King John*) have no prose at all, about half the others have at least one quarter of the dialogue in prose, and some have notably more: *1 Henry IV* and *2 Henry IV*, about half; *As You Like It*

and *Twelfth Night*, a little more than half; *Much Ado About Nothing*, more than three quarters; and *The Merry Wives of Windsor*, a little more than five sixths. We should remember that despite Molière's joke about M. Jourdain, who was amazed to learn that he spoke prose, most of us do not speak prose. Rather, we normally utter repetitive, shapeless, and often ungrammatical torrents; prose is something very different—a sort of literary imitation of speech at its most coherent.

Today we may think of prose as "natural" for drama; or even if we think that poetry is appropriate for high tragedy we may still think that prose is the right medium for comedy. Greek, Roman, and early English comedies, however, were written in verse. In fact, prose was not generally considered a literary medium in England until the late fifteenth century; Chaucer tells even his bawdy stories in verse. By the end of the 1580s, however, prose had established itself on the English comic stage. In tragedy, Marlowe made some use of prose, not simply in the speeches of clownish servants but even in the speech of a tragic hero, Doctor Faustus. Still, before Shakespeare, prose normally was used in the theater only for special circumstances: (1) letters and proclamations, to set them off from the poetic dialogue; (2) mad characters, to indicate that normal thinking has become disordered; and (3) low comedy, or speeches uttered by clowns even when they are not being comic. Shakespeare made use of these conventions, but he also went far beyond them. Sometimes he begins a scene in prose and then shifts into verse as the emotion is heightened; or conversely, he may shift from verse to prose when a speaker is lowering the emotional level, as when Brutus speaks in the Forum.

Shakespeare's prose usually is not prosaic. Hamlet's prose includes not only small talk with Rosencrantz and Guildenstern but also princely reflections on "What a piece of work is a man" (2.2.312). In conversation with Ophelia, he shifts from light talk in verse to a passionate prose denunciation of women (3.1.103), though the shift to prose here is perhaps also intended to suggest the possibility of madness. (Consult Brian Vickers, *The Artistry of Shakespeare's Prose* [1968].)

Poetry: Drama in rhyme in England goes back to the Middle Ages, but by Shakespeare's day rhyme no longer dominated poetic drama; a finer medium, blank verse (strictly speaking, unrhymed lines of ten syllables, with the stress on every second syllable) had been adopted. But before looking at unrhymed poetry, a few things should be said about the chief uses of rhyme in Shakespeare's plays. (1) A couplet (a pair of rhyming lines) is sometimes used to convey emotional heightening at the end of a blank verse speech; (2) characters sometimes speak a couplet as they leave the stage, suggesting closure; (3) except in the latest plays, scenes fairly often conclude with a couplet, and sometimes, as in *Richard II*, 2.1.145–46, the entrance of a new character within a scene is preceded by a couplet, which wraps up the earlier portion of that scene; (4) speeches of two characters occasionally are linked by rhyme, most notably in *Romeo and Juliet*, 1.5.95–108, where the lovers speak a sonnet between them; elsewhere a taunting reply occasionally rhymes with the previous speaker's last line; (5) speeches with sententious or gnomic remarks are sometimes in rhyme, as in the duke's speech in *Othello* (1.3.199–206); (6) speeches of sardonic mockery are sometimes in rhyme—for example, Iago's speech on women in *Othello* (2.1.146–58)—and they sometimes conclude with an emphatic couplet, as in Bolingbroke's speech on comforting words in *Richard II* (1.3.301–2); (7) some characters are associated with rhyme, such as the fairies in *A Midsummer Night's Dream*; (8) in the early plays, especially *The Comedy of Errors* and *The Taming of the Shrew*, comic scenes that in later plays would be in prose are in jingling rhymes; (9) prologues, choruses, plays-within-the-play, inscriptions, vows, epilogues, and so on are often in rhyme, and the songs in the plays are rhymed.

Neither prose nor rhyme immediately comes to mind when we first think of Shakespeare's medium: It is blank verse, unrhymed iambic pentameter. (In a mechanically exact line there are five iambic feet. An iambic foot consists of two syllables, the second accented, as in *away*; five feet make a pentameter line. Thus, a strict line of iambic pentameter contains ten syllables, the even syllables being stressed more heavily than the odd syllables. Fortunately, Shakespeare usually varies the line somewhat.) The first speech in *A Midsummer Night's Dream*, spoken by Duke Theseus to his betrothed, is an example of blank verse:

Now, fair Hippolyta, our nuptial hour
Draws on apace. Four happy days bring in
Another moon; but, O, methinks, how slow
This old moon wanes! She lingers my desires,
Like to a stepdame, or a dowager,
Long withering out a young man's revenue.   (1.1.1–6)

As this passage shows, Shakespeare's blank verse is not mechanically unvarying. Though the predominant foot is the iamb (as in *apace* or *desires*), there are numerous variations. In the first line the stress can be placed on "fair," as the regular metrical pattern suggests, but it is likely that "Now" gets almost as much emphasis; probably in the second line "Draws" is more heavily emphasized than "on," giving us a trochee (a stressed syllable followed by an unstressed one); and in the fourth line each word in the phrase "This old moon wanes" is probably stressed fairly heavily, conveying by two spondees (two feet, each of two stresses) the oppressive tedium that Theseus feels.

In Shakespeare's early plays much of the blank verse is end-stopped (that is, it has a heavy pause at the end of each line), but he later developed the ability to write iambic pentameter verse paragraphs (rather than lines) that give the illusion of speech. His chief techniques are (1) enjambing, i.e., running the thought beyond the single line, as in the first three lines of the speech just quoted; (2) occasionally replacing an iamb with another foot; (3) varying the position of the chief pause (the caesura) within a line; (4) adding an occasional unstressed syllable at the end of a line, traditionally called a feminine ending; (5) and beginning or ending a speech with a half line.

Shakespeare's mature blank verse has much of the rhythmic flexibility of his prose; both the language, though richly figurative and sometimes dense, and the syntax seem natural. It is also often highly appropriate to a particular character. Consider, for instance, this speech from *Hamlet*, in which Claudius, King of Denmark ("the Dane"), speaks to Laertes:

> And now, Laertes, what's the news with you?
> You told us of some suit. What is't, Laertes?
> You cannot speak of reason to the Dane
> And lose your voice. What wouldst thou beg, Laertes,
> That shall not be my offer, not thy asking?   (1.2.42–46)

Notice the short sentences and the repetition of the name "Laertes," to whom the speech is addressed. Notice, too, the shift from the royal "us" in the second line to the more intimate "my" in the last line, and from "you" in the first three lines to the more intimate "thou" and "thy" in the last two lines. Claudius knows how to ingratiate himself with Laertes.

For a second example of the flexibility of Shakespeare's blank verse, consider a passage from *Macbeth*. Distressed by the doctor's inability to cure Lady Macbeth and by the imminent battle, Macbeth addresses some of his remarks to the doctor and others to the servant who is arming him. The entire speech, with its pauses, interruptions, and irresolution (in "Pull't off, I say," Macbeth orders the servant to remove the armor that the servant has been putting on him), catches Macbeth's disintegration. (In the first line, *physic* means "medicine," and in the fourth and fifth lines, *cast the water* means "analyze the urine.")

> Throw physic to the dogs, I'll none of it.
> Come, put mine armor on. Give me my staff.
> Seyton, send out.—Doctor, the thanes fly from me.—
> Come, sir, dispatch. If thou couldst, doctor, cast
> The water of my land, find her disease
> And purge it to a sound and pristine health,
> I would applaud thee to the very echo,
> That should applaud again.—Pull't off, I say.—
> What rhubarb, senna, or what purgative drug,
> Would scour these English hence? Hear'st thou of them?
>
> (5.3.47–56)

Blank verse, then, can be much more than unrhymed iambic pentameter, and even within a single play Shakespeare's blank verse often consists of several styles, depending on the speaker and on the speaker's emotion at the moment.

The Play Text as a Collaboration

Shakespeare's fellow dramatist Ben Jonson reported that the actors said of Shakespeare, "In his writing, whatsoever he penned, he never blotted out line," i.e., never crossed out material and revised his work while composing. None of Shakespeare's plays survives in manuscript (with the possible exception of a scene in *Sir Thomas More*), so we cannot fully evaluate the comment, but in a few instances the published work clearly shows that he revised his manuscript. Consider the following passage (shown here in facsimile) from the best early text of *Romeo and Juliet*, the Second Quarto (1599):

Ro. Would I were fleepe and peace fo fweet to reft
The grey eyde morne fmiles on the frowning night,
Checkring the Eafterne Clouds with ftreaks of light,
And darkneffe fleckted like a drunkard reeles,
From forth daies pathway, made by *Tytans* wheeles.
Hence will I to my ghoftly Friers clofe cell,
His helpe to craue, and my deare hap to tell.

                                                Exit.

Enter Frier alone with a basket.   (night,
Fri. The grey-eyed morne fmiles on the frowning
Checking the Eafterne clowdes with ftreaks of light:
And fleckeld darkneffe like a drunkard reeles,
From forth daies path, and *Tytans* burning wheeles:
Now erethe fun aduance his burning eie,

Romeo rather elaborately tells us that the sun at dawn is
dispelling the night (morning is smiling, the eastern clouds
are checked with light, and the sun's chariot—Titan's
wheels—advances), and he will seek out his spiritual father,
the Friar. He exits and, oddly, the Friar enters and says pretty
much the same thing about the sun. Both speakers say that
"the gray-eyed morn smiles on the frowning night," but there
are small differences, perhaps having more to do with the
business of printing the book than with the author's
composition: For Romeo's "checkring," "fleckted," and
"pathway," we get the Friar's "checking," "fleckeld," and
"path." (Notice, by the way, the inconsistency in Elizabethan
spelling: Romeo's "clouds" become the Friar's "clowdes.")

Both versions must have been in the printer's copy, and it
seems safe to assume that both were in Shakespeare's manuscript. He must have written one version—let's say he first
wrote Romeo's closing lines for this scene—and then he
decided, no, it's better to give this lyrical passage to the
Friar, as the opening of a new scene, but he neglected to
delete the first version. Editors must make a choice, and they
may feel that the reasonable thing to do is to print the text as
Shakespeare intended it. But how can we know what he
intended? Almost all modern editors delete the lines from

Romeo's speech, and retain the Friar's lines. They don't do this because they know Shakespeare's intention, however. They give the lines to the Friar because the first published version (1597) of *Romeo and Juliet* gives only the Friar's version, and this text (though in many ways inferior to the 1599 text) is thought to derive from the memory of some actors, that is, it is thought to represent a performance, not just a script. Maybe during the course of rehearsals Shakespeare—an actor as well as an author—unilaterally decided that the Friar should speak the lines; if so (remember that we don't know this to be a fact) his final intention was to give the speech to the Friar. Maybe, however, the actors talked it over and settled on the Friar, with or without Shakespeare's approval. On the other hand, despite the 1597 version, one might argue (if only weakly) on behalf of giving the lines to Romeo rather than to the Friar, thus: (1) Romeo's comment on the coming of the daylight emphasizes his separation from Juliet, and (2) the figurative language seems more appropriate to Romeo than to the Friar. Having said this, in the Signet edition we have decided in this instance to draw on the evidence provided by earlier text and to give the lines to the Friar, on the grounds that since Q1 reflects a production, in the theater (at least on one occasion) the lines were spoken by the Friar.

A playwright sold a script to a theatrical company. The script thus belonged to the company, not the author, and author and company alike must have regarded this script not as a literary work but as the basis for a play that the actors would create on the stage. We speak of Shakespeare as the author of the plays, but readers should bear in mind that the texts they read, even when derived from a single text, such as the First Folio (1623), are inevitably the collaborative work not simply of Shakespeare with his company—doubtless during rehearsals the actors would suggest alterations—but also with other forces of the age. One force was governmental censorship. In 1606 parliament passed "an Act to restrain abuses of players," prohibiting the utterance of oaths and the name of God. So where the earliest text of *Othello* gives us "By heaven" (3.3.106), the first Folio gives "Alas," presumably reflecting the compliance of stage practice with the law. Similarly, the 1623 version of *King Lear* omits the oath "Fut" (probably from "By God's foot") at 1.2.142, again presumably reflecting the line as it was spoken on the stage. Editors who seek to give the reader the play that Shakespeare initially conceived—the "authentic" play conceived by the solitary Shakespeare—probably will restore the missing oaths and references to God. Other editors, who see the play as a collaborative work, a construction made not only by Shakespeare but also by actors and compositors and even government censors, may claim that what counts is the play as it was actually performed. Such editors regard the censored text as legitimate, since it is the play that was (presumably) finally put on. A performed text, they argue, has more historical reality than a text produced by an editor who has sought to get at what Shakespeare initially wrote. In this view, the text of a play is rather like the script of a film; the script is not the film, and the play text is not the performed play. Even if we want to talk about the play that Shakespeare "intended," we will find ourselves talking about a script that he handed over to a company with the intention that it be implemented by actors. The "intended" play is the one that the actors—we might almost say "society"—would help to construct.

Further, it is now widely held that a play is also the work of readers and spectators, who do not simply receive meaning, but who create it when they respond to the play. This idea is fully in accord with contemporary post-structuralist critical thinking, notably Roland Barthes's "The Death of the Author," in *Image-Music-Text* (1977) and Michel Foucault's "What Is an Author?," in *The Foucault Reader* (1984). The gist of the idea is that an author is not an isolated genius; rather, authors are subject to the politics and other social structures of their age. A dramatist especially is a worker in a collaborative project, working most obviously with actors—parts may be written for particular actors—but working also with the audience. Consider the words of Samuel Johnson, written to be spoken by the actor David Garrick at the opening of a theater in 1747:

The stage but echoes back the public voice;
The drama's laws, the drama's patrons give,
For we that live to please, must please to live.

The audience—the public taste as understood by the playwright—helps to determine what the play is. Moreover, even members of the public who are not part of the playwright's immediate audience may exert an influence through censorship. We have already glanced at governmental censorship, but there are also other kinds. Take one of Shakespeare's most beloved characters, Falstaff, who appears in three of Shakespeare's plays, the two parts of *Henry IV* and *The Merry Wives of Windsor*. He appears with this name in the earliest printed version of the first of these plays, *1 Henry IV*, but we know that Shakespeare originally called him (after an historical figure) Sir John Oldcastle. Oldcastle appears in Shakespeare's source (partly reprinted in the Signet edition of *1 Henry IV*), and a trace of the name survives in Shakespeare's play, 1.2.43–44, where Prince Hal punningly addresses Falstaff as "my old lad of the castle." But for some reason—perhaps because the family of the historical Oldcastle complained—Shakespeare had to change the name. In short, the play as we have it was (at least in this detail) subject to some sort of censorship. If we think that a text should present what we take to be the author's intention, we probably will want to replace *Falstaff* with *Oldcastle*. But if we recognize that a play is a collaboration, we may welcome the change, even if it was forced on Shakespeare. Somehow *Falstaff*, with its hint of *false-staff*, i.e., inadequate prop, seems just right for this fat knight who, to our delight, entertains the young prince with untruths. We can go as far as saying that, at least so far as a play is concerned, an insistence on the author's original intention (even if we could know it) can sometimes impoverish the text.

The tiny example of Falstaff's name illustrates the point that the text we read is inevitably only a version—something in effect produced by the collaboration of the playwright with his actors, audiences, compositors, and editors—of a fluid text that Shakespeare once wrote, just as the *Hamlet* that we see on the screen starring Kenneth Branagh is not the *Hamlet* that Shakespeare saw in an open-air playhouse starring Richard Burbage. *Hamlet* itself, as we shall note in a moment, also exists in several versions. It is not surprising that there is now much talk about the *instability* of Shakespeare's texts.

Because he was not only a playwright but was also an actor and a shareholder in a theatrical company, Shakespeare probably was much involved with the translation of the play from a manuscript to a stage production. He may or may not have done some rewriting during rehearsals, and he may or may not have been happy with cuts that were made. Some plays, notably *Hamlet* and *King Lear*, are so long that it is most unlikely that the texts we read were acted in their entirety. Further, for both of these plays we have more than one early text that demands consideration. In *Hamlet*, the Second Quarto (1604) includes some two hundred lines not found in the Folio (1623). Among the passages missing from the Folio are two of Hamlet's reflective speeches, the "dram of evil" speech (1.4.13–38) and "How all occasions do inform against me" (4.4.32–66). Since the Folio has more numerous and often fuller stage directions, it certainly looks as though in the Folio we get a theatrical version of the play, a text whose cuts were probably made—this is only a hunch, of course—not because Shakespeare was changing his conception of Hamlet but because the playhouse demanded a modified play. (The problem is complicated, since the Folio not only cuts some of the Quarto but adds some material. Various explanations have been offered.)

Or take an example from *King Lear*. In the First and Second Quarto (1608, 1619), the final speech of the play is given to Albany, Lear's surviving son-in-law, but in the First Folio version (1623), the speech is given to Edgar. The Quarto version is in accord with tradition—usually the highest-ranking character in a tragedy speaks the final words. Why does the Folio give the speech to Edgar? One possible answer is this: The Folio version omits some of Albany's speeches in earlier scenes, so perhaps it was decided (by Shakespeare? by the players?) not to give the final lines to so pale a character. In fact, the discrepancies are so many between the two texts, that some scholars argue we do not simply have texts showing different theatrical productions. Rather, these scholars say, Shakespeare substantially revised the play, and we really have two versions of *King Lear* (and of *Othello* also, say some)—two different plays—not simply two texts, each of which is in some ways imperfect.

In this view, the 1608 version of _Lear_ may derive from Shakespeare's manuscript, and the 1623 version may derive from his later revision. The Quartos have almost three hundred lines not in the Folio, and the Folio has about a hundred lines not in the Quartos. It used to be held that all the texts were imperfect in various ways and from various causes—some passages in the Quartos were thought to have been set from a manuscript that was not entirely legible, other passages were thought to have been set by a compositor who was new to setting plays, and still other passages were thought to have been provided by an actor who misremembered some of the lines. This traditional view held that an editor must draw on the Quartos and the Folio in order to get Shakespeare's "real" play. The new argument holds (although not without considerable strain) that we have two authentic plays, Shakespeare's early version (in the Quarto) and Shakespeare's—or his theatrical company's—revised version (in the Folio). Not only theatrical demands but also Shakespeare's own artistic sense, it is argued, called for extensive revisions. Even the titles vary: Q1 is called _True Chronicle Historie of the life and death of King Lear and his three Daughters_, whereas the Folio text is called _The Tragedie of King Lear_. To combine the two texts in order to produce what the editor thinks is the play that Shakespeare intended to write is, according to this view, to produce a text that is false to the history of the play. If the new view is correct, and we do have texts of two distinct versions of _Lear_ rather than two imperfect versions of one play, it supports in a textual way the poststructuralist view that we cannot possibly have an unmediated vision of (in this case) a play by Shakespeare; we can only recognize a plurality of visions.

Editing Texts

Though eighteen of his plays were published during his lifetime, Shakespeare seems never to have supervised their publication. There is nothing unusual here; when a playwright sold a play to a theatrical company he surrendered his ownership to it. Normally a company would not publish the play, because to publish it meant to allow competitors to acquire the piece. Some plays did get published: Apparently hard-up actors sometimes pieced together a play for a publisher; sometimes a company in need of money sold a play; and sometimes a company allowed publication of a play that no longer drew audiences. That Shakespeare did not concern himself with publication is not remarkable; of his contemporaries, only Ben Jonson carefully supervised the publication of his own plays.

In 1623, seven years after Shakespeare's death, John Heminges and Henry Condell (two senior members of Shakespeare's company, who had worked with him for about twenty years) collected his plays—published and unpublished—into a large volume, of a kind called a folio. (A folio is a volume consisting of large sheets that have been folded once, each sheet thus making two leaves, or four pages. The size of the page of course depends on the size of the sheet—a folio can range in height from twelve to sixteen inches, and in width from eight to eleven; the pages in the 1623 edition of Shakespeare, commonly called the First Folio, are approximately thirteen inches tall and eight inches wide.) The eighteen plays published during Shakespeare's lifetime had been issued one play per volume in small formats called quartos. (Each sheet in a quarto has been folded twice, making four leaves, or eight pages, each page being about nine inches tall and seven inches wide, roughly the size of a large paperback.)

Heminges and Condell suggest in an address "To the great variety of readers" that the republished plays are presented in better form than in the quartos:

> Before you were abused with diverse stolen and surreptitious copies, maimed and deformed by the frauds and stealths of injurious impostors that exposed them; even those, are now offered to your view cured and perfect of their limbs, and all the rest absolute in their numbers, as he [i.e., Shakespeare] conceived them.

There is a good deal of truth to this statement, but some of the quarto versions are better than others; some are in fact preferable to the Folio text.

Whoever was assigned to prepare the texts for publication

in the first Folio seems to have taken the job seriously and yet not to have performed it with uniform care. The sources of the texts seem to have been, in general, good unpublished copies or the best published copies. The first play in the collection, *The Tempest*, is divided into acts and scenes, has unusually full stage directions and descriptions of spectacle, and concludes with a list of the characters, but the editor was not able (or willing) to present all of the succeeding texts so fully dressed. Later texts occasionally show signs of carelessness: in one scene of *Much Ado About Nothing* the names of actors, instead of characters, appear as speech prefixes, as they had in the Quarto, which the Folio reprints; proofreading throughout the Folio is spotty and apparently was done without reference to the printer's copy; the pagination of *Hamlet* jumps from 156 to 257. Further, the proofreading was done while the presses continued to print, so that each play in each volume contains a mix of corrected and uncorrected pages.

Modern editors of Shakespeare must first select their copy; no problem if the play exists only in the Folio, but a considerable problem if the relationship between a Quarto and the Folio—or an early Quarto and a later one—is unclear. In the case of *Romeo and Juliet*, the First Quarto (Q1), published in 1597, is vastly inferior to the Second (Q2), published in 1599. The basis of Q1 apparently is a version put together from memory by some actors. Not surprisingly, it garbles many passages and is much shorter than Q2. On the other hand, occasionally Q1 makes better sense than Q2. For instance, near the end of the play, when the parents have assembled and learned of the deaths of Romeo and Juliet, in Q2 the Prince says (5.3.208–9),

> Come, *Montague;* for thou art early vp
> To see thy sonne and heire, now earling downe.

The last three words of this speech surely do not make sense, and many editors turn to Q1, which instead of "now earling downe" has "more early downe." Some modern editors take only "early" from Q1, and print "now early down"; others take "more early," and print "more early down." Further, Q1 (though, again, quite clearly a garbled and abbreviated text) includes some stage directions that are not found in Q2, and today many editors who base their text on Q2 are glad to add these stage directions, because the directions help to give us a sense of what the play looked like on Shakespeare's stage. Thus, in 4.3.58, after Juliet drinks the potion, Q1 gives us this stage direction, not in Q2: *"She falls upon her bed within the curtains."*

In short, an editor's decisions do not end with the choice of a single copy text. First of all, editors must reckon with Elizabethan spelling. If they are not producing a facsimile, they probably modernize the spelling, but ought they to preserve the old forms of words that apparently were pronounced quite unlike their modern forms—*lanthorn, alablaster*? If they preserve these forms are they really preserving Shakespeare's forms or perhaps those of a compositor in the printing house? What is one to do when one finds *lanthorn* and *lantern* in adjacent lines? (The editors of this series in general, but not invariably, assume that words should be spelled in their modern form, unless, for instance, a rhyme is involved.) Elizabethan punctuation, too, presents problems. For example, in the First Folio, the only text for the play, Macbeth rejects his wife's idea that he can wash the blood from his hand (2.2.60–62):

> No: this my Hand will rather
> The multitudinous Seas incarnadine,
> Making the Greene one, Red.

Obviously an editor will remove the superfluous capitals, and will probably alter the spelling to "incarnadine," but what about the comma before "Red"? If we retain the comma, Macbeth is calling the sea "the green one." If we drop the comma, Macbeth is saying that his bloody hand will make the sea ("the Green") *uniformly* red.

An editor will sometimes have to change more than spelling and punctuation. Macbeth says to his wife (1.7.46–47):

> I dare do all that may become a man,
> Who dares no more, is none.

For two centuries editors have agreed that the second line is unsatisfactory, and have emended "no" to "do": "Who dares do more is none." But when in the same play (4.2.21–22) Ross says that fearful persons

> Floate vpon a wilde and violent Sea
> Each way, and moue,

need we emend the passage? On the assumption that the compositor misread the manuscript, some editors emend "each way, and move" to "and move each way"; others emend "move" to "none" (i.e., "Each way and none"). Other editors, however, let the passage stand as in the original. The editors of the Signet Classic Shakespeare have restrained themselves from making abundant emendations. In their minds they hear Samuel Johnson on the dangers of emendation: "I have adopted the Roman sentiment, that it is more honorable to save a citizen than to kill an enemy." Some departures (in addition to spelling, punctuation, and lineation) from the copy text have of course been made, but the original readings are listed in a note following the play, so that readers can evaluate the changes for themselves.

Following tradition, the editors of the Signet Classic Shakespeare have prefaced each play with a list of characters, and throughout the play have regularized the names of the speakers. Thus, in our text of *Romeo and Juliet*, all speeches by Juliet's mother are prefixed "Lady Capulet," although the 1599 Quarto of the play, which provides our copy text, uses at various points seven speech tags for this one character: *Capu. Wi.* (i.e., Capulet's wife), *Ca. Wi., Wi., Wife, Old La.* (i.e., Old Lady), *La.,* and *Mo.* (i.e., Mother). Similarly, in *All's Well That Ends Well*, the character whom we regularly call "Countess" is in the Folio (the copy text) variously identified as *Mother, Countess, Old Countess, Lady,* and *Old Lady.* Admittedly there is some loss in regularizing, since the various prefixes may give us a hint of the way Shakespeare (or a scribe who copied Shakespeare's manuscript) was thinking of the character in a particular scene—for instance, as a mother, or as an old lady. But too much can be made of these differing prefixes, since the social relationships implied are *not* always relevant to the given scene.

We have also added line numbers and in many cases act and scene divisions as well as indications of locale at the beginning of scenes. The Folio divided most of the plays into acts and some into scenes. Early eighteenth-century editors increased the divisions. These divisions, which provide a convenient way of referring to passages in the plays, have been retained, but when not in the text chosen as the basis for the Signet Classic text they are enclosed within square brackets, [ ], to indicate that they are editorial additions. Similarly, though no play of Shakespeare's was equipped with indications of the locale at the heads of scene divisions, locales have here been added in square brackets for the convenience of readers, who lack the information that costumes, properties, gestures, and scenery afford to spectators. Spectators can tell at a glance they are in the throne room, but without an editorial indication the reader may be puzzled for a while. It should be mentioned, incidentally, that there are a few authentic stage directions—perhaps Shakespeare's, perhaps a prompter's—that suggest locales, such as *"Enter Brutus in his orchard,"* and *"They go up into the Senate house."* It is hoped that the bracketed additions in the Signet text will provide readers with the sort of help provided by these two authentic directions, but it is equally hoped that the reader will remember that the stage was not loaded with scenery.

Shakespeare on the Stage

Each volume in the Signet Classic Shakespeare includes a brief stage (and sometimes film) history of the play. When we read about earlier productions, we are likely to find them eccentric, obviously wrongheaded—for instance, Nahum Tate's version of *King Lear*, with a happy ending, which held the stage for about a century and a half, from the late seventeenth century until the end of the first quarter of the nineteenth. We see engravings of David Garrick, the greatest actor of the eighteenth century, in eighteenth-century garb as King Lear, and we smile, thinking how absurd the production must have been. If we are more thoughtful, we say, with the English novelist L. P. Hartley, "The past is a foreign country: they do things differently there." But if the eighteenth-century staging is a foreign country, what of the plays of the late sixteenth and seventeenth centuries? A foreign language, a foreign theater, a foreign audience.

Probably all viewers of Shakespeare's plays, beginning with Shakespeare himself, at times have been unhappy with the plays on the stage. Consider three comments about production that we find in the plays themselves, which suggest Shakespeare's concerns. The Chorus in *Henry V* complains that the heroic story cannot possibly be adequately staged:

> But pardon, gentles all,
> The flat unraisèd spirits that hath dared
> On this unworthy scaffold to bring forth
> So great an object. Can this cockpit hold
> The vasty fields of France? Or may we cram
> Within this wooden *O* the very casques
> That did affright the air at Agincourt?
>
> . . . .
>
> Piece out our imperfections with your thoughts.
>
> (Prologue 1.8–14,23)

Second, here are a few sentences (which may or may not represent Shakespeare's own views) from Hamlet's longish lecture to the players:

> Speak the speech, I pray you, as I pronounced it to you, trippingly on the tongue. But if you mouth it, as many of our players do, I had as lief the town crier spoke my lines. . . . O, it offends me to the soul to hear a robustious periwig-pated fellow tear a passion to tatters, to very rags, to split the ears of the groundlings. . . . And let those that play your clowns speak no more than is set down for them, for there be of them that will themselves laugh, to set on some quantity of barren spectators to laugh too, though in the meantime some necessary question of the play be then to be considered. That's villainous and shows a most pitiful ambition in the fool that uses it. (3.2.1–47)

Finally, we can quote again from the passage cited earlier in this introduction, concerning the boy actors who played the female roles. Cleopatra imagines with horror a theatrical version of her activities with Antony:

> The quick comedians
> Extemporally will stage us, and present
> Our Alexandrian revels: Antony
> Shall be brought drunken forth, and I shall see
> Some squeaking Cleopatra boy my greatness
> I' th' posture of a whore.   (5.2.216–21)

It is impossible to know how much weight to put on such passages—perhaps Shakespeare was just being modest about his theater's abilities—but it is easy enough to think that he was unhappy with some aspects of Elizabethan production. Probably no production can fully satisfy a playwright, and for that matter, few productions can fully satisfy *us;* we regret this or that cut, this or that way of costuming the play, this or that bit of business.

One's first thought may be this: Why don't they just do "authentic" Shakespeare, "straight" Shakespeare, the play as Shakespeare wrote it? But as we read the plays—words written to be performed—it sometimes becomes clear that we do not know *how* to perform them. For instance, in *Antony and Cleopatra* Antony, the Roman general who has succumbed to Cleopatra and to Egyptian ways, says, "The nobleness of life / Is to do thus" (1.1.36–37). But what is "thus"? Does Antony at this point embrace Cleopatra? Does he embrace and kiss her? (There are, by the way, very few scenes of kissing on Shakespeare's stage, possibly because boys played the female roles.) Or does he make a sweeping gesture, indicating the Egyptian way of life?

This is not an isolated example; the plays are filled with lines that call for gestures, but we are not sure what the gestures should be. *Interpretation* is inevitable. Consider a passage in *Hamlet*. In 3.1, Polonius persuades his daughter, Ophelia, to talk to Hamlet while Polonius and Claudius eavesdrop. The two men conceal themselves, and Hamlet encounters Ophelia. At 3.1.131 Hamlet suddenly says to her, "Where's your father?" Why does Hamlet, apparently out of nowhere—they have not been talking about Polonius—ask this question? Is this an example of the "antic disposition" (fantastic behavior) that Hamlet earlier (1.5.172) had told Horatio and others—including us—he would display? That is, is the question about the whereabouts of her father a seemingly irrational one, like his earlier question (3.1.103) to Ophelia, "Ha, ha! Are you honest?" Or, on the other hand, has Hamlet (as in many productions) suddenly glimpsed Polonius's foot protruding from beneath a drapery at the rear? That is, does Hamlet ask the question because he has suddenly seen something suspicious and now is testing Ophelia? (By the way, in productions that do give Hamlet a physical cue, it is almost always Polonius rather than Claudius who provides the clue. This itself is an act of inter- pretation on the part of the director.) Or (a third possibility) does Hamlet get a clue from Ophelia, who inadvertently betrays the spies by nervously glancing at their place of hiding? This is the interpretation used in the BBC television version, where Ophelia glances in fear toward the hiding place just after Hamlet says "Why wouldst thou be a breeder of sinners?" (121–22). Hamlet, realizing that he is being ob- served, glances here and there *before* he asks "Where's your father?" The question thus is a climax to what he has been doing while speaking the preceding lines. Or (a fourth inter- pretation) does Hamlet suddenly, without the aid of any clue whatsoever, intuitively (insightfully, mysteriously, wonder- fully) sense that someone is spying? Directors must decide, of course—and so must readers.

Recall, too, the preceding discussion of the texts of the plays, which argued that the texts—though they seem to be before us in permanent black on white—are unstable. The Signet text of *Hamlet*, which draws on the Second Quarto (1604) and the First Folio (1623) is considerably longer than any version staged in Shakespeare's time. Our version, even if spoken very briskly and played without any intermission, would take close to four hours, far beyond "the two hours' traffic of our stage" mentioned in the Prologue to *Romeo and Juliet*. (There are a few contemporary references to the dura- tion of a play, but none mentions more than three hours.) Of Shakespeare's plays, only *The Comedy of Errors*, *Macbeth*, and *The Tempest* can be done in less than three hours without cutting. And even if we take a play that exists only in a short text, *Macbeth*, we cannot claim that we are experiencing the very play that Shakespeare conceived, partly because some of the Witches' songs almost surely are non-Shakespearean additions, and partly because we are not willing to watch the play performed without an intermission and with boys in the female roles.

Further, as the earlier discussion of costumes mentioned, the plays apparently were given chiefly in contemporary, that is, in Elizabethan dress. If today we give them in the costumes that Shakespeare probably saw, the plays seem not contemporary but curiously dated. Yet if we use our own dress, we find lines of dialogue that are at odds with what we see; we may feel that the language, so clearly not our own, is inappropriate coming out of people in today's dress. A common solution, incidentally, has been to set the plays in the nineteenth century, on the grounds that this attractively distances the plays (gives them a degree of foreignness, allowing for interesting costumes) and yet doesn't put them into a museum world of Elizabethan England.

Inevitably our productions are adaptations, *our* adaptations, and inevitably they will look dated, not in a century but in twenty years, or perhaps even in a decade. Still, we cannot escape from our own conceptions. As the director Peter Brook has said, in *The Empty Space* (1968):

> It is not only the hair-styles, costumes and make-ups that look dated. All the different elements of staging—the shorthands of behavior that stand for emotions; gestures, gesticulations and tones of voice—are all fluctuating on an invisible stock exchange all the time. . . . A living theatre that thinks it can stand aloof from anything as trivial as fashion will wilt. (p. 16)

As Brook indicates, it is through today's hairstyles, costumes, makeup, gestures, gesticulations, tones of voice—this includes our *conception* of earlier hairstyles, costumes, and so forth if we stage the play in a period other than our own—that we inevitably stage the plays.

It is a truism that every age invents its own Shakespeare, just as, for instance, every age has invented its own classical world. Our view of ancient Greece, a slave-holding society in which even free Athenian women were severely circum-scribed, does not much resemble the Victorians' view of ancient Greece as a glorious democracy, just as, perhaps, our view of Victorianism itself does not much resemble theirs. We cannot claim that the Shakespeare on our stage is the true Shakespeare, but in our stage productions we find a Shakespeare that speaks to us, a Shakespeare that our ances-tors doubtless did not know but one that seems to us to be the true Shakespeare—at least for a while.

Our age is remarkable for the wide variety of kinds of staging that it uses for Shakespeare, but one development deserves special mention. This is the now common practice of race-blind or color-blind or nontraditional casting, which allows persons who are not white to play in Shakespeare. Previously blacks performing in Shakespeare were limited to a mere three roles, Othello, Aaron (in *Titus Andronicus*), and the Prince of Morocco (in *The Merchant of Venice*), and there were no roles at all for Asians. Indeed, African-Americans rarely could play even one of these three roles, since they were not welcome in white companies. Ira Aldridge (c.1806–1867), a black actor of undoubted talent, was forced to make his living by performing Shakespeare in England and in Europe, where he could play not only Othello but also—in whiteface—other tragic roles such as King Lear. Paul Robeson (1898–1976) made theatrical his-tory when he played Othello in London in 1930, and there was some talk about bringing the production to the United States, but there was more talk about whether American audiences would tolerate the sight of a black man—a real black man, not a white man in blackface—kissing and then killing a white woman. The idea was tried out in summer stock in 1942, the reviews were enthusiastic, and in the fol-lowing year Robeson opened on Broadway in a production that ran an astounding 296 performances. An occasional all-black company sometimes performed Shakespeare's plays, but otherwise blacks (and other minority members) were in effect shut out from performing Shakespeare. Only since about 1970 has it been common for nonwhites to play major roles along with whites. Thus, in a 1996–97 production of *Antony and Cleopatra*, a white Cleopatra, Vanessa Red-grave, played opposite a black Antony, David Harewood.

Multiracial casting is now especially common at the New York Shakespeare Festival, founded in 1954 by Joseph Papp, and in England, where even siblings such as Claudio and Isabella in *Measure for Measure* or Lear's three daughters may be of different races. Probably most viewers today soon stop worrying about the lack of realism, and move beyond the color of the performers' skin to the quality of the performance.

Nontraditional casting is not only a matter of color or race; it includes sex. In the past, occasionally a distinguished woman of the theater has taken on a male role—Sarah Bernhardt (1844–1923) as Hamlet is perhaps the most famous example—but such performances were widely regarded as eccentric. Although today there have been some performances involving cross-dressing (a drag *As You Like It* staged by the National Theatre in England in 1966 and in the United States in 1974 has achieved considerable fame in the annals of stage history), what is more interesting is the casting of women in roles that traditionally are male but that need not be. Thus, a 1993–94 English production of *Henry V* used a woman—*not* cross-dressed—in the role of the governor of Harfleur. According to Peter Holland, who reviewed the production in *Shakespeare Survey* 48 (1995), "having a female Governor of Harfleur feminized the city and provided a direct response to the horrendous threat of rape and murder that Henry had offered, his language and her body in direct connection and opposition" (p. 210). Ten years from now the device may not play so effectively, but today it speaks to us. Shakespeare, born in the Elizabethan Age, has been dead nearly four hundred years, yet he is, as Ben Jonson said, "not of an age but for all time." We must understand, however, that he is "for all time" precisely because each age finds in his abundance something for itself and something of itself.

And here we come back to two issues discussed earlier in this introduction—the instability of the text and, curiously, the Bacon/Oxford heresy concerning the authorship of the plays. *Of course* Shakespeare wrote the plays, and we should daily fall on our knees to thank him for them—and yet there is something to the idea that he is not their only author. Every editor, every director and actor, and every reader to some degree shapes them, too, for when we edit, direct, act, or read, we inevitably become Shakespeare's collaborator and re-create the plays. The plays, one might say, are so cunningly contrived that they guide our responses, tell us how we ought to feel, and make a mark on us, but (for better or for worse) we also make a mark on them.

—SYLVAN BARNET
Tufts University

Introduction

In the theater *Henry the Fifth* is renowned for its pageantry, battles and crowd scenes, its varied collection of minor characters, and the unquestioned dominance of its hero. After Shakespeare's day it first became popular as the theaters began to use ambitious stage settings and more elaborate stage management. Shakespeare's play was embellished in 1761 by a Coronation scene, and in 1839 with a moving "diorama"—an extensive panoramic view which moved across the back of the stage—that depicted the journey from Southampton to Harfleur. In recent years it has been performed in battle-dress against film sequences showing twentieth-century warfare or, as at Stratford-upon-Avon in 1964, with painstaking realism of gunsmoke and bloody shattered bodies. (Sir Laurence Olivier and Kenneth Branagh made it the subject of films.) For actors the play has always been hard work, with many changes of costume as pageantry is displaced by mobilization and then by warfare and hardship: and then there is another switch back to pageantry. But rewards are there, too, in the great number of parts that Shakespeare has individually realized for two or three episodes, or even a single scene: Mistress Quickly, Bardolph, Nym, the boy; Williams and Bates—or even a strangely effective gentleness in the one-line part of Court; Jamy, Gower, Macmorris; the Dauphin, Princess Katherine, the King of France, Montjoy, Burgundy. Press criticisms show that *Henry the Fifth* is the minor actors' opportunity; a boy or Mistress Quickly, a Princess or Burgundy can steal a large part of the notice.

Yet it also has an undoubted hero. For other history plays, the leading actor in a company might play the Bastard rather than King John, Falstaff or Hotspur rather than Prince Hal or Henry the Fourth—even Bolingbroke in preference to

Richard the Second. But here Fluellen and Pistol are the most considerable rivals to the hero, and neither is effectively present in more than six or seven scenes, or has more than incidental contact with the King.

Written in 1599, a year or so before *Hamlet*, *Henry the Fifth* was Shakespeare's last history play for ten years or more, and he appears to have taken no risks. Despite its crowd scenes and wide range of characters, it has a simple plot of wars, a battle and a peace, centered on its undoubted hero. A Chorus, before each act, encourages the audience's warmest responses, and invites its imagination to see two mighty monarchies, and follow Harry as a type of virtue, "the mirror of all Christian kings" (2.Prologue.6). For most of the play, the King appears publicly, in ceremonial consultation or address, or as leader of his army; his words are well ordered, and clearly and fully understood. When he surprises the French ambassador with defiance of the three traitors with a knowledge of their crimes, the audience has been prepared in advance so that its understanding suffers no shock. The minor characters are all dependent on Harry and yet make only occasional appearances in unconsecutive scenes, usually without the hero, so that the independent plot-interest they awaken is both small and quickly answered. Except for the French royal house, none already established has a place in the last long scene; but two entirely new characters are then introduced to eminence, Isabel and the Duke of Burgundy. The play's structure is firmly centered; its setting splendid, varied, broad. In its sweeping, general impression, and usually in performance, *Henry the Fifth* is a popular pageant play of the "star of England," and incidentally of his people and his victories.

But this view of Shakespeare's achievement will not satisfy many critics and scholars who have studied the play and resisted the confident tone of the Chorus. They can see it as a routine and unwieldy continuation of other histories, without the imaginative argumentation or consistency of earlier plays. Or, especially if they concentrate attention on the words of the hero, they can read it as a careful investigation of the human failings of a politician. (Professor Tillyard's book on the Histories, of which the relevant section is reprinted in the Commentaries, and Miss Honor Matthews' treatment of the play in her *Character and Symbol in Shakespeare's Plays* are eloquent advocates of these opposing views.) In the theater, too, the play can seem merely routine, especially in association with Shakespeare's other histories. When acted at Stratford-upon-Avon in 1951, as the fourth of a continuous series of plays, from *Richard II* and the two parts of *Henry IV*, it seemed something of an appendix. The stage designer was led to elaborate the single setting that had served for the other three plays with flags, drapes and properties. The official book on the season speaks of the play in these terms:

> By the time we reach *Henry V* the particular interest of the "presentation in cycle" is all but over.

When *Henry the Fifth* was performed at the same theater in 1964 in a longer series after the two parts of *Henry the Fourth* and before the three parts of *Henry the Sixth* and *Richard the Third*, its Harry ("the mirror of all Christian kings") was hailed as a plain man's king, a pacifist warrior or, fashionably, a self-questioning anti-hero. Shakespeare's ground plan for the hero-centered pageant-narrative can sustain very different edifices.

Indeed, in many small details of the play's structure Shakespeare seems to be guarding against too broad or relaxed a reception of the play. The comedy is carefully restricted, its incidents being short-lived and its characters severely limited in sensibility, that is in vocabulary and ideas. And on the other hand, Shakespeare used contrasts between consecutive scenes to sharpen the audience's appreciation: so Harry's "Once more unto the breach, dear friends . . .", confident that there is none "so mean and base" that has not a "noble luster" in his eyes (3.1.1ff.), is followed by Bardolph's mimicry and by thoughts of "a pot of ale, and safety" (3.2.1–13); such "friends" have to be driven to the breach by Fluellen calling them "dogs" and "cullions." The broad expanse of the stage-picture has no dark shadows in which attention can dwell and no individual issues on which it can concentrate; but, cunningly, its lines are kept sharp and agile. In particular Shakespeare has ensured by small details that the central figure can arouse the keenest perceptions.

The duologue of two bishops that prepares the audience for Harry's first appearance presents two differing qualities in the man without suggesting conflict: his "grace," or "celestial spirits," and his "policy" that makes even God's ministers circumspect towards him. His own early speeches easily command the responses he wishes from those presented with him, thus suggesting a superior awareness not fully explicit in his words; and for all their verbal control, they are fired by a wide range of ideas, thus hinting at a varied awareness stretching beyond the immediate context. His reply to the French ambassador (1.2.259ff.), for instance, gives jest for jest, mentions his "wilder days" with equal firmness as his present "majesty," and moves lightly from his own will ("I will keep my state . . . When I do rouse me . . . But I will rise there . . . I will dazzle") to the will of God ("But this lies all within the will of God . . . in whose name . . ."). These last transitions may also cause some of the audience to see Harry as a limited figure, apparently unaware of the size of the assumptions he makes; and so may the manner in which he speaks of widows, curses and tears with no slackened pace or tender epithet. Yet these incipient inquiries are never made a dramatic issue by presenting alternative courses, or by criticism of Harry on stage, or by a hint of his private thoughts, such as Shakespeare had already achieved for Prince Hal or Henry the Fourth and was to develop so fully in *Julius Caesar* and *Hamlet* written one or two years later. The Chorus is at hand to keep the picture fully animated and expectation forward, with:

> Now all the youth of England are on fire,
> And silken dalliance in the wardrobe lies.
>
> (2.Prologue.1–2)

So the predominant focus is maintained, a wide view of a pageant narrative.

But even the first act is not superficial. Because Shakespeare has not sharpened the focus by his usual devices as he could so effectively have done, this needs to be especially noticed. The audience's appreciation is quickened without bringing the hero closely and intimately to its attention; there is no soliloquy, no aside, no self-conscious or nervous speech, no sudden, unprepared exit or utterance, or transition of mood. The audience's view is centered on Harry and its perception is acute, but Harry is always the central figure of a group, and the audience knows him in the same kind of terms as it knows the other characters.

The second act, like the first, gives no occasion for an intense focus on Harry, but Shakespeare has ensured still greater clarity, and more deeply questioning responses. Among the noisy quarrels of Pistol and his fellows comes news that Falstaff is sick and broken in heart after Harry has banished him; and this, in turn, is followed by the contrasting affirmation, "The King is a good king . . . it must be as it may. . . . lambkins, we will live"; here the audience cannot give one simple emotional response. Then Harry in public discloses the treachery of three friends, elaborating formally on the evil hearts under their apparent goodness:

> thy fall hath left a kind of blot
> To mark the full-fraught man and best indued
> With some suspicion.   (2.2.138–40)

The audience is being made aware that the wide scene can be viewed in more than one way. Harry himself may be moved, for before pronouncing judgment he speaks a short sentence:

> I will weep for thee;
> For this revolt of thine, methinks, is like
> Another fall man.   (140–42)

This is not a clear intensification of the focus in a deeply revealing soliloquy, for the words are spoken formally for all to hear; but it makes sure that any questioning aroused by this incident may touch Harry as well as others. Then he concludes the scene securely, with a final conciseness that is habitual to him:

> Let us deliver
> Our puissance into the hand of God,
> Putting it straight in expedition.
> Cheerly to sea; the signs of war advance:
> No king of England, if not King of France! (189–93)

But now even this does not remain simple: Harry's confident committal into the "hand of God" is followed by the hostess' reflective account of Falstaff fumbling with the sheets and playing with flowers, and crying out "God, God, God!" three or four times:

> Now I, to comfort him, bid him 'a should not think of God; I hoped
> there was no need to trouble himself with any such thoughts yet.
> So 'a bade me lay more clothes on his feet.   (2.3.20ff.)

Harry went to France asserting that he went hand in hand with God; Falstaff is said to have gone "away and it had been any christom child"; and then Pistol leaves to follow the King:

> Let us to France, like horse-leeches, my boys,
> To suck, to suck, the very blood to suck!   (56–57)

Contrasts sharpen the wide view; and some of the audience, if they stopped to consider, would think they knew more of the over-all issues than any one of the dramatis personae.

Bickering at the French Court, differences among Harry's soldiers, the charm, absurdity and prim bawdiness of the French Princess learning English, all may cause the audience to question, in a general way, the motives and comprehension of the characters. And Harry's invocation of the "fleshed soldier, rough and hard of heart . . . With conscience wide as hell" as a threat to Harfleur (3.3.1–43), may heighten its sense of what is involved and cause it to question Harry's attitude to the brutality he is prepared to encourage. Then, as the battle of Agincourt approaches, his reply to Montjoy, the French Herald, shows all his earlier resource—vaunting wit, pride, modest self-blame, confidence in God, unhesitating threat of carnage, concise utterance. Expectation for the crisis of the action is heightened and wide, but in a new manner "objective" or watchful. The audience has seen more aspects of each figure in the picture than those figures seem to have seen themselves.

Yet the battle is prepared for in leisurely manner. The Chorus describes its setting with careful artistry, as in the multiple epithets of "cripple tardy-gaited night," or the Spenserian prettiness of "paly flames." Then Harry, disguised in a great cloak, wanders alone, meeting his various soldiers. He is no longer attended as a king, and speaking as a man in isolation he comes closer to the audience. Two very brief soliloquies are his first in the play. Then, talking to Williams, a tendentious, "ordinary" soldier, he considers the responsibility for life and death and deeds in a new vein:

> some (peradventure) had on them the guilt of premeditated and contrived murder; some, of beguiling virgins ... some, making the wars their bulwark, that have before gored the gentle bosom of peace with pillage and robbery. Now, if these men have defeated the law and outrun native punishment, though they can outstrip men, they have no wings to fly from God.   (4.1.165–73)

This is the voice of Hamlet

> That skull had a tongue in it, and could sing once. How the knave jowls it to the ground, as if 'twere Cain's jaw-bone, that did the first murder! This might be the pate of a politician, which this ass now o'erreaches, one that would circumvent God, might it not?
>   (5.1.76–81)

These thoughts were to stay in Shakespeare's mind as he wrote *Macbeth,* five or six years later:

> Faith, here's an equivocator, that could swear in both the scales against either scale; who committed treason enough for God's sake, yet could not equivocate to heaven.   (2.3.8–11)

Despite its length, Harry's meditative, elaborating prose has the conviction to keep Williams silent until its conclusion, when his only comment is simple agreement. For the audience, the unusual lack of concision, meter and pace gives Harry a new voice, helping to realize the new range of his thought and feeling which may well embody some of their own incipient comments on the action. As the soldiers move off and Harry is alone, the dramatic focus will be, for the first time, potentially intense and deep. There follows a questioning, yet formal, consideration of the cares of kingship, and a lyrical, yet still formal, consideration of a peasant's laboring life. This is yet another aspect of Harry's response, but he seems to shape his thoughts consciously and concludes as if presenting another concise summing-up in public. When Erpingham enters to call him to battle, the widest view seems about to be reestablished. But this valued messenger is sent away and Harry falls on his knees and prays:

> O God of battles, steel my soldiers' hearts.   (4.1.294)

He knows their weakness:

> Possess them not with fear! Take from them now
> The sense of reck'ning, or th' opposèd numbers
> Pluck their hearts from them.   (295–97)

Then he speaks of himself, urgently, repetitively, impulsively. He mentions precisely a fear which hitherto has not been made an issue anywhere on the surface of the drama:

> Not today, O Lord,
> O, not today, think not upon the fault
> My father made in compassing the crown!
> I Richard's body have interrèd new,
> And on it have bestowed more contrite tears
> Than from it issued forcèd drops of blood.
> Five hundred poor I have in yearly pay.   (297–303)

The expression of purpose—"to pardon blood"—is emphasized by word order and by meter, and twice the lines break before their end, to give urgency and weight to a new idea:

> Five hundred poor I have in yearly pay,
> Who twice a day their withered hands hold up
> Toward heaven, to pardon blood;
> And I have built two chantries,
> Where the sad and solemn priests sing still
> For Richard's soul. More will I do:
> Though all that I can do is nothing worth;
> Since that my penitence comes after all,
> Imploring pardon.   (303–11)

There is a half-line pause, then Gloucester enters and Harry is once more the leader, assured and ready:

> *Gloucester.* My liege!
> *King.* My brother Gloucester's voice? Ay.
>   I know thy errand; I will go with thee.
>   The day, my friends, and all things stay for me.   (311–14)

This sequence has shown Harry as king, son and man, conscious of his responsibility and that of other men in war as in peace, and acknowledging a fear within himself, an awareness that, though he may outstrip the judgment of men, he has "no wings to fly from God." As he prepared for battle a short moment of intense focus has revealed his inmost secrets, and his knowledge that no human help can redress the past.

It is possible to read Harry's prayer as another calculated maneuver—to judge, with Una Ellis-Fermor in her *Frontiers of Drama,* that:

> when he prays, . . . he is more than ever in the council chamber driving an astute bargain, a piece of shrewd diplomacy, between one king and another.

But this is to disregard the newly urgent style of utterance, and the considerable preparation for this moment. Harry had perhaps wept for the traitors as they reminded him that a "full-fraught" man may be suspected. He had earnestly commanded the archbishop to justify his title to the French crown with

> conscience washed
> As pure as sin with baptism.   (1.2.31–32)

Moreover the need for an honest heart and Harry's equal responsibility with all men are taken up in the following scenes in ways which can betray to the audience's intensified interest his deep concern with these issues.

His address to the soldiers before battle is not a spurring on of others, in the vein of "Once more unto the breach, dear friends, once more." Compared with that conjuring up of the blood before Harfleur, it is thoughtful:

> . . . if it be a sin to covet honor,
> I am the most offending soul alive.   (4.3.28–29)

Because it is their feast day, he remembers the two noble brothers, Crispin and Crispian, who during the Roman persecution served as shoemakers yet were still martyred for their obvious Christianity; and they become an image for his men in battle:

> We few, we happy few, we band of brothers;
> For he today that sheds his blood with me
> Shall be my brother; be he ne'er so vile,
> This day shall gentle his condition.   (60–63)

Harry covets honor in his heart and would have his soldiers do so with him; and this is his battle cry. In fight he is still valiant, gay almost with hardiness, angry, ruthless, efficient. He is again the Harry of the first three acts, ready in anger to kill all his prisoners. But afterwards there are further reminders of his inward knowledge and need. Perhaps the repeated insistence with which he gives all credit to God is one. Certainly when Fluellen, the robustly confident Welshman, claims brotherhood—

> I am your Majesty's countryman, I care not who know it. . . . I need not to be ashamed of your Majesty, praised be God, so long as your Majesty is an honest man—   (4.7.114–18)

Harry answers directly and simply, "God keep me so"—that is an "honest man"—and only then turns to public, urgent matters. Later, when Williams excuses his quarrel, his words must strike the monarch more deeply than the puzzled soldier could guess:

> All offenses, my lord, come from the heart: never came any from mine that might offend your Majesty.   (4.8.46–48)

Some of the audience, at least, will remember that this king has recognized an "offending" heart within himself. (As Shakespeare directed Harry to listen to Williams after battle, the seed for the epilogue to *The Tempest* may have been in his mind: "As you from crimes would pardoned be, Let your indulgence set me free.")

In that *Henry the Fifth* has a central scene of intense focus which shows the King acknowledging his guilt, it is obviously indebted to *Henry the Fourth, Part Two*. But Shakespeare has modified his purpose and his technique. Harry does not win peace like his father, only a recognition of the need for pardon; moreover, he remains a figure in the center of others. In this play, the predominantly wide view is reestablished and the audience's inward knowledge of Harry's personal crisis is used to deepen the view of the whole scene, and of the many other characters to whom, unlike Henry the Fourth, this king is dramatically related. Williams, Fluellen, Montjoy, and the soldiers are only the first to reenter the picture, the whole fifth act sustains and develops this experience.

It begins with the ludicrous unmasking of the braggart, Pistol, who is forced to eat Fluellen's leek. This is more than a comic counterpart to heroism, for he is left alone onstage and in a direct and immediate soliloquy he may briefly provoke empathetic sympathy:

> Old I do wax, and from my weary limbs
> Honor is cudgeled.   (5.1.87–88)

The moment is passed as he gathers confidence and decides to return to England to cheat and steal. And the audience's view is fully extended as the kings of France and England and their nobility fill the stage for the final scene in quiet and formal meeting. In a long, deliberate speech, the peacemaker, the Duke of Burgundy, describes France ravaged by war and a generation of her sons growing

> like savages—as soldiers will,
> That nothing do but meditate on blood—
>   (5.2.59–60)

The whole play, its action and consequences, passes in general review, seen this time with French eyes—or rather with a timeless concern with the arts and sciences of peace, and with natural affections. This new perspective is generalized, but as the two parties leave the stage to debate the terms of peace, Harry remains with Katherine, Princess of France, and her maid: here the dramatic interest is as narrow as before Agincourt. As Harry woos his bride, he speaks sometimes as if in soliloquy, for she cannot understand all he says. It is a complex scene: clearly this is to be a political, but also a personally felt, marriage; clearly Harry offers himself as a simple man, but he does so with wit and eloquence; clearly he is confident and a conqueror, but he is also suitor. And as he warms to his theme he speaks again, directly and with immediacy, of a "good heart":

> a good leg will fall, a straight back will stoop, a black beard will turn white, a curled pate will grow bald, a fair face will wither, a full eye will wax hollow: but a good heart, Kate, is the sun and the moon, or rather, the sun, and not the moon, for it shines bright and never changes, but keeps his course truly.   (163–70)

Katherine questions "Is is possible dat I sould love de ennemie of France?" And he can only answer with a riddle:

> No, it is not possible . . . but in loving me you should love the friend of France: for I love France so well, that I will not part with a village of it—I will have it all mine. And, Kate, when France is mine and I am yours, then yours is France, and you are mine. (176–82)

He gets the deserved response: "I cannot tell wat is dat," and the plain soldier is forced to attempt "false French." Yet now they speak more freely, and as Harry's blood "begins to flatter" him that he is loved, he speaks lightly of his father's ambition, which had held him in prayer before battle:

> Now beshrew my father's ambition! He was thinking of civil wars when he got me, therefore was I created with a stubborn outside, with an aspect of iron, that when I come to woo ladies, I fright them.   (233–37)

Too much should not be made of this reference; it shows a relaxation of mind, not a conscious change of attitude. Soon, against the "custom" of France, they kiss, and are silent together. And then, gently and with an intimate, relaxing jest, Harry acknowledges what has been given and taken, and understood without words:

> You have witchcraft in your lips, Kate: there is more eloquence in a sugar touch of them than in the tongues of the French Council . . .   (288–91)

The stage fills again, the relaxed mood being sustained by Burgundy's heavy teasing of the bridegroom. The latter still insists on receiving the cities of the bride's dowry and the title of Inheritor of France, but with a general "Amen," the contesting sides stand solemnly side by side in agreement. As the focus thus widens fully again, and steadies, there is another silence as Harry kisses Kate before them all, as his "sovereign Queen." But the view is also acute and questioning. Shakespeare has not attempted to show a love match, or a union in which the audience may be easily confident; and now the bride's mother reminds them frankly of:

> . . . fell jealousy,
> Which troubles oft the bed of blessed marriage.
>
> (375–76)

The long wooing scene—far more elaborate than at first seems to be required by the dramatic context—has served to show afresh and with an intermittent intensity the need for an honest heart, and the danger and embarrassment of relying on words alone; and, in the kiss, it suggested an inward understanding, peace, affection, unity that may be a greater solvent, a more powerful reorganizing power, than words or battles: the silence of the kiss is a shared silence in which the audience instinctively participates and must make its own judgment.

Representatives of two societies take up, with remembrances of past action and hopes and prayers for the future, their final positions of concord; and Harry, speaking formally within the wide picture, closes the play with a further pointer to the heart of all matters:

> . . . we'll take your oath,
> And all the peers', for surety of our leagues.

> Then shall I swear to Kate, and you to me,
> *And may our oaths well kept and prosp'rous be!**(383–86)

Shakespeare has finished his long series of history plays by presenting a group of people standing together: behind appearances and oaths there is need for an "honest heart"; within the wide range the audience is invited to search for signs of inward peace, good faith, affection, trust, of that which "never changes, but keeps his course truly." When the stage empties and the Chorus announces the end of the action, he also speaks of later times when all France was lost and England bled again. If this play has received its intended "acceptance," it will not be destructive or irrelevant to remind the audience that the final, peaceful grouping was neither fully honest nor fully permanent.

Henry the Fifth is a hero-centered historical pageant that presents a clear narrative and varied characters. In that, it differs from Shakespeare's earlier histories, with their concern with political necessity or "commodity," with rebellion, power and conscience, and with God's providence. But it was not an easy, or routine, declension from a more serious drama. The play tries to relate the personal, instinctive and affectionate truth of human relationships, exemplified in the meeting of Kate and Harry, with warfare, politics and national rivalries; and it has effected this in the wide range of characters that is such an important aid to the full acceptance of this play. Mistress Quickly's account of Falstaff's death, Fluellen's incongruous loyalty and familiarity with his king, Williams' defense of his honest heart, Pistol's recognition of the end of his campaign, and Kate and Harry's kiss, all represent the necessary element of human understanding, as eloquent as Burgundy's general evocation of the virtues of peace. The audience's involvement in these moments is of a different nature from its involvement in the narrative of war and politics, and is of pervasive, because unthinking, importance in the reception of the play as a whole.

—JOHN RUSSELL BROWN
University of Michigan

* Editor's italics.

[Dramatis Personae

Chorus
King Henry the Fifth
Dukes of Gloucester and Bedford, brothers of the
    King
Duke of Exeter, uncle of the King
Duke of York, cousin of the King
Earls of Salisbury, Westmoreland, Warwick, and
    Cambridge
Archbishop of Canterbury
Bishop of Ely
Lord Scroop
Sir Thomas Grey
Sir Thomas Erpingham
Gower, Fluellen, Macmorris, Jamy, officers in the
    English army
John Bates, Alexander Court, Michael Williams, sol-
    diers in the English army
Pistol, Nym, Bardolph
Boy
An English Herald
Charles the Sixth, King of France
Lewis, the Dauphin
Dukes of Burgundy, Orleans, Bourbon, and Bretagne
The Constable of France
Rambures and Grandpré, French lords
Governor of Harfleur
Montjoy, a French herald
Ambassadors to King Henry
Isabel, Queen of France
Katherine, daughter of the French King and Queen
Alice, an attendant to Katherine
Hostess Quickly of an Eastcheap tavern, married to
    Pistol
Lords, Ladies, Officers, Soldiers, Citizens, Messengers
    and Attendants

Scene: England; France]

The Life of Henry the Fifth

Enter Prologue.

O for a Muse of fire,°¹ that would ascend
The brightest heaven of invention:°
A kingdom for a stage, princes to act,
And monarchs to behold the swelling° scene!
Then should the warlike Harry, like himself,°   *5*
Assume the port of Mars,° and at his heels
(Leashed in, like hounds) should famine, sword, and
    fire
Crouch for employment. But pardon, gentles° all,
The flat unraisèd spirits° that hath dared
On this unworthy scaffold° to bring forth   *10*
So great an object. Can this cockpit hold
The vasty fields of France? Or may we cram
Within this wooden *O*° the very casques°
That did affright the air at Agincourt?
O, pardon—since a crooked figure° may   *15*
Attest in little place a million;

¹The degree sign (°) indicates a footnote, which is keyed to the text by
line number. Text references are printed in **boldface** type; the annotation
follows in roman type.
1 Prologue   1 **fire** (1) most airy (sublime) of the four elements (2) warlike nature (cf. line 6 below and 2 Prologue 1)   2 **invention** imaginative
creation   4 **swelling** stately   5 **like himself** (1) incomparable (2)
worthy of himself   6 **port of Mars** bearing of the god of war   8 **gentles** gentlefolk   9 **flat unraisèd spirits** i.e., dull, uninspired actors and
playwright   10 **scaffold** stage (technical term)   13 **wooden *O*** small
wooden circle; i.e., the theater of the King's Men (at the first performance, this was probably the Curtain)   13 **very casques** i.e., helmets,
even without the men who wore them   15 **crooked figure** i.e., a nought,
that could change 100,000 into 1,000,000

And let us, ciphers° to this great accompt,°
On your imaginary° forces work.
Suppose within the girdle of these walls
20   Are now confined two mighty monarchies,
Whose high, uprearèd and abutting fronts°
The perilous narrow ocean parts asunder.°
Piece out our imperfections with your thoughts:
Into a thousand parts divide one man
25   And make imaginary puissance.°
Think, when we talk of horses, that you see them
Printing their proud° hoofs i' th' receiving earth;
For 'tis your thoughts that now must deck our kings,
Carry them° here and there, jumping o'er times,
30   Turning th' accomplishment of many years
Into an hourglass; for the which supply,°
Admit me Chorus to this history;
Who, Prologue-like, your humble patience pray,
Gently to hear, kindly to judge our play.   *Exit.*

17 **ciphers** nothings   17 **accompt** (1) sum total (2) story   18 **imaginary** imaginative   21 **fronts** frontiers   21–22 **high ... asunder** i.e., the cliffs of Dover and Calais, on opposite sides of the English Channel   25 **puissance** armed force (a trisyllable)   27 **proud** spirited   29 **them** i.e., thoughts (?), kings (?)   31 **for the which supply** to help you in which

ACT 1

*Enter the two Bishops [the Archbishop] of
Canterbury and [the Bishop of] Ely.*

Canterbury. My lord, I'll tell you, that self° bill is
    urged
  Which in th' eleventh year of the last king's reign°
  Was like,° and had indeed against us passed
  But that the scambling° and unquiet time
  Did push it out of farther question.   *5*

Ely. But how, my lord, shall we resist it now?

Canterbury. It must be thought on. If it pass against
    us,
  We lose the better half of our possession;
  For all the temporal° lands which men devout
  By testament have given to the Church   *10*
  Would they strip from us; being valued thus—
  As much as would maintain, to the King's honor,
  Full fifteen earls and fifteen hundred knights,
  Six thousand and two hundred good esquires,
  And to relief of lazars,° and weak age   *15*
  Of indigent faint souls, past corporal toil,

1.1.1 **self** same 2 **eleventh ... reign** i.e., 1410 3 **like** likely (to be
passed) 4 **scambling** scuffling, disordered 9 **temporal** secular (as
opposed to sacred) 15 **lazars** lepers

A hundred almshouses right well supplied;
And to the coffers of the King beside,
A thousand pounds by th' year. Thus runs the bill.

Ely. This would drink deep.

20 *Canterbury.*   'Twould drink the cup and all.

Ely. But what prevention?

Canterbury. The King is full of grace and fair regard.°

Ely. And a true lover of the holy Church.

Canterbury. The courses of his youth promised it not.
25   The breath no sooner left his father's body
    But that his wildness, mortified° in him,
    Seemed to die too; yea, at that very moment
    Consideration° like an angel came
    And whipped th' offending Adam° out of him,
30   Leaving his body as a paradise
    T' envelop and contain celestial spirits.
    Never was such a sudden scholar made;
    Never came reformation in a flood
    With such a heady currance° scouring faults;
35   Nor never Hydra-headed° willfulness
    So soon did lose his seat°—and all at once—
    As in this king.

Ely.   We are blessèd in the change.

Canterbury. Hear him but reason° in divinity,
    And, all-admiring, with an inward wish
40   You would desire the King were made a prelate;
    Hear him debate of commonwealth affairs,
    You would say it hath been all in all° his study;
    List° his discourse of war, and you shall hear
    A fearful battle rend'red you in music;°

---

22 **regard** repute   26 **mortified** dead (a religious usage)   28 **Consideration** meditation   29 **whipped th' offending Adam** drove original sin   34 **heady currance** headlong current   35 **Hydra-headed** Hydra was a mythological beast with nine heads, growing two more for every one cut off   36 **seat** throne   38 **reason** debate   42 **all in all** all things in all respects   43 **List** listen to   44 **rend'red you in music** recounted with harmonious and stirring eloquence

Turn him to any cause of policy,°   45
The Gordian knot° of it he will unloose,
Familiar as his garter; that when he speaks,
The air, a chartered libertine,° is still,
And the mute wonder° lurketh in men's ears
To steal his sweet and honeyed sentences;°   50
So that the art and practic part of life
Must be the mistress to this theoric;°
Which is a wonder how his Grace° should glean it,
Since his addiction was to courses vain,
His companies° unlettered, rude, and shallow,   55
His hours filled up with riots, banquets, sports;
And never noted in him any study,
Any retirement, any sequestration
From open haunts and popularity.°

Ely. The strawberry grows underneath the nettle,   60
And wholesome berries thrive and ripen best
Neighbored by fruit of baser quality;
And so the Prince obscured his contemplation°
Under the veil of wildness, which (no doubt)
Grew like the summer grass, fastest by night,   65
Unseen, yet crescive in his faculty.°

Canterbury. It must be so, for miracles are ceased;°
And therefore we must needs admit the means°
How things are perfected.

Ely.   But, my good lord,
How now for mitigation of this bill   70

---

45 **cause of policy** political problem 46 **Gordian knot** (tied by
Gordius when chosen King of Gordium; the oracle declared that whoever
loosened it would rule Asia; Alexander the Great cut through it with his
sword) 48 **chartered libertine** one licensed to go his own way
49 **wonder** wonderer 50 **sentences** sayings 51–52 **art ... theoric**
practice and experience must have taught him theory 53 **Grace**
Majesty (a formal title) 55 **companies** companions 59 **open haunts
and popularity** public places and familiarity 63 **contemplation** study
of life 66 **crescive in his faculty** growing because that is its nature 67 **miracles are ceased** (protestants believed miracles ceased to
occur after the revelation of Christ) 68 **means** i.e., natural cause

Urged by the commons?° Doth his Majesty
Incline to it, or no?

Canterbury.   He seems indifferent;°
Or rather swaying more upon our part
Than cherishing th' exhibiters° against us;
75 For I have made an offer to his Majesty—
Upon our spiritual Convocation,°
And in regard of causes° now in hand,
Which I have opened° to his Grace at large,
As touching France—to give a greater sum
80 Than ever at one time the clergy yet
Did to his predecessors part withal.

Ely. How did this offer seem received, my lord?

Canterbury. With good acceptance of his Majesty;
Save that there was not time enough to hear,
85 As I perceived his Grace would fain have done,
The severals and unhidden passages°
Of his true titles to some certain dukedoms,
And generally to the crown and seat of France,
Derived from Edward, his great-grandfather.

90 *Ely.* What was th' impediment that broke this off?

Canterbury. The French ambassador upon that instant
Craved audience; and the hour I think is come
To give him hearing. Is it four o'clock?

Ely. It is.

95 *Canterbury.* Then go we in to know his embassy;
Which I could with a ready guess declare
Before the Frenchman speak a word of it.

Ely. I'll wait upon you, and I long to hear it.   *Exeunt.*

---

71 **commons** House of Commons in the parliament of England   72 **indifferent** impartial   74 **exhibiters** presenters of the bill   76 **Convocation** formal meeting of the clergy   77 **causes** affairs   78 **opened**
revealed   86 **severals and unhidden passages** details and clear (obvious)
lines of descent

[Scene 2. *The presence chamber in the palace.*]

Enter the King, Humphrey [Duke of Gloucester],
Bedford, Clarence, Warwick, Westmoreland, and
Exeter, [with Attendants].

King. Where is my gracious Lord of Canterbury?

Exeter. Not here in presence.

King.　　　　　　　　　　Send for him, good uncle.

Westmoreland. Shall we call in th' ambassador, my
　liege?

King. Not yet, my cousin.° We would be resolved,°
　Before we hear him, of some things of weight　　　　5
　That task° our thoughts concerning us and France.

Enter two Bishops [the Archbishop of
Canterbury and the Bishop of Ely].

Canterbury. God and his angels guard your sacred
　throne,
　And make you long become it!

King.　　　　　　　　　　Sure we thank you.
　My learnèd lord, we pray you to proceed,
　And justly and religiously unfold　　　　　　　　10
　Why the Law Salique, that they have in France,
　Or should or° should not bar us in our claim.
　And God forbid, my dear and faithful lord,
　That you should fashion, wrest, or bow your read-
　　ing,°
　Or nicely charge your understanding soul　　　　15
　With opening titles miscreate,° whose right°

1.2.4 **cousin** kinsman　4 **be resolved** have doubts removed　6 **task**
burden　12 **Or ... or** either ... or　14 **reading** interpretation
15–16 **nicely ... miscreate** by subtle reasoning lay to the charge of your
soul—that knows right and wrong—the fault of advancing illegitimate
claims　16 **right** claim

Suits not in native colors with the truth;°
For God doth know how many now in health
Shall drop their blood in approbation°
20   Of what your reverence shall incite us to.
Therefore take heed how you impawn° our person,
How you awake our sleeping sword of war.
We charge you in the name of God, take heed;
For never two such kingdoms did contend
25   Without much fall of blood, whose guiltless drops
Are every one a woe, a sore complaint
'Gainst him whose wrongs° gives edge unto the
        swords
That makes such waste in brief mortality.
Under this conjuration, speak my lord:
30   For we will hear, note, and believe in heart
That what you speak is in your conscience washed
As pure as sin with baptism.

Canterbury. Then hear me, gracious Sovereign, and
        you peers,
That owe yourselves, your lives, and services
35   To this imperial throne. There is no bar
To make° against your Highness' claim to France
But this which they produce from Pharamond:°
"In terram Salicam mulieres ne succedant";
"No woman shall succeed in Salique land."
40   Which Salique land the French unjustly gloze°
To be the realm of France, and Pharamond
The founder of this law and female bar.
Yet their own authors faithfully affirm
That the land Salique is in Germany,
45   Between the floods of Sala and of Elbe;
Where Charles the Great having subdued the
        Saxons,
There left behind and settled certain French;
Who, holding in disdain the German women
For some dishonest manners° of their life,

17 **Suits . . . truth** i.e., plainly told would not be taken as true   19 **approbation** support   21 **impawn** pledge, hazard   27 **wrongs** wrongdoings   36 **make** i.e., be made   37 **Pharamond** legendary king of Salian Franks   40 **gloze** interpret   49 **dishonest manners** unchaste conduct

Established then this law: to wit, no female   50
Should be inheritrix in Salique land;
Which Salique (as I said) 'twixt Elbe and Sala
Is at this day in Germany, called Meisen.
Then doth it well appear the Salique Law
Was not devisèd for the realm of France;   55
Nor did the French possess the Salique land
Until four hundred one and twenty years
After defunction° of King Pharamond,
Idly supposed the founder of this law,
Who died within the year of our redemption   60
Four hundred twenty-six; and Charles the Great
Subdued the Saxons, and did seat the French
Beyond the river Sala, in the year
Eight hundred five. Besides, their writers say,
King Pepin,° which deposèd Childeric,   65
Did, as heir general,° being descended
Of Blithild, which was daughter to King Clothair,
Make claim and title to the crown of France.
Hugh Capet also—who usurped the crown
Of Charles the Duke of Lorraine, sole heir male   70
Of the true line and stock of Charles the Great—
To find° his title with some shows of truth,
Though in pure truth it was corrupt and naught,
Conveyed° himself as heir to th' Lady Lingard,
Daughter to Charlemain,° who was the son   75
To Lewis the Emperor, and Lewis the son
Of Charles the Great. Also King Lewis the Tenth,°
Who was sole heir to the usurper Capet,
Could not keep quiet in his conscience,
Wearing the crown of France, till satisfied   80
That fair Queen Isabel, his grandmother,
Was lineal° of the Lady Ermengard,
Daughter to Charles the foresaid Duke of Lorraine;
By the which marriage the line of Charles the Great
Was reunited to the crown of France.   85

58 **defunction** discharge, death   65 **Pepin** King of Franks   66 **general** through male or female line of descent   72 **find** provide   74 **Conveyed** passed off   75 **Charlemain** (Holinshed's error for Charles the Bold)   77 **Tenth** (Holinshed's error for Ninth)   82 **lineal** lineally descended

So that, as clear as is the summer's sun,
King Pepin's title and Hugh Capet's claim,
King Lewis his satisfaction,° all appear
To hold in right and title of the female:
90 So do the kings of France unto this day.
Howbeit they would hold up this Salique Law
To bar your Highness claiming from the female,
And rather choose to hide them in a net
Than amply to imbar their crooked titles°
95 Usurped from you and your progenitors.

King. May I with right and conscience make this
   claim?

Canterbury. The sin upon my head, dread Sovereign!
For in the Book of Numbers is it writ:
When the man dies, let the inheritance
100 Descend unto the daughter. Gracious lord,
Stand for your own, unwind your bloody flag,
Look back into your mighty ancestors;
Go, my dread lord, to your great-grandsire's° tomb,
From whom you claim; invoke his warlike spirit,
105 And your great-uncle's, Edward the Black Prince,
Who on the French ground played a tragedy,°
Making defeat on the full power° of France,
Whiles his most mighty father on a hill
Stood smiling, to behold his lion's whelp
110 Forage in blood of French nobility.
O noble English, that could entertain
With half their forces° the full pride of France,
And let another half stand laughing by,
All out of work, and cold for° action!

115 *Ely.* Awake remembrance of these valiant dead
And with your puissant arm renew their feats.

---

88 **his satisfaction** (see line 80)   93–94 **to hide . . . titles** to take refuge
in a tangle of sophistical arguments than make the most of (bar in,
secure) their own false claims (by admitting female succession)   103
great-grandsire's i.e., Edward III's (whose mother, Isabella, was
daughter of Philip IV of France)   106 **a tragedy** i.e., battle of
Crécy   107 **power** army   112 **half their forces** (one third was held in
reserve with the King)   114 **for** for lack of

You are their heir; you sit upon their throne;
The blood and courage that renownèd them
Runs in your veins: and my thrice-puissant° liege
Is in the very May-morn of his youth   120
Ripe for exploits and mighty enterprises.

Exeter. Your brother kings and monarchs of the earth
Do all expect that you should rouse yourself,
As did the former lions of your blood.

Westmoreland. They know your Grace hath° cause
  and means and might;   125
So hath your Highness. Never king of England
Had nobles richer and more loyal subjects,
Whose hearts have left their bodies here in England
And lie pavilioned in the fields of France.

Canterbury. O, let their bodies follow, my dear liege,   130
With blood, and sword and fire, to win your right!
In aid whereof we of the spirituality
Will raise your Highness such a mighty sum
As never did the clergy at one time
Bring in to any of your ancestors.   135

King. We must not only arm t' invade the French,
But lay down our proportions° to defend
Against the Scot, who will make road° upon us
With all advantages.°

Canterbury. They of those marches,° gracious Sov-
  ereign,   140
Shall be a wall sufficient to defend
Our inland° from the pilfering borderers.

King. We do not mean the coursing° snatchers only;
But fear the main intendment° of the Scot,
Who hath been still° a giddy neighbor to us;   145
For you shall read that my great-grandfather

---

119 **thrice-puissant** i.e., for the three reasons just stated   125 **hath**
(accented)   137 **lay down our proportions** estimate the size of our
forces   138 **road** raid   139 **With all advantages** at every favorable
opportunity, with everything in their favor   140 **marches** border
country   142 **inland** heart of the country   143 **coursing** marauding
144 **main intendment** general purpose   145 **still** always

Never went with his forces into France
But that the Scot on his unfurnished° kingdom
Came pouring like the tide into a breach,
150   With ample and brim fullness of his force,
Galling the gleanèd° land with hot assays,
Girding with grievous siege castles and towns;
That England, being empty of defense,
Hath shook and trembled at th' ill neighborhood.°

Canterbury. She hath been then more feared° than
155   harmed, my liege;
For hear her but exampled° by herself:
When all her chivalry hath been in France,
And she a mourning widow of her nobles,
She hath herself not only well defended
160   But taken and impounded as a stray°
The King of Scots;° whom she did send to France
To fill King Edward's fame with prisoner kings,
And make her chronicle as rich with praise
As is the ooze and bottom° of the sea
165   With sunken wrack° and sumless treasuries.

Ely. But there's a saying very old and true—
            "If that you will France win,
            Then with Scotland first begin."
For once the eagle (England) being in prey,°
170   To her unguarded nest the weasel (Scot)
Comes sneaking, and so sucks her princely eggs
(Playing the mouse in absence of the cat)
To tame° and havoc more than she can eat.

Exeter. It follows then, the cat must stay at home;
175   Yet that is but a crushed° necessity,
Since we have locks to safeguard necessaries,
And pretty traps to catch the petty thieves.

---

148 **unfurnished** undefended   151 **gleanèd** i.e., stripped of defenders
154 **neighborhood** neighborliness   155 **feared** alarmed   156 **exampled** furnished with a precedent   160 **stray** animal found wandering out of bounds   161 **King of Scots** i.e., David II   164 **ooze and bottom** oozy bottom   165 **wrack** wreck   169 **in prey** engaged upon preying   173 **tame** broach (as a weasel breaks into eggs to suck their meat)   175 **crushed** strained, needless

While that the armèd hand doth fight abroad,
Th' advisèd° head defends itself at home;
For government, though high, and low, and lower,   *180*
Put into parts,° doth keep in one consent,°
Congreeing° in a full and natural close,°
Like music.

Canterbury.   Therefore doth heaven divide
The state° of man in divers functions,
Setting endeavor in continual motion;°   *185*
To which is fixèd, as an aim or butt,
Obedience; for so work the honeybees,
Creatures that by a rule in nature° teach
The act° of order to a peopled kingdom.
They have a king, and officers of sorts,°   *190*
Where some like magistrates correct° at home,
Others like merchants venture trade abroad,
Others like soldiers armèd in their stings
Make boot upon° the summer's velvet buds,
Which pillage they with merry march bring home   *195*
To the tent-royal of their emperor—
Who, busied in his majesty, surveys
The singing masons building roofs of gold,
The civil citizens kneading up the honey,
The poor mechanic° porters crowding in   *200*
Their heavy burdens at his narrow gate,
The sad-eyed justice, with his surly° hum,
Delivering o'er to executors° pale
The lazy yawning drone. I this infer,°
That many things, having full reference°   *205*
To one consent, may work contrariously;
As many arrows loosèd several ways°

179 **advisèd** prudent   181 **parts** (1) members of the body politic (2)
melodies of the various instruments in concerted music   181 **consent**
(1) agreement (2) harmony   182 **Congreeing** agreeing   182 **close** (1)
union (2) conclusion of a piece of music   184 **state** estate, kingdom
185 **Setting ... motion** giving a perpetual stimulus to effort   188 **in
nature** instinctive   189 **act** operation   190 **sorts** various kinds
191 **correct** administer justice   194 **Make boot upon** plunder
200 **mechanic** engaged in manual labor   202 **surly** stern   203 **executors** executioners   204 **infer** adduce   205 **reference** relation   207 **loosèd
several ways** shot from various places

Come to one mark, as many ways meet in one
  town,
As many fresh streams meet in one salt sea,
210 As many lines close in the dial's center,
So may a thousand actions, once afoot,
End in one purpose, and be all well borne°
Without defeat. Therefore to France, my liege!
Divide your happy England into four,
215 Whereof take you one quarter into France,
And you withal shall make all Gallia shake.
If we, with thrice such powers left at home,
Cannot defend our own doors from the dog,
Let us be worried, and our nation lose
220 The name of hardiness and policy.°

King. Call in the messengers sent from the Dauphin.
                    [*Exeunt some Attendants.*]
Now are we well resolved,° and by God's help
And yours, the noble sinews of our power,
France being ours,° we'll bend it to our awe,°
225 Or break it all to pieces. Or there we'll sit,
Ruling in large and ample empery°
O'er France and all her (almost) kingly dukedoms,
Or lay these bones in an unworthy urn,°
Tombless, with no remembrance° over them.
230 Either our history shall with full mouth
Speak freely of our acts, or else our grave,
Like Turkish mute,° shall have a tongueless mouth,
Not worshipped° with a waxen° epitaph.

Enter Ambassadors of France [and Attendants].

Now are we well prepared to know the pleasure
235 Of our fair cousin Dauphin; for we hear
Your greeting is from him, not from the King.

---

212 **borne** carried out   220 **policy** statesmanship   222 **resolved** (1) convinced (2) determined   224 **ours** i.e., by right of inheritance   224 **bend it to our awe** subdue it to our authority   226 **empery** dominion   228 **urn** grave   229 **remembrance** memorial inscription   232 **Turkish mute** (certain slaves in the Turkish royal household had their tongues cut out to ensure secrecy)   233 **worshipped** honored   233 **waxen** easily effaced

Ambassador. May't please your Majesty to give us
    leave
  Freely to render what we have in charge;
  Or shall we sparingly° show you far off
  The Dauphin's meaning, and our embassy?   240

King. We are no tyrant, but a Christian king,
  Unto whose grace° our passion is as subject
  As is our wretches fett'red in our prisons;
  Therefore with frank and with uncurbèd plainness,
  Tell us the Dauphin's mind.

Ambassador.   Thus then, in few:°   245
  Your Highness, lately sending into France,
  Did claim some certain dukedoms, in the right
  Of your great predecessor, King Edward the Third.
  In answer of which claim, the Prince our master
  Says that you savor too much of your youth,   250
  And bids you be advised:° There's naught in
    France
  That can be with a nimble galliard° won;
  You cannot revel into dukedoms there.
  He therefore sends you, meeter for your spirit,
  This tun° of treasure; and in lieu of this,   255
  Desires you let the dukedoms that you claim
  Hear no more of you. This the Dauphin speaks.

King. What treasure, uncle?

Exeter.   Tennis balls, my liege.

King. We are glad the Dauphin is so pleasant° with
    us—
  His present, and your pains, we thank you for.   260
  When we have matched our rackets to these balls,
  We will in France° (by God's grace) play a set
  Shall strike his father's crown° into the hazard.°

239 **sparingly** with reserve, discreetly   242 **grace** gracious disposition   245 **few** few words   251 **be advised** take care   252 **galliard**
lively dance   255 **tun** cask   259 **pleasant** jocular, merry   262
France (1) tennis court (2) the country   263 **crown** (1) coin (stake
money) (2) throne and power   263 **hazard** (1) opening in the walls of
an old-fashioned tennis court; the ball entering it became "dead" and a
point was scored (2) peril, jeopardy

Tell him he hath made a match with such a wran-
　　gler°
265　That all the courts° of France will be disturbed
　　With chases.° And we understand him well,
　　How he comes o'er us with° our wilder days,
　　Not measuring what use we made of them.
　　We never valued this poor seat° of England,
270　And therefore, living hence,° did give ourself
　　To barbarous license; as 'tis ever common
　　That men are merriest when they are from home.
　　But tell the Dauphin I will keep my state,°
　　Be like a king, and show my sail of greatness,°
275　When I do rouse me in my throne of France.
　　For that I have laid by my majesty,
　　And plodded like a man for working days;°
　　But I will rise there with so full a glory
　　That I will dazzle all the eyes of France,
280　Yea, strike the Dauphin blind to look on us.°
　　And tell the pleasant prince this mock of his
　　Hath turned his balls to gunstones,° and his soul
　　Shall stand sore chargèd for the wasteful vengeance
　　That shall fly with them; for many a thousand
　　　widows
　　Shall this his mock mock out of their dear hus-
285　　bands,
　　Mock mothers from their sons, mock castles down;
　　And some are yet ungotten and unborn
　　That shall have cause to curse the Dauphin's
　　　scorn.°

264 **wrangler** (1) adversary (2) disputant   265 **courts** (1) tennis courts
(2) courts of princes   266 **chases** (1) bouncings twice of tennis ball
(scoring points) (2) pursuits   267 **comes o'er us with** affects superiority over us by reason of   269 **seat** throne (lines 269–72 are
ironical)   270 **hence** i.e., away from the court   273 **state** position of
power   274 **show my sail of greatness** demean myself proud-
ly   276–77 **For that ... working days** i.e., to be able to achieve this I
have divested myself of greatness and learned what it is to live as a
laboring man   278–80 **But I will ... look on us** (cf. *1 Henry IV*
1.2.217–39)   282 **gunstones** stones used for cannonballs   288 **scorn**
taunt

But this lies all within° the will of God,
To whom I do appeal, and in whose name,   290
Tell you the Dauphin, I am coming on
To venge me as I may, and to put forth
My rightful hand in a well-hallowed cause.
So get you hence in peace. And tell the Dauphin
His jest will savor but of shallow wit,   295
When thousands weep more than did laugh at it.
Convey them with safe conduct. Fare you well.
               Exeunt Ambassadors [and Attendants].

Exeter. This was a merry message.

King. We hope to make the sender blush at it.
  Therefore, my lords, omit no happy hour°   300
  That may give furth'rance to our expedition;°
  For we have now no thought in us but France,
  Save those to God, that run before° our business.
  Therefore let our proportions° for these wars
  Be soon collected, and all things thought upon   305
  That may with reasonable swiftness add
  More feathers to our wings; for, God before,°
  We'll chide this Dauphin at his father's door.
  Therefore let every man now task his thought
  That this fair action may on foot° be brought.   310
               Exeunt.

289 **lies all within** depends wholly upon   300 **omit no happy hour**
lose no favorable occasion   301 **expedition** enterprise   303 **run before** i.e., as prayers precede   304 **proportions** forces and sup-
plies   307 **God before** God leading us   310 **on foot** in active
operation

[ACT 2]

Flourish.° Enter Chorus.

Now all the youth of England are on fire,
And silken dalliance in the wardrobe lies;°
Now thrive the armorers, and honor's thought
Reigns solely° in the breast of every man.
5 They sell the pasture now, to buy the horse;
Following the mirror° of all Christian kings
With wingèd heels, as English Mercuries.°
For now sits Expectation in the air
And hides a sword, from hilts° unto the point,
10 With crowns imperial, crowns and coronets
Promised to Harry and his followers.
The French, advised by good intelligence°
Of this most dreadful preparation,
Shake in their fear, and with pale policy°
15 Seek to divert the English purposes.
O England, model° to thy inward greatness,
Like little body with a mighty heart,
What mightst thou do, that honor would thee do,
Were all thy children kind and natural!°

---

2 Prologue s.d. **Flourish** trumpet fanfare 2 **silken dalliance in the
wardrobe lies** i.e., pastimes and luxuries are laid aside like
clothes 4 **solely** alone 6 **mirror** model 7 **Mercuries** (in classical
mythology Mercury, or Hermes, was the gods' messenger: he was pictured as wearing winged helmet and sandals) 9 **hilts** hilt (plural for singular, as frequently) 12 **advised by good intelligence** informed by
efficient espionage 14 **pale policy** contrivance inspired by
fear 16 **model** form 19 **kind and natural** loving and naturally
affectionate

But see, thy fault° France° hath in thee found
　out—　　　　　　　　　　　　　　　　　　　　20
A nest of hollow° bosoms—which he fills
With treacherous crowns;° and three corrupted
　men—
One, Richard Earl of Cambridge, and the second,
Henry Lord Scroop of Masham, and the third,
Sir Thomas Grey, knight, of Northumberland—　　25
Have, for the gilt° of France (O guilt indeed!),
Confirmed conspiracy with fearful France,
And by their hands this grace° of kings must die,
If hell and treason hold their promises,
Ere he take ship for France, and in Southampton.　30
Linger your patience on, and we'll digest
Th' abuse of distance;° force° a play:—
The sum is paid; the traitors are agreed;
The King is set from London; and the scene
Is now transported, gentles, to Southampton.　　35
There is the playhouse now, there must you sit,
And thence to France shall we convey you safe
And bring you back, charming the narrow seas°
To give you gentle pass;° for, if we may,
We'll not offend one stomach° with our play.　　40
But, till the King come forth, and not till then,
Unto Southampton do we shift our scene.　　*Exit.*

---

20 **fault** imperfection　20 **France** the King of France　21 **hollow** (1)
false (2) empty　22 **crowns** coins　26 **gilt** i.e., golden crowns
28 **grace** ornament　31–32 **digest/Th' abuse of distance** dispose of
the wrong done to fact in moving from place to place in the play's
action　32 **force** cram full　38 **charming the narrow seas** laying
spells on the English Channel　39 **pass** passage　40 **offend one
stomach** (1) displease anyone (2) make anyone seasick

[Scene 1. *London. A street.*]

Enter Corporal Nym and Lieutenant Bardolph.

Bardolph. Well met, Corporal Nym.

Nym. Good morrow, Lieutenant° Bardolph.

Bardolph. What, are Ancient° Pistol and you friends
yet?

5   *Nym.* For my part, I care not; I say little; but when
time shall serve,° there shall be smiles—but that
shall be as it may. I dare not fight; but I will wink°
and hold out mine iron.° It is a simple one; but
what though? It will toast cheese, and it will endure
10   cold,° as another man's sword will—and there's
an end.°

Bardolph. I will bestow° a breakfast to make you
friends, and we'll be all three sworn brothers° to
France. Let 't be so, good Corporal Nym.

15   *Nym.* Faith, I will live so long as I may, that's the
certain of it; and when I cannot live any longer,
I will do as I may.° That is my rest,° that is the
rendezvous° of it.

Bardolph. It is certain, Corporal, that he is married

2.1.2 **Lieutenant** (Bardolph was a Corporal in *2 Henry IV* and Nym calls
him so again at 3.2.3, below)   3 **Ancient** Ensign, Standard Bearer
6 **serve** be opportune   7 **wink** (1) shut my eyes (2) give a meaningful
look   8 **iron** sword   9–10 **will endure cold** does not mind being
naked   10–11 **there's an end** that's all there is to it   12 **bestow** treat
you to   13 **sworn brothers** comrades pledged to share each other's
fortunes (cf. 3.2.45–46)   17 **I will do as I may** (cf. the proverb, "He
that cannot do as he would must do as he may")   17 **rest** when I stand
to win or lose (the stakes in a game of primero, the loss of which brings
about the end of the game)   18 **rendezvous** last resort

to Nell Quickly, and certainly she did you wrong,   *20*
for you were troth-plight° to her.

Nym. I cannot tell. Things must be as they may; men
may sleep, and they may have their throats about
them at that time, and some say knives have edges.
It must be as it may; though patience be a tired   *25*
mare, yet she will plod;° there must be conclusions.
Well, I cannot tell.

        Enter Pistol and [Hostess] Quickly.

Bardolph. Here comes Ancient Pistol and his wife.
Good Corporal, be patient here. How now, mine
host Pistol?   *30.*

Pistol. Base tyke, call'st thou me host?
Now by this hand I swear I scorn the term;
Nor shall my Nell keep lodgers!

Hostess. No, by my troth, not long; for we cannot
lodge and board a dozen or fourteen gentlewomen   *35*
that live honestly° by the prick of their needles, but
it will be thought we keep a bawdy house straight.
[*Nym draws his sword.*] O well-a-day, Lady, if he
be not hewn now! We shall see willful adultery
and murder committed.   [*Pistol draws.*]   *40*

Bardolph. Good Lieutenant—good Corporal—offer
nothing here.

Nym. Pish!

Pistol. Pish for thee, Iceland dog;° thou prick-eared
cur of Iceland!   *45*

Hostess. Good Corporal Nym, show thy valor, and put
up your sword.°

---

21 **troth-plight** betrothed (more binding than a modern engagement)   25–26 **patience be a tired mare, yet she will plod** patience is
wearisome, yet it achieves its purpose in the end   36 **honestly** (1)
decently (2) chastely ("prick" of the same line sustains the bawdy allusion)   44 **Iceland dog** white sharp-eared dog, so shaggy that neither its
face nor body can be seen (a favorite lapdog)   46–47 **show thy valor,
and put up your sword** (unintentionally apposite, for Nym had such
little valor that he could not fight)

Nym. Will you shog off?° I would have you solus.°

Pistol. "Solus," egregious° dog? O viper vile!
50   The "solus" in thy most marvelous face!
      The "solus" in thy teeth, and in thy throat,
      And in thy hateful lungs, yea, in thy maw,° perdy!°
      And, which is worse, within thy nasty mouth!
      I do retort the "solus" in thy bowels;
55   For I can take,° and Pistol's cock is up,°
      And flashing fire will follow.

Nym. I am not Barbason;° you cannot conjure° me;
      I have an humor to knock you indifferently° well.
      If you grow foul with me, Pistol, I will scour you
60   with my rapier,° as I may, in fair terms.° If you
      would walk off, I would prick your guts a little ·in
      good terms,° as I may, and that's the humor° of it.

Pistol. O braggard vile, and damnèd furious wight,°
      The grave doth gape,° and doting° death is near;
65   Therefore exhale!°

Bardolph. Hear me, hear me what I say! He that
      strikes the first stroke, I'll run him up to the hilts,°
      as I am a soldier.   [*Draws.*]

Pistol. An oath of mickle° might, and fury shall abate.
                    [*Pistol and Nym sheathe their swords.*]
70   Give me thy fist, thy forefoot° to me give.

---

48 **shog off** move off (slang)   48 **solus** alone (Pistol takes it to mean
single, i.e., unmarried; or, ignorant of Latin, some great insult)   49
egregious outsized   52 **maw** stomach   52 **perdy** by God   55 **take**
(1) cause harm to befall (by his elaborate exorcism or curse) (2) strike (3)
take fire ˙ 55 **cock is up** is cocked for firing (punning on his name)
57 **Barbason** name of a fiend   57 **conjure** exorcise   58 **indifferently**
fairly   59–60 **If you grow . . . my rapier** (a pistol was said to be "foul"
after firing, and was normally cleaned with a ̄ramrod or scouring
rod)   60 **in fair terms** fairly (a fashionable cliché)   61–62 **in good
terms** on a good footing (another fashionable cliché)   62 **humor** fancy,
inclination (yet another cliché)   63 **wight** person   64 **gape** (1) open
(2) greedily desire   64 **doting** loving, fond   65 **exhale** draw forth   67
run him up to the hilts drive the whole sword blade into him   69
mickle great (already, in Shakespeare's day, archaistic)   70 **forefoot**
paw

   Thy spirits are most tall.°

Nym. I will cut thy throat one time or other in fair
   terms, that is the humor of it.

Pistol. Couple a gorge!°
   That is the word. I thee defy° again.   75
   O hound of Crete,° think'st thou my spouse to get?
   No; to the spital° go,
   And from the powd'ring tub° of infamy
   Fetch forth the lazar kite of Cressid's kind,°
   Doll Tearsheet,° she by name, and her espouse.   80
   I have, and I will hold, the quondam° Quickly
   For the only she;° and—pauca,° there's enough.
   Go to!

                      Enter the Boy.

Boy. Mine host Pistol, you must come to my master°
   —and your hostess. He is very sick and would to   85
   bed. Good Bardolph, put thy face° between his
   sheets, and do the office of a warming pan. Faith,
   he's very ill.

Bardolph. Away, you rogue!

Hostess. By my troth, he'll yield the crow a pudding°   90
   one of these days. The King has killed his heart.°
   Good husband, come home presently.°   *Exit.*

Bardolph. Come, shall I make you two friends? We

71 **tall** courageous   74 **Couple a gorge** cut the throat (a comic version
of the French, *couper la gorge,* appropriate to the coming campaign)   75 **defy** challenge   76 **hound of Crete** (another shaggy dog;
cf. line 44, note)   77 **spital** hospital   78 **powd'ring tub** pickling vat
(frequently applied to the sweating tub used for curing venereal
disease)   79 **lazar kite of Cressid's kind** leprous whore (a stock
phrase; a kite is a bird of prey)   80 **Doll Tearsheet** (cf. *2 Henry 4,*
2.3.165–68 and 5.4)   81 **quondam** former   82 **only she** one woman
in the world   82 **pauca** few words (Latin, *pauca verba*)   84 **my
master** i.e., Falstaff (the boy is the page given to Falstaff by Prince Hal, *2
Henry 4,* 1.2)   86 **thy face** (Bardolph's was red like fire)   90 **he'll
yield the crow a pudding** i.e., the boy will make food (**pudding** =
stuffed intestines) for crows on the gallows (proverbial)   91 **The King
has killed his heart** (by rejecting Falstaff; cf. *2 Henry 4,* 5.5.51–77)
92 **presently** immediately

must to France together; why the devil should we
95 keep knives to cut one another's throats?

Pistol. Let floods o'erswell, and fiends for food howl
on!°

Nym. You'll pay me the eight shillings I won of you
at betting?

Pistol. Base is the slave that pays.°

100 *Nym.* That now I will have; that's the humor of it.

Pistol. As manhood shall compound.° Push° home.
                                    [*They*] *draw.*

Bardolph. By this sword, he 'that makes the first
thrust, I'll kill him! By this sword, I will.   [*Draws.*]

Pistol. "Sword" is an oath, and oaths must have their
course.   [*Sheathes his sword.*]

105 *Bardolph.* Corporal Nym, and° thou wilt be friends,
be friends; and thou wilt not, why then be enemies
with me too. Prithee put up.°

Nym. I shall have my eight shillings I won of you at
betting?

110 *Pistol.* A noble° shalt thou have, and present° pay;
And liquor likewise will I give to thee,
And friendship shall combine, and brotherhood.
I'll live by Nym, and Nym shall live by me.
Is not this just? For I shall sutler° be
115 Unto the camp, and profits will accrue.
Give me thy hand.   [*Nym sheathes his sword.*]

Nym. I shall have my noble?

Pistol. In cash, most justly paid.

96 **Let floods . . . howl on** let riot thrive and the devils be deprived of
their prey   99 **Base is the slave that pays** (a corruption of the proverb,
"The poor man always pays")   101 **manhood shall compound** valor
decides   101 **Push** thrust (of a sword)   105 **and** if   107 **put up**
sheathe   110 **noble** coin worth six shillings and eight pence   110
present immediate   114 **sutler** seller of provisions to a camp or gar-
rison

Nym. Well then, that's the humor of 't.

              Enter Hostess.

Hostess. As ever you come of women, come in   *120*
    quickly to Sir John. Ah, poor heart! he is so shaked
    of a burning quotidian tertian° that it is most la-
    mentable to behold. Sweet men, come to him.

Nym. The King hath run bad humors° on the knight;
    that's the even° of it.   *125*

Pistol. Nym, thou hast spoke the right;
    His heart is fracted and corroborate.°

Nym. The King is a good king, but it must be as it
    may: he passes some humors, and careers.°

Pistol. Let us condole the knight; for, lambkins, we
    will live.   *[Exeunt.]* *130*

           [Scene 2. *Southampton.*]

     Enter Exeter, Bedford, and Westmoreland.

Bedford. Fore God, his Grace is bold to trust these
    traitors.

Exeter. They shall be apprehended by and by.°

Westmoreland. How smooth and even° they do bear
    themselves,
    As if allegiance in their bosoms sat,
    Crowned with faith and constant loyalty!   *5*

---

122 **quotidian tertian** two kinds of intermittent fevers, the first recur-
ring daily, the second every third day (a nonsensical phrase) 124 **run
bad humors** vented his ill humor 125 **even** truth 127 **fracted and
corroborate** broken and joined together (?) 129 **passes some humors,
and careers** indulges some whims and liveliness 2.2.2 **apprehended
by and by** arrested soon 3 **even** unruffled

Bedford. The King hath note° of all that they intend,
   By interception which they dream not of.

Exeter. Nay, but the man that was his bedfellow,°
   Whom he hath dulled and cloyed° with gracious
      favors
10   That he should, for a foreign purse, so sell
   His Sovereign's life to death and treachery!

   Sound trumpets. Enter the King, Scroop, Cam-
      bridge, and Grey, [Lords, and Attendants].

King. Now sits the wind fair, and we will aboard.
   My Lord of Cambridge, and my kind Lord of
      Masham,
   And you, my gentle knight, give me your thoughts:
15   Think you not that the pow'rs we bear with us
   Will cut their passage through the force of France,
   Doing the execution and the act
   For which we have in head° assembled them?

Scroop. No doubt, my liege, if each man do his best.

20 *King.* I doubt not that, since we are well persuaded
   We carry not a heart with us from hence
   That grows° not in a fair consent° with ours,
   Nor leave not one behind that doth not wish
   Success and conquest to attend on us.

Cambridge. Never was monarch better feared and
25   loved
   Than is your Majesty. There's not, I think, a sub-
      ject
   That sits in heart-grief and uneasiness
   Under the sweet shade° of your government.

Grey. True. Those that were your father's enemies
30   Have steeped their galls° in honey, and do serve
      you

6 **note** knowledge   8 **bedfellow** i.e., Scroop   9 **dulled and cloyed**
bored and overindulged   18 **in head** as an organized force   22 **grows**
lives   22 **consent** agreement   28 **shade** protection   30 **galls** bitter-
ness

    With hearts create° of duty, and of zeal.

King. We therefore have great cause of thankfulness,
    And shall forget the office° of our hand
    Sooner than quittance° of desert and merit
    According to the weight and worthiness.   35

Scroop. So service shall with steelèd sinews toil,
    And labor shall refresh itself with hope,
    To do your Grace incessant services.

King. We judge no less. Uncle of Exeter,
    Enlarge° the man committed yesterday   40
    That railed against our person. We consider
    It was excess of wine that set him on,
    And on his more advice,° we pardon him.

Scroop. That's mercy, but too much security:°
    Let him be punished, Sovereign, lest example   45
    Breed (by his sufferance)° more of such a kind.

King. O, let us yet° be merciful!

Cambridge. So may your Highness, and yet punish
    too.

Grey. Sir,
    You show great mercy if you give him life   50
    After the taste° of much correction.

King. Alas, your too much love and care of me
    Are heavy orisons° 'gainst this poor wretch!
    If little faults proceeding on distemper°
    Shall not be winked° at, how shall we stretch° our
       eye   55
    When capital° crimes, chewed, swallowed, and di-
       gested,
    Appear before us? We'll yet enlarge that man,

---

31 **create** created 33 **office** proper function 34 **quittance** requital
40 **Enlarge** set at liberty 43 **on his more advice** on maturer
reflection 44 **security** want of caution 46 **by his sufferance** by not
checking him 47 **yet** now as always 51 **taste** experience 53 **heavy
orisons** weighty pleas 54 **proceeding on distemper** i.e., committed
when drunk 55 **winked** connived 55 **stretch** open wide 56 **capital** punishable by death

Though Cambridge, Scroop, and Grey, in their
 dear° care
And tender preservation of our person,
Would have him punished. And now to our French
60 causes.°
Who are the late° commissioners?

Cambridge. I one, my lord.
 Your Highness bade me ask for it° today.

Scroop. So did you me, my liege.

65 *Grey.* And I, my royal Sovereign.

King. Then, Richard Earl of Cambridge, there is
 yours;
There yours, Lord Scroop of Masham; and, sir
 knight,
Grey of Northumberland, this same is yours:
Read them, and know I know your worthiness.
70 My Lord of Westmoreland, and uncle Exeter,
We will aboard tonight.—Why, how now, gentle-
 men?
What see you in those papers that you lose
So much complexion?°—Look ye, how they
 change!
Their cheeks are paper.—Why, what read you
 there
75 That have so cowarded and chased your blood
Out of appearance?°

Cambridge.   I do confess my fault,
 And do submit me to your Highness' mercy.

Grey, Scroop. To which we all appeal.

King. The mercy that was quick in us but late,
80 By your own counsel is suppressed and killed.
You must not dare (for shame) to talk of mercy,
For your own reasons turn into your bosoms,

---

58 **dear** (1) deeply felt (2) dire 60 **causes** affairs 61 **late** recently appointed 63 **it** i.e., the written commission 73 **complexion** color 76 **appearance** sight

As dogs upon their masters, worrying you.
See you, my princes and my noble peers,
These English monsters! My Lord of Cambridge
 here—   85
You know how apt our love was to accord°
To furnish him with all appertinents
Belonging to his honor; and this man
Hath, for a few light crowns, lightly° conspired
And sworn unto the practices° of France   90
To kill us here in Hampton; to the which
This knight, no less for bounty bound to us
Than Cambridge is, hath likewise sworn. But O,
What shall I say to thee, Lord Scroop, thou cruel,
Ingrateful, savage, and inhuman creature?   95
Thou that didst bear the key of all my counsels,
That knew'st the very bottom of my soul,
That (almost) mightst have coined me into gold,
Wouldst thou have practiced on me for thy use?°
May it be possible that foreign hire   100
Could out of thee extract one spark of evil
That might annoy my finger? 'Tis so strange
That, though the truth of it stands off as gross°
As black and white, my eye will scarcely see it.
Treason and murder ever kept together,   105
As two yoke-devils° sworn to either's purpose,
Working so grossly in a natural cause
That admiration did not hoop at them;°
But thou ('gainst all proportion)° didst bring in
Wonder to wait on treason and on murder;   110
And whatsoever cunning fiend it was
That wrought upon thee so preposterously°
Hath got the voice° in hell for excellence;
And other devils that suggest° by treasons

---

86 **accord** agree   89 **light . . . lightly** trivial . . . readily   90 **practices**
intrigues   99 **practiced on me for thy use** plotted against me for your
own profit   103 **off as gross** out as plain   106 **yoke-devils** fellow-
devils   107–08 **so grossly . . . at them** so obviously in a matter natural
to them that no one cried out in wonder   109 **proportion** pro-
priety   112 **preposterously** unnaturally   113 **voice** vote   114 **suggest** tempt

115   Do botch and bungle up damnation
       With patches, colors, and with forms being fetched
       From glist'ring semblances of piety;°
       But he that tempered° thee bade thee stand up,°
       Gave thee no instance why thou shouldst do
          treason,
120   Unless to dub° thee with the name of traitor.
       If that same demon that hath gulled thee thus
       Should with his lion gait° walk the whole world,
       He might return to vasty Tartar° back
       And tell the legions,° "I can never win
125   A soul so easy as that Englishman's."
       O, how hast thou with jealousy infected°
       The sweetness of affiance!° Show° men dutiful?
       Why, so didst thou. Seem they grave and learned?
       Why, so didst thou. Come they of noble family?
130   Why, so didst thou. Seem they religious?
       Why, so didst thou. Or are they spare in diet,
       Free from gross passion, or of mirth or anger,
       Constant in spirit, not swerving with the blood,°
       Garnished and decked in modest complement,°
135   Not working with the eye without the ear,°
       And but in purgèd judgment trusting neither?
       Such and so finely bolted° didst thou seem;
       And thus thy fall hath left a kind of blot
       To mark the full-fraught° man and best indued°
140   With some suspicion. I will weep for thee;
       For this revolt of thine, methinks, is like
       Another fall of man. Their faults are open.°
       Arrest them to the answer° of the law;

115–17 **Do botch ... piety** disguise the fact of damnation with folly, false pretexts and behavior borrowed from bright outward manifestations of piety   118 **tempered** worked upon   118 **stand up** make a stand straightforwardly   120 **dub** invest (with a title)   122 **lion gait** (cf. 1 Peter 5:8 "your adversary, the devil, as a roaring lion walketh about, seeking whom he may devour")   123 **Tartar** Tartarus hell   124 **legions** i.e., of devils   126 **jealousy infected** suspicion tainted   127 **affiance** confidence   127 **Show** seen   133 **swerving with the blood** erring after the flesh   134 **modest complement** unostentatious demeanor   135 **Not working with the eye without the ear** i.e., listening as well as seeing   137 **bolted** sifted (as flour)   139 **Full-fraught** completely gifted   139 **indued** endowed   142 **open** patent   143 **answer** punishment

And God acquit° them of their practices!

Exeter. I arrest thee of high treason by the name of   *145*
Richard Earl of Cambridge.

    I arrest thee of high treason by the name of
Henry Lord Scroop of Masham.

    I arrest thee of high treason by the name of
Thomas Grey, knight, of Northumberland.   *150*

Scroop. Our purposes God justly hath discovered,
And I repent my fault more than my death—
Which I beseech your Highness to forgive,
Although my body pay the price of it.

Cambridge. For me, the gold of France did not se-
duce,   *155*
Although I did admit it as a motive
The sooner to effect what I intended.
But God be thankèd for prevention,°
Which I in sufferance° heartily will rejoice,°
Beseeching God, and you, to pardon me.   *160*

Grey. Never did faithful subject more rejoice
At the discovery of most dangerous treason
Than I do at this hour joy o'er myself,
Prevented from a damnèd enterprise.
My fault, but not my body, pardon, Sovereign.   *165*

King. God quit° you in His mercy! Hear your sen-
tence.
You have conspired against our royal person,
Joined with an enemy proclaimed, and from his
coffers
Received the golden earnest° of our death;
Wherein you would have sold your king to slaugh-
ter,   *170*
His princes and his peers to servitude,
His subjects to oppression and contempt,
And his whole kingdom into desolation.
Touching our person, seek we no revenge,

144 **acquit** requite   158 **prevention** (four syllables)   159 **sufferance**
suffering the penalty   159 **rejoice** i.e., rejoice at   166 **quit** ab-
solve   169 **golden earnest** advance payment

175 But we our kingdom's safety must so tender,°
    Whose ruin you have sought, that to her laws
    We do deliver you. Get you therefore hence
    (Poor miserable wretches) to your death;
    The taste° whereof God of His mercy give
180 You patience to endure, and true repentance
    Of all your dear° offenses! Bear them hence.

        Exeunt [Cambridge, Scroop, and Grey, guarded].

    Now, lords, for France; the enterprise whereof
    Shall be to you as us, like° glorious.
    We doubt not of a fair and lucky war,
185 Since God so graciously hath brought to light
    This dangerous treason, lurking in our way
    To hinder our beginnings. We doubt not now
    But every rub° is smoothèd on our way.
    Then, forth, dear countrymen. Let us deliver
190 Our puissance° into the hand of God,
    Putting it straight in expedition.°
    Cheerly to sea; the signs of war advance:°
    No king of England, if not King of France!

                    Flourish. [Exeunt.]

    [Scene 3. *London. Before a tavern.*]

    Enter Pistol, Nym, Bardolph, Boy, and Hostess.

Hostess. Prithee, honey-sweet husband, let me bring
    thee to Staines.°

Pistol. No; for my manly heart doth earn.°

175 **tender** care for   179 **taste** experience   181 **dear** dire   183 **like**
equally   188 **rub** obstacle   190 **puissance** armed force   191 **expedition** motion   192 **the signs of war advance** raise up the banners
2.3.2 **Staines** (on the road to Southampton)   3 **earn** grieve

Bardolph, be blithe; Nym, rouse thy vaunting
  veins;°

Boy, bristle thy courage up; for Falstaff he is dead,   5
And we must earn therefore.

Bardolph. Would I were with him, wheresome'er he is,
either in heaven or in hell!

Hostess. Nay sure, he's not in hell! He's in Arthur's
bosom,° if ever man went to Arthur's bosom. 'A°   10
made a finer end,° and went away and° it had
been any christom child.° 'A parted ev'n just between twelve and one, ev'n at the turning o' th'
tide.° For after I saw him fumble with the sheets,
and play with flowers, and smile upon his finger's   15
end, I knew there was but one way; for his nose
was as sharp as a pen,° and 'a babbled° of green
fields. "How now, Sir John?" quoth I. "What man?
Be o' good cheer." So 'a cried out "God, God, God!"
three or four times. Now I, to comfort him, bid him   20
'a should not think of God; I hoped there
was no need to trouble himself with any such
thoughts yet. So 'a bade me lay more clothes on
his feet. I put my hand into the bed, and felt them,
and they were as cold as any stone. Then I felt to   25

---

4 **vaunting veins** rising spirits   9–10 **Arthur's bosom** (a mistake for
Abraham's bosom)   10 **'A** he   11 **finer end** i.e., than going to
hell   11 **and** as if   12 **christom child** infant in christening robe (the
proper form was "chrisom"), innocent babe   13–14 **at the turning o'
th' tide** (according to popular belief, persons near the sea died at the turn
of the tide)   14–17 **fumble . . . nose was as sharp as a pen** (traditionally accepted signs of the imminence of death)   17 **'a babbled** (the
Folio has "a Table," which seems meaningless to most readers. Lewis
Theobald's conjecture, in 1726, that a compositor misread the copy's "a
babld" has been widely accepted. One might argue that the compositor
misread "a talkd," but "babbled" is more appropriate than "talked" to the
childishness referred to earlier in the speech of an old man's last
moments. Recently the Folio reading has been defended, though not con-
vincingly. One student, for example, takes "Table" in the sense of "picture" or "tableau," and paraphrases thus: Falstaff's nose was sharp as the
pointed stakes of a pinfold, in a picture of green fields. Various interpretations are usefully surveyed in E. G. Fogel, *Shakespeare Quarterly* IX.
[1958]: 485–92; but Theobald's conjecture seems better sense and better
Shakespeare)

his knees, and so upward, and upward, and all was as cold as any stone.

Nym. They say he cried out of° sack.

Hostess. Ay, that 'a did.

30   *Bardolph.* And of women.

Hostess. Nay, that 'a did not.

Boy. Yes, that 'a did, and said they were devils incarnate.°

Hostess. 'A could never abide carnation;° 'twas a
35   color he never liked.

Boy. 'A said once, the devil would have him about women.

Hostess. 'A did in some sort, indeed, handle° women; but then he was rheumatic,° and talked of the
40   Whore of Babylon.°

Boy. Do you not remember 'a saw a flea stick upon Bardolph's nose, and 'a said it was a black soul burning in hell?

Bardolph. Well, the fuel° is gone that maintained that
45   fire: that's all the riches I got in his service.

Nym. Shall we shog?° The King will be gone from Southampton.

Pistol. Come, let's away. My love, give me thy lips. Look to my chattels and my movables.
50   Let senses rule. The word is "Pitch and pay."°
Trust none;
For oaths are straws, men's faiths are wafer-cakes,°

---

28 **cried out of** complained loudly of   32–33 **incarnate** in human shape   34 **carnation** flesh color   38 **handle** speak of   39 **rheumatic** (perhaps a mistake for "lunatic": probably pronounced "rome-atic"; see next note)   39–40 **the Whore of Babylon** (1) the "scarlet woman" of Revelation 17:4–5 (2) the Church of Rome   44 **fuel** i.e., liquor provided by Falstaff   46 **shog** move off   50 **Let senses rule. The word is "Pitch and pay"** keep your wits about you. The motto is "Cash down"   52 **wafer cakes** i.e., easily broken

And Hold-fast is the only dog,° my duck.
Therefore Caveto° be thy counselor.
Go, clear thy crystals.° Yokefellows in arms,   55
Let us to France, like horse-leeches, my boys,
To suck, to suck, the very blood to suck!

Boy. And that's but unwholesome food, they say.

Pistol. Touch her soft mouth, and march.

Bardolph. Farewell, hostess.   [*Kisses her.*] 60

Nym. I cannot kiss, that is the humor of it; but adieu!

Pistol. Let housewifery° appear; keep close,° I thee
    command.

Hostess. Farewell! Adieu!   *Exeunt.*

[Scene 4. *France. The French King's palace.*]

*Flourish. Enter the French King, the Dauphin,
the Dukes of Berri and Bretagne, [the Constable,
and others].*

King. Thus comes the English with full power upon
    us,
And more than carefully it us concerns
To answer royally in our defenses.
Therefore the Dukes of Berri and of Bretagne,
Of Brabant and of Orleans, shall make forth,   5
And you, Prince Dauphin, with all swift dispatch
To line° and new repair our towns of war
With men of courage, and with means defendant;

---

53 **Hold-fast is the only dog** (cf. the proverb, "Brag is a good dog, but
Hold-fast is a better") 54 **Caveto** take care 55 **clear thy crystals**
wipe your eyes 62 **housewifery** good housekeeping 62 **keep close**
stay at home 2.4.7 **line** fortify

For England his approaches makes as fierce
10   As waters to the sucking of a gulf.°
It fits us then to be as provident
As fear may teach us out of late examples°
Left by the fatal and neglected° English
Upon our fields.

Dauphin. My most redoubted father,
15   It is most meet we arm us 'gainst the foe;
For peace itself should not so dull a kingdom
(Though war nor no known quarrel were in question)
But that defenses, musters, preparations
Should be maintained, assembled, and collected,°
20   As were a war in expectation.
Therefore I say, 'tis meet we all go forth
To view the sick and feeble parts of France;
And let us do it with no show of fear—
No, with no more than if we heard that England
25   Were busied with a Whitsun morris dance;°
For, my good liege, she is so idly kinged,
Her scepter so fantastically borne,°
By a vain, giddy, shallow, humorous° youth,
That fear attends° her not.

Constable.   O peace, Prince Dauphin!
30   You are too much mistaken in this king.
Question your Grace the late ambassadors,
With what great state he heard their embassy,
How well supplied with noble counselors,
How modest in exception,° and withal
35   How terrible in constant resolution;
And you shall find his vanities forespent°

---

10 **gulf** whirlpool   12 **late examples** i.e., battles of Crécy (1346) and Poitiers (1356)   13 **fatal and neglected** fatally underestimated   19 **maintained, assembled, and collected** (these verbs refer singly to the nouns of the previous line, in order)   25 **Whitsun morris dance** folk dance celebrating the coming of summer   27 **Her scepter so fantastically borne** her royal power so freakishly exercised   28 **humorous** capricious   29 **attends** accompanies   34 **exception** expressing disapproval   36 **forespent** already used up

Were but the outside of the Roman Brutus,°
Covering discretion with a coat of folly;
As gardeners do with ordure hide those roots
That shall first spring and be most delicate.   40

Dauphin. Well, 'tis not so, my Lord High Constable!
But though we think it so, it is no matter;
In cases of defense, 'tis best to weigh
The enemy more mighty than he seems;
So the proportions of defense are filled,   45
Which of a weak and niggardly projection°
Doth, like a miser, spoil his coat with scanting°
A little cloth.

King.   Think we King Harry strong;
And, princes, look you strongly arm to meet him.
The kindred of him hath been fleshed° upon us;   50
And he is bred out of that bloody strain°
That haunted° us in our familiar paths;
Witness our too much memorable shame
When Crécy battle fatally was struck,
And all our princes captived, by the hand   55
Of that black name, Edward, Black Prince of
     Wales;
Whiles that his mountain sire°—on mountain
     standing,
Up in the air, crowned with the golden sun—
Saw his heroical seed,° and smiled to see him
Mangle the work of nature, and deface   60
The patterns° that by God and by French fathers
Had twenty years been made. This is a stem
Of that victorious stock; and let us fear
The native mightiness and fate° of him.

37 **Brutus** (Lucius Junius Brutus feigned stupidity in order to escape
repressive action when planning to free Rome from the Tarquin
tyranny) 45–46 **So the proportions ... niggardly projection** in this
way the defending forces are fully mustered which if on a weak and
sparing scheme 47 **scanting** stinting 50 **fleshed** (1) encouraged by a
foretaste of success (2) initiated to bloodshed 51 **strain** stock 52
haunted pursued 57 **mountain sire** father of more than human proportions 59 **seed** issue, son 61 **patterns** i.e., examples of Frenchmen 64 **fate** what he is destined to achieve

Enter a Messenger.

Messenger. Ambassadors from Harry, King of Eng-
65   land,
          Do crave admittance to your Majesty.

King. We'll give them present° audience. Go, and bring
          them.   [*Exeunt Messenger and certain Lords.*]
          You see this chase is hotly followed, friends.

Dauphin. Turn head,° and stop pursuit; for coward
          dogs
          Most spend their mouths° when what they seem to
70   threaten
          Runs far before them. Good my Sovereign,
          Take up the English short, and let them know
          Of what a monarchy you are the head.
          Self-love,° my liege, is not so vile a sin
          As self-neglecting.

Enter [Lords, with] Exeter [and Train].

75 **King.**   From our brother of England?

Exeter. From him, and thus he greets your Majesty:
          He wills you, in the name of God Almighty,
          That you divest yourself, and lay apart
          The borrowed glories that by gift of heaven,
80   By law of nature and of nations, 'longs
          To him and to his heirs—namely, the crown
          And all wide-stretchèd honors that pertain
          By custom, and the ordinance of times,°
          Unto the crown of France. That you may know
85   'Tis no sinister nor no awkward° claim,
          Picked from the wormholes° of long-vanished days,
          Nor from the dust of old oblivion raked,
          He sends you this most memorable line,° [*giving a
          paper*]

---

67 **present** immediate 69 **Turn head** stand at bay (like stags) 70
spend their mouths give cry 74 **Self-love** i.e., in praising one-
self 83 **ordinance of times** established usage 85 **no sinister nor no
awkward** neither irregular nor illegitimate 86 **Picked from the
wormholes** ingeniously derived from neglected (worm-eaten) books
88 **memorable line** noteworthy pedigree

In every branch truly demonstrative;
Willing you overlook° this pedigree;   90
And when you find him evenly° derived
From his most famed of famous ancestors,
Edward the Third, he bids you then resign
Your crown and kingdom, indirectly° held
From him, the native° and true challenger.   95

King. Or else what follows?

Exeter. Bloody constraint; for if you hide the crown
    Even in your hearts, there will he rake for it.
    Therefore in fierce tempest is he coming,
    In thunder and in earthquake, like a Jove;   100
    That if requiring° fail, he will compel;
    And bids you, in the bowels of the Lord,°
    Deliver up the crown, and to take mercy
    On the poor souls for whom this hungry war
    Opens his vasty jaws; and on your head   105
    Turning the widows' tears, the orphans' cries,
    The dead men's blood, the pining maidens' groans,
    For husbands, fathers, and betrothèd lovers
    That shall be swallowed in this controversy.
    This is his claim, his threat'ning, and my message;   110
    Unless the Dauphin be in presence here,
    To whom expressly I bring greeting too.

King. For us, we will consider of this further.
    Tomorrow shall you bear our full intent
    Back to our brother of England.

Dauphin.   For the Dauphin,   115
    I stand here for him: what to him from England?

Exeter. Scorn and defiance, slight regard, contempt,
    And anything that may not misbecome
    The mighty sender, doth he prize you at.
    Thus says my King: and if your father's Highness   120
    Do not, in grant of all demands at large,

90 **Willing you overlook** desiring you to peruse   91 **evenly** directly
94 **indirectly** wrongfully   95 **native** rightful   101 **requiring** demand
102 **in the bowels of the Lord** (a phrase found in Holinshed, and
derived from Philippians 1:8)

Sweeten the bitter mock you sent his Majesty,
He'll call you to so hot an answer of it
That caves and womby vaultages° of France
125 Shall chide your trespass, and return your mock
In second accent of his ordinance.°

Dauphin. Say: if my father render fair return,
It is against my will; for I desire
Nothing but odds with England. To that end,
130 As matching to his youth and vanity,
I did present him with the Paris balls.°

Exeter. He'll make your Paris Louvre shake for it,
Were it the mistress° court of mighty Europe;
And be assured, you'll find a difference,
135 As we his subjects have in wonder found,
Between the promise of his greener° days
And these he masters now. Now he weighs° time
Even to the utmost grain: that you shall read
In your own losses, if he stay in France.

140 *King.* Tomorrow shall you know our mind at full.

                              Flourish.

Exeter. Dispatch us with all speed, lest that our king
Come here himself to question our delay;
For he is footed in this land already.

King. You shall be soon dispatched, with fair conditions.
145 A night is but small breath and little pause
To answer matters of this consequence.   *Exeunt.*

---

124 **womby vaultages** hollow caverns   126 **second accent of his ordinance** echo of his cannon   131 **Paris balls** tennis balls   133 **mistress** chief   136 **greener** more inexperienced   137 **weighs** values

ACT [3]

Thus with imagined° wing our swift scene flies,
In motion of no less celerity
Than that of thought. Suppose that you have seen
The well-appointed King at Hampton pier
Embark his royalty; and his brave° fleet   5
With silken streamers the young Phoebus fanning.°
Play with your fancies, and in them behold
Upon the hempen tackle shipboys climbing;
Hear the shrill whistle° which doth order give
To sounds confused; behold the threaden sails,   10
Borne with th' invisible and creeping wind,
Draw the huge bottoms° through the furrowed sea,
Breasting the lofty surge. O, do but think
You stand upon the rivage,° and behold
A city on th' inconstant billows dancing;   15
For so appears this fleet majestical,
Holding due course to Harfleur. Follow, follow!
Grapple your minds to sternage of° this navy,
And leave your England, as dead midnight, still,
Guarded with grandsires, babies, and old women,   20
Either past or not arrived to pith° and puissance;
For who is he whose chin is but enriched
With one appearing hair that will not follow
These culled and choice-drawn° cavaliers to
    France?

3 Prologue 1 **imagined** of imagination 5 **brave** splendid 6 **the young Phoebus fanning** seen fluttering against the rising sun 9 **whistle** (blown by the master of a ship) 12 **bottoms** ships 14 **rivage** shore 18 **to sternage of** astern 21 **pith** strength 24 **choice-drawn** chosen with special care

25   Work, work your thoughts, and therein see a siege:
     Behold the ordinance° on their carriages,
     With fatal mouths gaping on girded° Harfleur.
     Suppose th' ambassador from the French comes
         back;
     Tells Harry that the King doth offer him
30   Katherine his daughter, and with her to dowry
     Some petty and unprofitable dukedoms.
     The offer likes not; and the nimble gunner
     With linstock° now the devilish cannon touches,°
                     Alarum, and chambers° go off.
     And down goes all before them. Still be kind,
35   And eke out our performance with your mind.   *Exit.*

[Scene 1. *France. Harfleur.*]

Enter the King, Exeter, Bedford, and Gloucester.
Alarum. [Enter Soldiers carrying] scaling ladders
at Harfleur.

King. Once more unto the breach, dear friends, once
         more;
     Or close the wall up with our English dead!
     In peace there's nothing so becomes a man
     As modest stillness° and humility;
5   But when the blast of war blows in our ears,
     Then imitate the action of the tiger:
     Stiffen the sinews, conjure up the blood,
     Disguise fair nature with hard-favored rage;
     Then lend the eye a terrible aspect:
10   Let it pry through the portage° of the head

26 **ordinance** ordnance, cannon   27 **girded** besieged   33 **linstock**
staff holding lighted match   33 **touches** touches off, fires   33s.d.
chambers small pieces of ordnance (usually for ceremonial
purposes)   3.1.4 **stillness** silence, stainedness (?)   10 **portage** portholes

Like the brass cannon; let the brow o'erwhelm it
As fearfully as doth a gallèd° rock
O'erhang and jutty his confounded° base,
Swilled° with the wild and wasteful ocean.
Now set the teeth, and stretch the nostril wide,   15
Hold hard the breath, and bend up° every spirit
To his full height! On, on, you noble English,
Whose blood is fet° from fathers of war-proof;°
Fathers that like so many Alexanders°
Have in these parts from morn till even fought   20
And sheathed their swords for lack of argument.°
Dishonor° not your mothers; now attest
That those whom you called fathers did beget you!
Be copy now to men of grosser blood
And teach them how to war! And you, good
    yeomen,   25
Whose limbs were made in England, show us here
The mettle of your pasture.° Let us swear
That you are worth your breeding; which I doubt
    not,
For there is none of you so mean and base
That hath not noble luster in your eyes.   30
I see you stand like greyhounds in the slips,°
Straining upon the start. The game's afoot!
Follow your spirit; and upon this charge,°
Cry, "God for Harry, England and Saint George!"
        [*Exeunt.*] *Alarum, and chambers go off.*

---

12 **gallèd** sea-beaten   13 **confounded** demolished   14 **Swilled** greedily
swallowed   16 **bend up** strain   18 **fet** fetched   18 **war-proof** proved
in war   19 **Alexanders** i.e., sighing for more worlds to conquer
21 **argument** i.e., opponents   22 **Dishonor** i.e., by throwing doubts on
your paternity   27 **mettle of your pasture** fine quality of your
rearing   31 **slips** leashes   33 **upon this charge** as you charge

[Scene 2. *Harfleur.*]

Enter Nym, Bardolph, Pistol, and Boy.

Bardolph. On, on, on, on, on, to the breach, to the breach!

Nym. Pray thee, Corporal, stay; the knocks are too hot; and, for mine own part, I have not a case° of
5   lives. The humor of it is too hot; that is the very plain-song° of it.

Pistol. The plain-song is most just; for humors do abound.
     Knocks go and come; God's vassals drop and die;
                    And sword and shield
10   In bloody field
                    Doth win immortal fame.

Boy. Would I were in an alehouse in London! I would give all my fame for a pot of ale, and safety.

Pistol. And I:
15   If wishes would prevail with me,
                My purpose should not fail with me,
                    But thither would I hie.

Boy.   As duly, but not as truly,°
                As bird doth sing on bough.

                Enter Fluellen.

20 *Fluellen.* Up to the breach, you dogs! Avaunt, you cullions!°

Pistol. Be merciful, great Duke, to men of mold!°

3.2.4 **case** set 6 **plain-song** simple air without variations, i.e., simple truth 18 **truly** (1) honorably (2) in tune 21 **cullions** base fellows 22 **mold** clay

Abate thy rage, abate thy manly rage,
Abate thy rage, great Duke!
Good bawcock, bate thy rage! Use lenity, sweet
  chuck!°   25

Nym. These be good° humors. Your honor wins bad
  humors.°   *Exit [with all but Boy].*

Boy. As young as I am, I have observed these three
  swashers. I am boy to them all three; but all they
  three, though they would serve me, could not be   30
  man to me; for indeed three such antics° do not
  amount to a man. For Bardolph, he is white-liv-
  ered° and red-faced; by the means whereof 'a faces
  it out, but fights not. For Pistol, he hath a killing
  tongue and a quiet sword; by the means whereof 'a   35
  breaks words,° and keeps whole weapons. For
  Nym, he hath heard that men of few words are the
  best men, and therefore he scorns to say his
  prayers, lest 'a should be thought a coward; but his
  few bad words are matched with as few good deeds,   40
  for 'a never broke any man's head but his own, and
  that was against a post when he was drunk. They
  will steal anything, and call it purchase.° Bardolph
  stole a lute-case, bore it twelve leagues, and sold it
  for three halfpence. Nym and Bardolph are sworn   45
  brothers in filching; and in Calais they stole a fire-
  shovel. I knew by that piece of service the men
  would carry coals.° They would have me as familiar with men's pockets as their gloves or their
  handkerchers; which makes much against my man-   50
  hood, if I should take from another's pocket to put
  into mine; for it is plain pocketing up of wrongs.°
  I must leave them, and seek some better service.

25 **bawcock ... sweet chuck** (ingratiating familiarities) 26 **good**
(ironical) 26–27 **Your honor wins bad humors** valor is dangerous (so
he runs off) 31 **antics** buffoons 32–33 **white-livered** cowardly 36
breaks words (1) breaks promises (2) exchanges words 43 **purchase**
booty (thieves' slang) 48 **carry coals** (1) do dirty work (2) submit to
insult 52 **pocketing up of wrongs** (1) receiving stolen goods (2) submitting to insult

Their villainy goes against my weak stomach,° and
55 therefore I must cast it up.°   *Exit.*

Enter Gower [and Fluellen].

Gower. Captain Fluellen, you must come presently°
to the mines; the Duke of Gloucester would speak
with you.

Fluellen. To the mines? Tell you the Duke, it is not
60 so good to come to the mines; for look you, the
mines is not according to the disciplines of the
war.° The concavities of it is not sufficient; for look
you, th' athversary, you may discuss° unto the
Duke, look you, is digt himself four yard under the
65 countermines.° By Cheshu, I think 'a will plow°
up all, if there is not better directions.

Gower. The Duke of Gloucester, to whom the order
of the siege is given, is altogether directed by an
Irishman, a very valiant gentleman, i' faith.

70 *Fluellen.* It is Captain Macmorris, is it not?

Gower. I think it be.

Fluellen. By Cheshu, he is an ass, as in the world! I
will verify as much in his beard.° He has no more
directions in the true disciplines of the wars, look
75 you, of the Roman disciplines, than is a puppy-dog.

Enter Macmorris and Captain Jamy.

Gower. Here 'a comes, and the Scots captain, Captain
Jamy, with him.

Fluellen. Captain Jamy is a marvelous falorous gentleman, that is certain, and of great expedition° and

---

54 **goes against my weak stomach** (1) is against my disposition (2) makes
me sick   55 **cast it up** (1) run from their service (2) be sick   56
presently immediately   61–62 **disciplines of the war** military
experience   63 **discuss** declare   64–65 **four yard under the countermines** countermines four yards under the mines   65 **plow** (the first of
Fluellen's dialect substitutions of "p" for "b")   73 **verify as much in his
beard** prove it to his face   79 **expedition** readiness in disputation (rhetorical term)

knowledge in th' aunchient wars, upon my particu-   80
lar° knowledge of his directions. By Cheshu, he will
maintain his argument as well as any military man
in the world in the disciplines of the pristine wars
of the Romans.

Jamy. I say gud day, Captain Fluellen.   85

Fluellen. God-den to your worship, good Captain
James.

Gower. How now, Captain Macmorris? Have you quit
the mines? Have the pioners° given o'er?

Macmorris. By Chrish, law, tish ill done! The work   90
ish give over, the trumpet sound the retreat. By my
hand I swear, and my father's soul, the work ish
ill done! It ish give over. I would have blowed up
the town, so Chrish save me, law, in an hour. O,
tish ill done, tish ill done! By my hand, tish ill done!   95

Fluellen. Captain Macmorris, I beseech you now, will
you voutsafe me, look you, a few disputations with
you, as partly touching or concerning the disciplines of the war, the Roman wars?—in the way of
argument, look you, and friendly communication;   100
partly to satisfy my opinion, and partly for the satisfaction, look you, of my mind—as touching the
direction of the military discipline, that is the point.

Jamy. It sall be vary gud, gud feith, gud captens bath,
and I sall quit° you with gud leve, as I may pick   105
occasion. That sall I, mary.°

Macmorris. It is no time to discourse, so Chrish save
me! The day is hot, and the weather, and the wars,
and the King, and the Dukes; it is no time to discourse; the town is beseeched,° and the trumpet call   110
us to the breach, and we talk, and, be Chrish, do
nothing; 'tis shame for us all, so God sa' me, 'tis
shame to stand still, it is shame, by my hand! And

80–81 **particular** personal   89 **pioners** pioneers, miners   105 **quit**
answer   106 **mary** (Jamy's pronunciation of "marry," a mild oath, from
"By the Virgin Mary")   110 **beseeched** (for "besieged")

there is throats to be cut, and works to be done,
115   and there ish nothing done, so Chrish sa' me, law!

Jamy. By the mess, ere theise eyes of mine take themselves to slomber, I'll do gud service, or I'll lig i'
th' grund for it! Ay or go to death! And I'll pay't
as valorously as I may, that sall I suerly do, that
120   is the breff and the long. Mary, I wad full fain
heard some question 'tween you tway.

Fluellen. Captain Macmorris, I think, look you, under
your correction, there is not many of your nation—

Macmorris. Of my nation? What ish my nation? Ish
125   a villain, and a basterd, and a knave, and a rascal.
What ish my nation? Who talks of my nation?

Fluellen. Look you, if you take the matter otherwise
than is meant, Captain Macmorris, peradventure I
shall think you do not use me with that affability
130   as in discretion you ought to use me, look you, being as good a man as yourself, both in the disciplines of war, and in the derivation of my birth, and
in other particularities.

Macmorris. I do not know you so good a man as my-
135   self; so Chrish save me, I will cut off your head!

Gower. Gentlemen both, you will° mistake each
other.

Jamy. Ah, that's a foul fault!   *A parley* [*sounded*].

Gower. The town sounds a parley.

140   *Fluellen.* Captain Macmorris, when there is more better opportunity to be required,° look you, I will be
so bold as to tell you I know the disciplines of war;
and there is an end.   *Exit* [*with others*].

136 **will** are determined to   141 **to be required** serves

[Scene 3. *Before the gates of Harfleur.*]

Enter the King [Henry] and all his Train
before the gates.

King. How yet resolves the Governor of the town?
 This is the latest parle we will admit:
 Therefore to our best mercy give yourselves,
 Or, like to men proud of destruction,°
 Defy us to our worst; for, as I am a soldier,   *5*
 A name that in my thoughts becomes me best,
 If I begin the batt'ry once again,
 I will not leave the half-achieved Harfleur
 Till in her ashes she lie buried.
 The gates of mercy shall be all shut up,   *10*
 And the fleshed° soldier, rough and hard of heart,
 In liberty of bloody hand shall range
 With conscience wide as hell, mowing like grass
 Your fresh fair virgins and your flow'ring infants.
 What is it then to me if impious war,   *15*
 Arrayed in flames like to the prince of fiends,
 Do with his smirched complexion all fell° feats
 Enlinked to waste and desolation?
 What is't to me, when you yourselves are cause,
 If your pure maidens fall into the hand   *20*
 Of hot and forcing violation?
 What rein can hold licentious wickedness
 When down the hill he holds his fierce career?°
 We may as bootless spend our vain command
 Upon th' enragèd soldiers in their spoil°   *25*
 As sends precepts° to the leviathan°
 To come ashore. Therefore, you men of Harfleur,

3.3.4 **proud of destruction** glorying in death 11 **fleshed** initiated in
slaughter 17 **fell** savage 23 **career** gallop 25 **spoil** plundering
26 **precepts** written instructions 26 **leviathan** legendary aquatic
animal of enormous size (common in Hebrew poetry)

Take pity of your town and of your people
Whiles yet my soldiers are in my command,
30   Whiles yet the cool and temperate wind of grace
O'erblows the filthy and contagious clouds
Of heady murder, spoil, and villainy.
If not—why, in a moment look to see
The blind° and bloody soldier with foul hand
35   Defile the locks of your shrill-shrieking daughters;
Your fathers taken by the silver beards,
And their most reverend heads dashed to the walls;
Your naked infants spitted upon pikes,
Whiles the mad mothers with their howls confused
40   Do break the clouds, as did the wives of Jewry
At Herod's bloody-hunting slaughtermen.
What say you? Will you yield, and this avoid?
Or, guilty in defense,° be thus destroyed?

Enter Governor [on the wall].

Governor. Our expectation hath this day an end;
45   The Dauphin, whom of succors we entreated,
Returns us that his powers are yet not ready
To raise so great a siege. Therefore, great King,
We yield our town and lives to thy soft mercy.
Enter our gates, dispose of us and ours,
50   For we no longer are defensible.°

King. Open your gates. Come, uncle Exeter,
Go you and enter Harfleur; there remain
And fortify it strongly 'gainst the French.
Use mercy to them all. For us, dear uncle,
55   The winter coming on, and sickness growing
Upon our soldiers, we will retire to Calais.
Tonight in Harfleur will we be your guest;
Tomorrow for the march are we addrest.°
                    Flourish, and enter the town.

34 **blind** reckless 43 **guilty in defense** to blame for holding
out 50 **defensible** able to make a defense 58 **addrest** prepared

[Scene 4. *Rouen. A room in the palace.*]

Enter Katherine and [*Alice,*] *an old Gentlewoman.*

Katherine. Alice, tu as été en Angleterre, et tu parles
bien le langage.

Alice. Un peu, madame.

Katherine. Je te prie m'enseignez; il faut que j'ap-
prenne à parler. Comment appelez-vous la main en   5
Anglais?

Alice. La main? Elle est appelée de hand.

Katherine. De hand. Et les doigts?

Alice. Les doigts? Ma foi, j'oublie les doigts; mais je
me souviendrai. Les doigts? Je pense qu'ils sont   10
appelés de fingres; oui, de fingres.

Katherine. La main, de hand; les doigts, le fingres. Je
pense que je suis le bon écolier; j'ai gagné deux
mots d'Anglais vitement. Comment appelez-vous
les ongles?   15

Alice. Les ongles? Nous les appelons de nails.

3.4 (translated) *Katherine.* Alice, you have been in England and speak
the language well.
Alice. A little, my lady.
Katherine. I pray you, teach me; I have to learn to speak it. What do you
call *la main* in English?
Alice. La main? It is called de hand.
Katherine. De hand. And *les doigts?*
Alice. Les doigts? Oh dear, I forget *les doigts;* but I shall remember. *Les
doigts?* I think that they are called de fingres; yes, de fingres.
Katherine. La main, de hand; *les doigts, le* fingres. I think that I am an apt
scholar; I have learned two words of English quickly. What do you call
les ongles?
Alice. Les ongles? We call them de nails.

Katherine. De nails. Ecoutez; dites-moi si je parle bien: de hand, de fingres, et de nails.

Alice. C'est bien dit, madame; il est fort bon Anglais.

20 *Katherine.* Dites-moi l'Anglais pour le bras.

Alice. De arm, madame.

Katherine. Et le coude.

Alice. D'elbow.

Katherine. D'elbow. Je m'en fais la répétition de
25 tous les mots que vous m'avez appris dès à présent.

Alice. Il est trop difficile, madame, comme je pense.

Katherine. Excusez-moi, Alice; écoutez: d'hand, de fingre, de nails, d'arma, de bilbow.

Alice. D'elbow, madame.

30 *Katherine.* O Seigneur Dieu, je m'en oublie! D'elbow. Comment appelez-vous le col?

Alice. De nick, madame.

Katherine. De nick. Et le menton?

Alice. De chin.

Katherine. De nails. Listen; tell me if I speak correctly: de hand, de fin-gres, and de nails.
Alice. Well said, my lady; it is very good English.
Katherine. Tell me the English for *le bras.*
Alice. De arm, my lady.
Katherine. And *le coude.*
Alice. D' elbow.
Katherine. D' elbow. I shall repeat all the words you have taught me so far.
Alice. It is too hard, my lady, I think.
Katherine. Pardon me, Alice; listen: d' hand, de fingre, de nails, d' arma, de bilbow.
Alice. D' elbow, my lady.
Katherine. O dear Lord, I forget. D' elbow. What do you call *le col?*
Alice. De nick, my lady.
Katherine. De nick. And *le menton?*
Alice. De chin.

Katherine. De sin. Le col, de nick; le menton, de sin.   35

Alice. Oui. Sauf votre honneur, en vérité, vous pro-
noncez les mots aussi droit que les natifs d'Angleterre.

Katherine. Je ne doute point d'apprendre, par la grace
de Dieu, et en peu de temps.   40

Alice. N'avez-vous pas déjà oublié ce que je vous ai
enseigné?

Katherine. Non, je réciterai à vous promptement: d'
hand, de fingre, de mails—

Alice. De nails, madame.   45

Katherine. De nails, de arm, de ilbow—

Alice. Sauf votre honneur, d' elbow.

Katherine. Ainsi dis-je; d' elbow, de nick, et de sin.
Comment appelez-vous le pied et la robe?

Alice. Le foot, madame; et le count.   50

Katherine. Le foot et le count! O Seigneur Dieu! Ils
sont les mots de son mauvais, corruptible, gros, et
impudique, et non pour les dames d'honneur d'user:
je ne voudrais prononcer ces mots devant les

Katherine. De sin. *Le col,* de nick; *le menton,* de sin.
Alice. Yes. By your leave, indeed you pronounce the words just like a
native of England.
Katherine. I have no doubt that I shall learn, with God's help, and in little
time.
Alice. Have you not already forgotten what I have taught you?
Katherine. No, I shall recite to you now: d' hand, de fingre, de mails—
Alice. De nails, my lady.
Katherine. De nails, de arm, de ilbow—
Alice. By your leave, d' elbow.
Katherine. That's what I said; d' elbow, de nick, and de sin. What do you
call *le pied* and *la robe?*
Alice. The foot, my lady; and the count. [editor's note: these words are
similar in sound to the French equivalents of the English "four-letter"
words; "count" is an attempt at "gown"]
Katherine. The foot and the count! O dear Lord! Those are bad
words, wicked, vulgar, and indecent, and respectable ladies don't
use them. I wouldn't utter those words before French gentlemen

55   seigneurs de France pour tout le monde. Foh, le
        ·foot et le count! Néanmoins, je réciterai une autre
        fois ma leçon ensemble: d' hand, de fingre, de
        nails, d' arm, d' elbow, de nick, de sin, de foot,
        le count.   .

60 *Alice.* Excellent, madame!

    Katherine. C'est assez pour une fois: allons-nous à
        diner.   *Exit [with Alice].*

            [Scene 5. *Rouen. A room in the palace.*]

        *Enter the King of France, the Dauphin, [Bretagne,]
            the Constable of France, and others.*

    King. 'Tis certain he hath passed the river Somme.

    Constable. And if he be not fought withal, my lord,
        Let us not live in France; let us quit all
        And give our vineyards to a barbarous people.

5   *Dauphin.* O Dieu vivant! Shall a few sprays of us,°
        The emptying° of our father's luxury,
        Our scions, put in wild and savage stock,°
        Spirt° up so suddenly into the clouds
        And overlook their grafters?

    Bretagne. Normans, but bastard Normans, Norman
10   bastards!
        Mort Dieu! Ma vie! if they march along

        for the whole world. Fie, the foot and the count! Still, I shall recite
        once more my whole lesson: d' hand, de fingre, de nails, d' arm, d'
        elbow, de sin, de foot, the count.
        Alice. Excellent, my lady.
        Katherine. That's enough for one session: let's go to dinner.
        3.5.5 **sprays of us** offshoots, bastards 6 **emptying** expenditure
        7 **scions, put in wild and savage stock** i.e., Norman French mating with
        Anglo-Saxon ("scions" are shoots, for grafting) 8 **Spirt** sprout, shoot

Unfought withal, but I will sell my dukedom
To buy a slobb'ry° and a dirty farm
In that nook-shotten° isle of Albion.°

Constable. Dieu de batailles! where have they this
        mettle?   15
Is not their climate foggy, raw, and dull,
On whom, as in despite, the sun looks pale,
Killing their fruit with frowns? Can sodden° water,
A drench for sur-reined jades, their barley broth,°
Decoct° their cold blood to such valiant heat?   20
And shall our quick blood, spirited with wine,
Seem frosty? O, for honor of our land,
Let us not hang like roping° icicles
Upon our houses' thatch, whiles a more frosty
        people
Sweat drops of gallant youth in our rich fields—   25
"Poor" we call them° in their native lords!

Dauphin. By faith and honor,
Our madams mock at us and plainly say
Our mettle is bred out,° and they will give
Their bodies to the lust of English youth,   30
To new-store France with bastard warriors.

Bretagne. They bid us to the English dancing schools
And teach lavoltas° high, and swift corantos,°
Saying our grace° is only in our heels,°
And that we are most lofty° runaways.   35

King. Where is Montjoy, the herald? Speed him
        hence;
Let him greet England with our sharp defiance.

---

13 **slobb'ry** waterlogged   14 **nook-shotten** full of odd angles, shapeless   14 **Albion** (an ancient poetical name for Britain, alluding to
the white cliffs visible from France)   18 **sodden** boiled   19 **drench
for sur-reined jades, their barley broth** medicinal draught (or mash)
given to overridden nags, (which is much the same as) their beer
20 **Decoct** warm up   23 **roping** hanging down together like
rope   26 **them** i.e., the "rich fields" of France   29 **bred out** exhausted,
degenerate   33 **lavoltas** dances with high leaps   33 **corantos** dances
with a running step   34 **grace** virtue, saving grace (?)   34 **our heels**
(1) dancing (2) running away   35 **lofty** stately, pompous

Up, Princes, and with spirit of honor edged
More sharper than your swords, hie to the field.
40   Charles Delabreth, High Constable of France,
You Dukes of Orleans, Bourbon, and of Berri,
Alençon, Brabant, Bar, and Burgundy;
Jacques Chatillon, Rambures, Vaudemont,
Beaumont, Grandpré, Roussi, and Faulconbridge,
45   Foix, Lestrale, Bouciqualt, and Charolois,
High dukes, great princes, barons, lords, and
knights,
For your great seats° now quit you of great shames:
Bar Harry England, that sweeps through our land
With pennons painted in the blood of Harfleur;
50   Rush on his host, as doth the melted snow
Upon the valleys whose low vassal seat
The Alps doth spit and void his° rheum upon.
Go down upon him—you have power enough—
And in a captive chariot into Rouen
Bring him our prisoner.

55   *Constable.*   This becomes the great.
Sorry am I his numbers are so few,
His soldiers sick, and famished in their march;
For I am sure, when he shall see our army,
He'll drop his heart into the sink° of fear
60   And, for achievement,° offer us his ransom.

King. Therefore, Lord Constable, haste on Montjoy,
And let him say to England that we send
To know what willing ransom he will give.
Prince Dauphin, you shall stay with us in Rouen.

65   *Dauphin.* Not so, I do beseech your Majesty.

King. Be patient, for you shall remain with us.
Now forth, Lord Constable, and Princes all,
And quickly bring us word of England's fall.

                                        Exeunt.

---

47 **seats** estates   52 **his** i.e., the Alps's   59 **sink** pit   60 **achievement** acquisition (i.e., for France)

[Scene 6. *France. The English camp in Picardy.*]

Enter Captains, English and Welsh:
Gower and Fluellen.

Gower. How now, Captain Fluellen, come you from the bridge?°

Fluellen. I assure you, there is very excellent services° committed at the bridge.

Gower. Is the Duke of Exeter safe?   5

Fluellen. The Duke of Exeter is as magnanimous as Agamemnon, and a man that I love and honor with my soul, and my heart, and my duty, and my live, and my living, and my uttermost power. He is not —God be praised and blessed!—any hurt in the   10 world, but keeps the bridge most valiantly, with excellent discipline. There is an aunchient lieutenant° there at the pridge, I think in my very conscience he is as valiant a man as Mark Anthony, and he is a man of no estimation in the world, but I did see him   15 do as gallant service.

Gower. What do you call him?

Fluellen. He is called Aunchient Pistol.

Gower. I know him not.

Enter Pistol.

Fluellen. Here is the man.   20

Pistol. Captain, I thee beseech to do me favors;
The Duke of Exeter doth love thee well.

3.6.2 **the bridge** (over the Ternoise, captured on October 23, 1415, two days before the battle of Agincourt)   3 **services** exploits   12 **aunchient lieutenant** sublieutenant

Fluellen. Ay, I praise God; and I have merited some
    love at his hands.

25 *Pistol.* Bardolph, a soldier firm and sound of heart,
    And of buxom° valor, hath by cruel fate,
    And giddy Fortune's furious fickle wheel—
    That goddess blind,
    That stands upon the rolling restless stone—

30 *Fluellen.* By your patience, Aunchient Pistol. Fortune
    is painted blind, with a muffler afore her eyes, to
    signify to you that Fortune is blind; and she is
    painted also with a wheel, to signify to you, which
    is the moral of it, that she is turning and incon-
35   stant, and mutability, and variation; and her foot,
    look you, is fixed upon a spherical stone, which
    rolls, and rolls, and rolls. In good truth, the poet
    makes a most excellent description of it; Fortune
    is an excellent moral.°

40 *Pistol.* Fortune is Bardolph's foe, and frowns on him;
    For he hath stol'n a pax,° and hangèd must 'a be—
    A damnèd death!
    Let gallows gape for dog; let man go free,
    And let not hemp his windpipe suffocate.
45   But Exeter hath given the doom° of death
    For pax of little price.
    Therefore, go speak—the Duke will hear thy voice;
    And let not Bardolph's vital thread be cut
    With edge of penny cord, and vile reproach.
50   Speak, Captain, for his life, and I will thee requite.

Fluellen. Aunchient Pistol, I do partly understand
    your meaning.

Pistol. Why then, rejoice therefore!

Fluellen. Certainly, Aunchient, it is not a thing to
55   rejoice at; for if, look you, he were my brother, I
    would desire the Duke to use his good pleasure,

26 **buxom** lively 39 **moral** symbolical figure 41 **pax** tablet depict-
ing the crucifixion, kissed by priest and then communicants at
Mass 45 **doom** sentence

and put him to execution; for discipline ought to be used.

Pistol. Die and be damned! and figo° for thy friendship!

Fluellen. It is well.   60

Pistol. The fig of Spain!°   *Exit.*

Fluellen. Very good.

Gower. Why, this is an arrant° counterfeit rascal! I remember him now—a bawd, a cutpurse.

Fluellen. I'll assure you, 'a utt'red as prave words at   65
the pridge, as you shall see in a summer's day. But it is very well. What he has spoke to me, that is well, I warrant you, when time is serve.

Gower. Why, 'tis a gull,° a fool, a rogue, that now and then goes to the wars, to grace himself at his   70
return into London, under the form of a soldier. And such fellows are perfect in the great commanders' names, and they will learn you by rote where services° were done: at such and such a sconce,° at such a breach, at such a convoy; who came off°   75
bravely, who was shot, who disgraced, what terms the enemy stood on° and this they con° perfectly in the phrase of war, which they trick up with new-tuned oaths;° and what a beard of the general's cut° and a horrid suit of the camp will do among   80
foaming bottles and ale-washed wits is wonderful to be thought on. But you must learn to know such slanders of the age, or else you may be marvelously mistook.

---

59 figo (Spanish for) fig (see next note)   **61 fig of Spain** contemptuous and obscene gesture made by thrusting the thumb between the fingers or into the mouth   **63 arrant** out-and-out   **69 gull** simpleton   **74 services** exploits   **74 sconce** small fort or earthwork   **75 came off** got clear   **76–77 what terms the enemy stood on** what the position of the enemy depended on   **77 con** learn   **78–79 trick up with new-tuned oaths** adorn with newly phrased oaths   **79–80 of the general's cut** shaped in the same fashion as the general's

85 *Fluellen.* I tell you what, Captain Gower: I do per-
     ceive he is not the man that he would gladly make
     show to the world he is. If I find a hole in his coat,°
     I will tell him my mind. [Drum within.] Hark you,
     the King is coming, and I must speak with him
90   from the pridge.

       Drum and Colors. Enter the King and his poor
              Soldiers [and Gloucester].
       God bless your Majesty!

     King. How now, Fluellen, cam'st thou from the
     bridge?

     Fluellen. Ay, so please your Majesty: the Duke of
95   Exeter has very gallantly maintained the pridge; the
     French is gone off, look you, and there is gallant
     and most prave passages.° Marry, th' athversary
     was have possession of the pridge, but he is en-
     forced to retire, and the Duke of Exeter is master
100 of the pridge. I can tell your Majesty, the Duke
     is a prave man.

     King. What men have you lost, Fluellen?

     Fluellen. The perdition of th' athversary hath been
     very great, reasonable great: marry, for my part, I
105 think the Duke hath lost never a man, but one that
     is like to be executed for robbing a church—one
     Bardolph, if your Majesty know the man. His face
     is all bubukles and whelks,° and knobs, and flames
     o' fire, and his lips blows at his nose, and it is like
110 a coal of fire, sometimes plue and sometimes red;
     but his nose is executed,° and his° fire's out.

     King. We would have all such offenders so cut off;°
     and we give express charge that in our marches
     through the country there be nothing compelled

---

87 **a hole in his coat** some fault in him   97 **passages** i.e., of
arms   108 **bubukles and whelks** abscesses-and-carbuncles (a confusion of two words) and pimples   111 **executed** i.e., slit (as he stood in
the pillory before being hanged)   111 **his** its   112 **cut off** put to death

from the villages, nothing taken but paid for; none   *115*
of the French upbraided or abused in disdainful
language; for when lenity and cruelty play for a
kingdom, the gentler gamester is the soonest win-
ner.

> *Tucket.° Enter Montjoy.*

Montjoy. You know me by my habit.°   *120*

King. Well then, I know thee. What shall I know of
thee?

Montjoy. My master's mind.

King. Unfold it.

Montjoy. Thus says my King: Say thou to Harry of   *125*
England, though we seemed dead, we did but sleep.
Advantage° is a better soldier than rashness. Tell
him, we could have rebuked him at Harfleur, but
that we thought not good to bruise an injury° till it
were full ripe. Now we speak upon our cue, and   *130*
our voice is imperial: England shall repent his folly,
see his weakness, and admire our sufferance.° Bid
him therefore consider of his ransom, which must
proportion the losses we have borne, the subjects
we have lost, the disgrace we have digested; which   *135*
in weight to re-answer, his pettiness would bow
under.° For our losses, his exchequer is too poor;
for th' effusion of our blood, the muster of his
kingdom too faint a number; and for our disgrace,
his own person kneeling at our feet but a weak and   *140*
worthless satisfaction. To this add defiance; and
tell him for conclusion, he hath betrayed his followers, whose condemnation is pronounced. So far
my King and master; so much my office.

King. What is thy name? I know thy quality.   *145*

119s.d. **Tucket** a personal trumpet call   120 **habit** i.e., the herald's
tabard   127 **Advantage** favorable opportunity   129 **bruise an injury**
squeeze out a festering wound   132 **admire our sufferance** wonder at
our patience   136–37 **in weight … bow under** to compensate in full
would be too much for his small resources

Montjoy. Montjoy.°

King.   Thou dost thy office fairly. Turn thee back,
    And tell thy King, I do not seek him now,
    But could be willing to march on to Calais
150   Without impeachment;° for, to say the sooth,
    Though 'tis no wisdom to confess so much
    Unto an enemy of craft and vantage,°
    My people are with sickness much enfeebled,
    My numbers lessened; and those few I have
155   Almost no better than so many French,
    Who when they were in health, I tell thee, herald,
    I thought upon one pair of English legs
    Did march three Frenchmen. Yet forgive me, God,
    That I do brag thus! This your air of France
160   Hath blown that vice in me. I must repent.
    Go therefore tell thy master, here I am;
    My ransom is this frail and worthless trunk;
    My army but a weak and sickly guard;
    Yet, God before, tell him we will come on,
165   Though France himself and such another neighbor
    Stand in our way. There's for thy labor, Montjoy.
                        [*Gives a purse.*]
    Go bid thy master well advise himself:
    If we may pass, we will; if we be hind'red,
    We shall your tawny ground with your red blood
170   Discolor; and so, Montjoy, fare you well.
    The sum of all our answer is but this:
    We would not seek a battle as we are,
    Nor, as we are, we say we will not shun it.
    So tell your master.

175 *Montjoy.* I shall deliver so. Thanks to your Highness.
                                  [*Exit.*]

Gloucester. I hope they will not come upon us now.

King. We are in God's hand, brother, not in theirs.
    March to the bridge, it now draws toward night;

146 **Montjoy** (title of chief herald of France, not his name)   150
impeachment hindrance   152 **craft and vantage** cunning and superiority

Beyond the river we'll encamp ourselves,
And on tomorrow bid them march away.   *Exeunt.* 180

[Scene 7. *France. The French camp, near
Agincourt.*]

*Enter the Constable of France, the Lord Rambures,
Orleans, Dauphin, with others.*

Constable. Tut! I have the best armor of the world.
Would it were day!

Orleans. You have an excellent armor; but let my
horse have his due.

Constable. It is the best horse of Europe.   5

Orleans. Will it never be morning?

Dauphin. My Lord of Orleans, and my Lord High
Constable, you talk of horse and armor?

Orleans. You are as well provided of both as any
prince in the world.   10

Dauphin. What a long night is this! I will not change
my horse with any that treads but on four pasterns.
Ça, ha! He bounds from the earth, as if his entrails
were hairs;° le cheval volant, the Pegasus, chez les
narines de feu!° When I bestride him, I soar, I am   15
a hawk; he trots the air; the earth sings when he
touches it. The basest horn of his hoof is more
musical than the pipe of Hermes.°

Orleans. He's of the color of the nutmeg.

3.7.13–14 **as if his entrails were hairs** i.e., as if he were a tennis ball (or
perhaps "hairs" = hares)   14–15 **le cheval . . . de feu** the flying horse,
Pegasus, with fiery nostrils   17–18 **The basest horn . . . pipe of
Hermes** (the winged horse, Pegasus, struck Mount Helicon with his hoof
and the fountain of the Muses sprang forth; Hermes, alias Mercury,
invented the pipe and charmed to sleep Argus of the hundred eyes)

20 *Dauphin.* And of the heat of the ginger. It is a beast
      for Perseus:° he is pure air and fire; and the dull
      elements of earth and water never appear in him,
      but only in patient stillness while his rider mounts
      him. He is indeed a horse, and all other jades° you
25   may call beasts.

    Constable. Indeed, my lord, it is a most absolute and
      excellent horse.

    Dauphin. It is the prince of palfreys;° his neigh is like
      the bidding of a monarch, and his countenance en-
30   forces homage.

    Orleans. No more, cousin.

    Dauphin. Nay, the man hath no wit that cannot, from
      the rising of the lark to the lodging of the lamb,
      vary° deservèd praise on my palfrey; it is a theme
35   as fluent as the sea. Turn the sands into eloquent
      tongues, and my horse is argument° for them all.
      'Tis a subject for a sovereign to reason° on, and
      for a sovereign's sovereign to ride on; and for the
      world, familiar to us and unknown, to lay apart
40   their particular functions, and wonder at him. I
      once writ a sonnet in his praise and began thus,
      "Wonder of nature!"

    Orleans. I have heard a sonnet begin so to one's
      mistress.

45 *Dauphin.* Then did they imitate that which I com-
      posed to my courser, for my horse is my mistress.

    Orleans. Your mistress bears well.°

    Dauphin. Me well, which is the prescript° praise and
      perfection of a good and particular° mistress.

---

21 **Perseus** (Pegasus sprang from the blood of the gorgon, Medusa,
when Perseus cut off her head) 24 **jades** nags 28 **palfreys** saddle
horses (too light for use in battle) 34 **vary** express in different
ways 36 **argument** subject 37 **reason** discourse 47 **bears well**
carries her rider well 48 **prescript** prescribed 49 **particular** private

Constable. Nay, for methought yesterday your mis- 50
tress shrewdly° shook your back.

Dauphin. So perhaps did yours.

Constable. Mine was not bridled.°

Dauphin. O, then belike she was old and gentle, and
you rode like a kern° of Ireland, your French hose° 55
off, and in your strait strossers.°

Constable. You have good judgment in horsemanship.°

Dauphin. Be warned by me then: they that ride so,
and ride not warily, fall into foul bogs. I had rather 60
have my horse to my mistress.

Constable. I had as lief have my mistress a jade.°

Dauphin. I tell thee, Constable, my mistress wears his
own hair.°

Constable. I could make as true a boast as that, if I 65
had a sow to my mistress.

Dauphin. "Le chien est retourné à son propre vomis-
sement, et la truie lavée au bourbier."° Thou mak'st
use of anything.

Constable. Yet do I not use my horse for my mistress, 70
or any such proverb so little kin to the purpose.

Rambures. My Lord Constable, the armor that I saw
in your tent tonight—are those stars or suns upon
it?

Constable. Stars, my lord. 75

Dauphin. Some of them will fall tomorrow, I hope.

---

51 **shrewdly** (1) severely (2) shrewishly (cf. line 53)   53 **bridled** (as (1) a
horse (2) a shrew compelled to wear a bridle)   55 **kern** lightly armed Irish
foot soldier   55 **French hose** loose, wide breeches   56 **strait strossers**
tight trousers (i.e., bare-legged)   57–58 **horsemanship** (with a pun on
"whores-manship")   62 **jade** (1) poor horse (2) loose woman   63–64
wears his own hair i.e., doesn't need a (fashionable) wig   67–68
Le chien . . . bourbier cf. 2 Peter 2:22 "The dog is turned to his own vomit
again, and the sow that was washed to her wallowing in the mire"

Constable. And yet my sky shall not want.

Dauphin. That may be, for you bear a many super-
fluously, and 'twere more honor some were away.

80 *Constable.* Ev'n as your horse bears your praises, who
would trot as well, were some of your brags dis-
mounted.

Dauphin. Would I were able to load him with his
desert! Will it never be day? I will trot tomorrow a
85 mile, and my way shall be paved with English faces.

Constable. I will not say so, for fear I should be faced
out of my way;° but I would it were morning, for
I would fain be about the ears of the English.

Rambures. Who will go to hazard° with me for twenty
90 prisoners?

Constable. You must first go yourself to hazard, ere
you have them.

Dauphin. 'Tis midnight; I'll go arm myself.   *Exit.*

Orleans. The Dauphin longs for morning.

95 *Rambures.* He longs to eat the English.

Constable. I think he will eat all he kills.

Orleans. By the white hand of my lady, he's a gallant
prince.

Constable. Swear by her foot, that she may tread out°
100 the oath.

Orleans. He is simply the most active gentleman of
France.

Constable. Doing is activity, and he will still be
doing.°

105 *Orleans.* He never did harm, that I heard of.

86–87 **faced out of my way** (1) put out of countenance (2) driven
off   89 **go to hazard** take a wager   99 **tread out** (1) obliterate (2)
treat with contempt   104 **doing** having sexual intercourse

Constable. Nor will do none tomorrow; he will keep
  that good name still.

Orleans. I know him to be valiant.

Constable. I was told that, by one that knows him
  better than you.   *110*

Orleans. What's he?

Constable. Marry, he told me so himself, and he said
  he cared not who knew it.

Orleans. He needs not; it is no hidden virtue in him.

Constable. By my faith, sir, but it is! Never anybody   *115*
  saw it but his lackey;° 'tis a hooded valor, and when
  it appears, it will bate.°

Orleans. Ill will never said well.

Constable. I will cap that proverb with "There is
  flattery in friendship."   *120*

Orleans. And I will take up that with "Give the devil
  his due."

Constable. Well placed! There stands your friend for
  the devil. Have at the very eye of that proverb with
  "A pox of the devil!"   *125*

Orleans. You are the better at proverbs, by how much
  "a fool's bolt is soon shot."

Constable. You have shot over.°

Orleans. 'Tis not the first time you were overshot.°

                   Enter a Messenger.

Messenger. My Lord High Constable, the English lie   *130*
  within fifteen hundred paces of your tents.

Constable. Who hath measured the ground?

116 **but his lackey** i.e., he has beaten no one but his foot-
boy 116–17 **hooded valor . . . will bate** valor like a hawk hooded before action, which flutters and beats its wings when its hood is
removed   117 **bate** (1) beat its wings (2) become dejected   128 **over**
beyond the mark   129 **overshot** (1) wide of the mark (2) beaten in
shooting

Messenger. The Lord Grandpré.

Constable. A valiant and most expert gentleman.
135   Would it were day! Alas, poor Harry of England!
He longs not for the dawning, as we do.

Orleans. What a wretched and peevish° fellow is this
King of England, to mope with his fat-brained followers so far out of his knowledge!

140 *Constable.* If the English had any apprehension,° they
would run away.

Orleans. That they lack; for if their heads had any
intellectual armor, they could never wear such
heavy headpieces.

145 *Rambures.* That island of England breeds very valiant
creatures: their mastiffs are of unmatchable
courage.

Orleans. Foolish curs, that run winking° into the
mouth of a Russian bear, and have their heads
150   crushed like rotten apples! You may as well say,
that's a valiant flea, that dare eat his breakfast on
the lip of a lion.

Constable. Just, just! And the men do sympathize
with the mastiffs in robustious and rough coming
155   on, leaving their wits with their wives: and then
give them great meals of beef, and iron and steel;
they will eat like wolves and fight like devils.

Orleans. Ay, but these English are shrewdly° out of
beef.

160 *Constable.* Then shall we find tomorrow they have
only stomachs° to eat, and none to fight. Now is
it time to arm; come, shall we about it?

Orleans. It is now two o'clock; but let me see—by
ten
We shall have each a hundred Englishmen.   *Exeunt.*

---

137 **peevish** senseless   140 **apprehension** understanding, grasp of mind
148 **winking** with eyes shut   158 **shrewdly** very much   161 **stomachs**
disposition

ACT [4]

Chorus.

Now entertain conjecture of a time
When creeping murmur and the poring° dark
Fills the wide vessel of the universe.
From camp to camp, through the foul womb of night,
The hum of either army stilly° sounds;   5
That the fixed sentinels almost receive
The secret whispers of each other's watch.
Fire answers fire, and through their paly° flames
Each battle° sees the other's umbered° face.
Steed threatens steed, in high and boastful neighs   10
Piercing the night's dull ear; and from the tents
The armorers accomplishing° the knights,
With busy hammers closing rivets up,
Give dreadful note° of preparation.
The country cocks do crow, the clocks do toll;   15
And the third hour of drowsy morning named.
Proud of their numbers, and secure° in soul,
The confident and over-lusty° French
Do the low-rated English play° at dice;
And chide the cripple tardy-gaited night   20
Who like a foul and ugly witch doth limp
So tediously away. The poor condemnèd English,

4 Prologue 2 **poring** eye-straining 5 **stilly** softly 8 **paly** pale
(poetic) 9 **battle** army 9 **umbered** shadowed 12 **accomplishing**
equipping 14 **note** indication 17 **secure** confident 18 **over-lusty**
too lively 19 **play** play for

Like sacrifices, by their watchful° fires
Sit patiently, and inly ruminate
The morning's danger; and their gesture° sad,
Investing° lank-lean cheeks and war-worn coats,
Presenteth them unto the gazing moon
So many horrid ghosts. O, now, who will behold
The royal captain of this ruined band
Walking from watch to watch, from tent to tent,
Let him cry, "Praise and glory on his head!"
For forth he goes and visits all his host,
Bids them good morrow with a modest smile,
And calls them brothers, friends, and countrymen.
Upon his royal face there is no note
How dread an army hath enrounded him;
Nor doth he dedicate one jot of color
Unto° the weary and all-watchèd° night;
But freshly looks, and overbears attaint°
With cheerful semblance and sweet majesty;
That every wretch, pining and pale before,
Beholding him, plucks comfort from his looks.
A largess universal, like the sun,
His liberal eye doth give to everyone,
Thawing cold fear, that mean and gentle all
Behold, as may unworthiness define,°
A little touch of Harry in the night.
And so our scene must to the battle fly;
Where (O for pity!) we shall much disgrace,
With four or five most vile and ragged foils°
Right ill-disposed in brawl ridiculous,
The name of Agincourt. Yet sit and see,
Minding true things by what their mock'ries° be.

Exit.

---

23 **watchful** used for keeping watch   25 **gesture** bearing   26 **Investing** accompanying   37–38 **dedicate one jot of color/Unto** look pale on account of   38 **all-watchèd** entirely spent in watches   39 **overbears attaint** overcomes any sign of exhaustion   46 **as may unworthiness define** as far as our unworthy selves can present it   50 **foils** light fencing weapons   53 **mock'ries** imitations

[Scene 1. *France. The English camp at Agincourt.*]

Enter the King, Bedford, and Gloucester.

King. Gloucester, 'tis true that we are in great danger;
  The greater therefore should our courage be.
  Good morrow, brother Bedford. God Almighty!
  There is some soul of goodness in things evil,
  Would men observingly distill it out;   5
  For our bad neighbor makes us early stirrers,
  Which is both healthful, and good husbandry.°
  Besides, they are our outward° consciences,
  And preachers to us all, admonishing
  That we should dress us° fairly for our end.   10
  Thus may we gather honey from the weed
  And make a moral° of the devil himself.

Enter Erpingham.

  Good morrow, old Sir Thomas Erpingham:
  A good soft pillow for that good white head
  Were better than a churlish turf of France.   15

Erpingham. Not so, my liege. This lodging likes me
    better,
  Since I may say, "Now lie I like a king."

King. 'Tis good for men to love their present pains
  Upon° example: so the spirit is eased;
  And when the mind is quick'ned, out of doubt   20
  The organs,° though defunct° and dead before,
  Break up their drowsy grave, and newly° move
  With casted slough and fresh legerity.°

4.1.7 **husbandry** careful management   8 **outward** i.e., not our own
inner   10 **dress us** prepare ourselves   12 **moral** improving lesson
19 **Upon** in pursuance of   21 **organs** parts of the body   21 **defunct**
out of use   22 **newly** (a snake is torpid before casting its slough)
23 **legerity** nimbleness

Lend me thy cloak, Sir Thomas. Brothers, both,
25   Commend me to the princes in our camp;
Do my good morrow to them, and anon
Desire them all to my pavilion.

Gloucester. We shall, my liege.

Erpingham. Shall I attend your Grace?

King.   No, my good knight.
30   Go with my brothers to my lords of England.
I and my bosom must debate awhile,
And then I would no other company.

Erpingham. The Lord in heaven bless thee, noble
Harry!   *Exeunt [all but the King].*

King. God-a-mercy, old heart! thou speak'st cheerfully.

Enter Pistol.

35   *Pistol.* Qui va là?°

King. A friend.

Pistol. Discuss° unto me; art thou officer,
Or art thou base, common, and popular?°

King. I am a gentleman of a company.

40   *Pistol.* Trail'st thou the puissant pike?°

King. Even so. What are you?

Pistol. As good a gentleman as the Emperor.

King. Then you are a better than the King.

Pistol. The King's a bawcock,° and a heart of gold,
45   A lad of life, an imp° of fame,
Of parents good, of fist most valiant.
I kiss his dirty shoe, and from heartstring

35 **Qui va là** who goes there   37 **Discuss** declare   38 **popular** vulgar
40 **Trail'st thou the puissant pike?** i.e., are you an infantryman? (a
pike was held below its head, the butt trailing behind on the ground)
44 **bawcock** fine fellow (familiar term)   45 **imp** child

I love the lovely bully.° What is thy name?

King. Harry le Roy.

Pistol. Le Roy? A Cornish name. Art thou of Cornish   50
    crew?

King. No, I am a Welshman.

Pistol. Know'st thou Fluellen?

King. Yes.

Pistol. Tell him I'll knock his leek about his pate
    Upon Saint Davy's day.°   55

King. Do not you wear your dagger in your cap that
    day, lest he knock that about yours.

Pistol. Art thou his friend?

King. And his kinsman too.

Pistol. The figo° for thee then!   60

King. I thank you. God be with you!

Pistol. My name is Pistol called.   *Exit.*

King. It sorts° well with your fierceness.
                              Manet° King [aside].

Enter Fluellen and Gower.

Gower. Captain Fluellen!

Fluellen. So! in the name of Jesu Christ, speak fewer.°   65
    It is the greatest admiration in the universal world,
    when the true and aunchient prerogatifes and laws
    of the wars is not kept. If you would take the pains
    but to examine the wars of Pompey the Great, you
    shall find, I warrant you, that there is no tiddle   70
    taddle nor pibble babble in Pompey's camp; I war-
    rant you, you shall find the ceremonies of the wars,

48 **bully** fine fellow (familiar, endearing term)   55 **Saint Davy's day**
March 1   60 **figo** fig (Spanish), contemptuous and obscene gesture
63 **sorts** suits (the Elizabethan pistol was notably noisy and ineffective)   63s.d. **Manet** remains (Latin)   65 **fewer** less

and the cares of it, and the forms of it, and the
sobriety of it, and the modesty° of it, to be other-
75   wise.

Gower. Why, the enemy is loud; you hear him all
night.

Fluellen. If the enemy is an ass and a fool and a
prating coxcomb, is it meet, think you, that we
80   should also, look you, be an ass and a fool and a
prating coxcomb, in your own conscience now?

Gower. I will speak lower.

Fluellen. I pray you, and beseech you that you will.
                                    Exit [*with Gower*].

King. Though it appear a little out of fashion,°
85   There is much care and valor in this Welshman.

     Enter three Soldiers: John Bates, Alexander Court,
             and Michael Williams.

Court. Brother John Bates, is not that the morning
which breaks yonder?

Bates. I think it be; but we have no great cause to
desire the approach of day.

90   *Williams.* We see yonder the beginning of the day, but
I think we shall never see the end of it. Who goes
there?

King. A friend.

Williams. Under what captain serve you?

95   *King.* Under Sir Thomas Erpingham.

Williams. A good old commander, and a most kind
gentleman. I pray you, what thinks he of our
estate?°

King. Even as men wracked upon a sand, that look to
100   be washed off the next tide.

74 **modesty** moderation   84 **out of fashion** odd   98 **estate** state, condition

Bates. He hath not told his thought to the King?

King. No; nor it is not meet he should. For though I
speak it to you, I think the King is but a man, as
I am: the violet smells to him, as it doth to me; the
element shows° to him, as it doth to me; all his   *105*
senses have but human conditions.° His ceremo-
nies° laid by, in his nakedness he appears but a man;
and though his affections are higher mounted than
ours, yet when they stoop,° they stoop with the like
wing: therefore, when he sees reason of° fears, as   *110*
we do, his fears, out of doubt, be of the same rel-
ish as ours are. Yet, in reason, no man should possess him with any appearance of fear, lest he, by
showing it, should dishearten his army.

Bates. He may show what outward courage he will;   *115*
but I believe, as cold a night as 'tis, he could wish
himself in Thames up to the neck; and so I would
he were, and I by him, at all adventures,° so we
were quit here.°

King. By my troth, I will speak my conscience° of the   *120*
King: I think he would not wish himself anywhere
but where he is.

Bates. Then I would he were here alone; so should he
be sure to be ransomed, and a many poor men's
lives saved.   *125*

King. I dare say you love him not so ill to wish him
here alone; howsoever you speak this to feel other
men's minds. Methinks I could not die anywhere so
contented as in the King's company, his cause being just and his quarrel honorable.   *130*

Williams. That's more than we know.

Bates. Ay, or more than we should seek after; for we

---

105 **element shows** sky appears 106 **conditions** characteristics 106–
07 **ceremonies** accompaniments of royalty 109 **stoop** (used of a
hawk swooping down on its prey) 110 **of** for 118 **at all adventures**
whatever the consequences 119 **quit here** done with this job 120
conscience inmost thought

know enough if we know we are the King's subjects: if his cause be wrong, our obedience to the
135   King wipes the crime of it out of us.

Williams. But if the cause be not good, the King himself hath a heavy reckoning to make, when all those
legs and arms and heads, chopped off in a battle,
shall join together at the latter day and cry all,
140   "We died at such a place," some swearing, some
crying for a surgeon, some upon their wives left
poor behind them, some upon the debts they owe,
some upon their children rawly° left. I am afeard
there are few die well° that die in a battle; for how
145   can they charitably dispose of anything when blood
is their argument? Now, if these men do not die
well, it will be a black matter for the King that led
them to it; who to disobey, were against all proportion of subjection.°

150   *King.* So, if a son that is by his father sent about
merchandise do sinfully miscarry° upon the sea, the
imputation of his wickedness, by your rule, should
be imposed upon his father that sent him; or if a
servant, under his master's command transporting
155   a sum of money, be assailed by robbers and die in
many irreconciled° iniquities, you may call the business of the master the author of the servant's
damnation. But this is not so. The king is not
bound to answer° the particular endings of his sol-
160   diers, the father of his son, nor the master of his
servant; for they purpose not their death when they
purpose not their services. Besides, there is no king, be
his cause never so spotless, if it come to the arbi-
trament of swords, can try it out with all unspotted
165   soldiers: some (peradventure) have on them the
guilt of premeditated and contrived murder; some,

143 **rawly** (1) unprepared (2) at immature age   144 **well** i.e., a Christian death   148–49 **proportion of subjection** due relation of subject to
monarch   151 **sinfully miscarry** perish in his sins   156 **irreconciled**
not atoned for   159 **answer** render account for

of beguiling virgins with the broken seals° of perjury; some, making the wars their bulwark,° that
have before gored the gentle bosom of peace with
pillage and robbery. Now, if these men have de-   170
feated the law and outrun native° punishment,
though they can outstrip men, they have no wings
to fly from God. War is his beadle,° war is his vengeance; so that here men are punished for before-
breach° of the King's laws in now the King's quar-   175
rel. Where they feared the death, they have borne
life away; and where they would be safe, they
perish. Then if they die unprovided,° no more is
the King guilty of their damnation than he was
before guilty of those impieties for the which they   180
are now visited.° Every subject's duty is the King's,
but every subject's soul is his own. Therefore should
every soldier in the wars do as every sick man in
his bed—wash every mote out of his conscience;
and dying so, death is to him advantage; or not dy-   185
ing, the time was blessedly lost wherein such preparation was gained; and in him that escapes, it were
not sin to think that, making God so free° an offer,
He let him outlive that day, to see His greatness,
and to teach others how they should prepare.   190

Williams. 'Tis certain, every man that dies ill, the ill
upon his own head; the King is not to answer it.

Bates. I do not desire he should answer for me, and
yet I determine to fight lustily for him.

King. I myself heard the King say he would not be   195
ransomed.

Williams. Ay, he said so, to make us fight cheerfully;
but when our throats are cut, he may be ransomed,
and we ne'er the wiser.

---

167 **seals** sealed covenants 168 **bulwark** defense (against pursuing
justice) 171 **native** rightful 173 **beadle** parish officer for punishing
petty offenders 174–75 **before-breach** previous breach 178 **unprovided** unprepared 181 **visited** punished 188 **free** complete, whole-
hearted

200 *King.* If I live to see it, I will never trust his word
after.

Williams. You pay him° then! That's a perilous shot
out of an elder-gun,° that a poor and a private°
displeasure can do against a monarch! You may
205 as well go about to turn the sun to ice with fanning
in his face. with a peacock's feather. You'll never
trust his word after! Come, 'tis a foolish saying.

King. Your reproof is something too round;° I should
be angry with you, if the time were convenient.

210 *Williams.* Let it be a quarrel between us, if you live.

King. I embrace it.

Williams. How shall I know thee again?

King. Give me any gage° of thine, and I will wear it
in my bonnet. Then, if ever thou dar'st acknowl-
215 edge it, I will make it my quarrel.

Williams. Here's my glove. Give me another of thine.

King. There.

Williams. This will I also wear in my cap. If ever
thou come to me and say, after tomorrow, "This is
220 my glove," by this hand, I will take° thee a box on
the ear.

King. If ever I live to see it, I will challenge it.

Williams. Thou dar'st as well be hanged.

King. Well, I will do it, though I take thee in the
225 King's company.

Williams. Keep thy word. Fare thee well.

Bates. Be friends, you English fools, be friends! We
have French quarrels enow, if you could tell how
to reckon.

---

202 **pay him** pay him out   203 **elder-gun** popgun (child's toy)   203
private single and common man's   208 **round** plainspoken   213 **gage**
pledge   220 **take** strike

King. Indeed the French may lay twenty French   230
    crowns° to one they will beat us, for they bear
    them on their shoulders;° but it is no English trea-
    son° to cut French crowns, and tomorrow the King
    himself will be a clipper.   *Exeunt Soldiers.*
    "Upon the King! Let us our lives, our souls,   235
    Our debts, our careful° wives,
    Our children, and our sins, lay on the King!"
    We must bear all. O hard condition,
    Twin-born with greatness, subject to the breath°
    Of every fool, whose sense no more can feel   240
    But his own wringing!° What infinite heart's-ease
    Must kings neglect that private men enjoy!
    And what have kings that privates have not too,
    Save ceremony, save general ceremony?
    And what art thou, thou idol Ceremony?   245
    What kind of god art thou, that suffer'st more
    Of mortal griefs than do thy worshippers?
    What are thy rents? What are thy comings-in?
    O Ceremony, show me but thy worth!
    What is thy soul of adoration?°   250
    Art thou aught else but place, degree, and form,°
    Creating awe and fear in other men?
    Wherein thou art less happy, being feared,
    Than they in fearing.
    What drink'st thou oft, instead of homage sweet,   255
    But poisoned flattery? O, be sick, great greatness,
    And bid thy ceremony give thee cure!
    Thinks thou the fiery fever will go out
    With titles blown° from adulation?
    Will it give place to flexure° and low bending?   260
    Canst thou, when thou command'st the beggar's
        knee,

231 **crowns** (1) coins, worth about six shillings each (2) heads
231–32 **for they bear them on their shoulders** i.e., the French can lay
such bets because (1) they so outnumber the English (2) they are still
alive   232–33 **treason** (it was a treasonable offense to debase the
coinage by "clipping," or paring the edges of coins, to take their
gold)   236 **careful**   anxious   239 **breath**   speech   241 **wringing**
stomachache   250 **thy soul of adoration** the real nature of thy
worship   251 **form**   good order   259 **blown**   inflated   260 **flexure**
obsequious bowing

Command the health of it? No, thou proud dream,
That play'st so subtlety with a king's repose.
I am a king that find° thee; and I know
265 'Tis not the balm, the scepter, and the ball,°
The sword, the mace, the crown imperial,
The intertissued robe of gold and pearl,
The farcèd° title running fore the king,
The throne he sits on, nor the tide of pomp
270 That beats upon the high shore° of this world—
No, not all these, thrice-gorgeous ceremony,
Not all these, laid in bed majestical,
Can sleep so soundly as the wretched slave,
Who, with a body filled, and vacant mind,
275 Gets him to rest, crammed with distressful° bread;
Never sees horrid night, the child of hell;
But like a lackey,° from the rise to set,
Sweats in the eye of Phoebus,° and all night
Sleeps in Elysium;° next day after dawn,
280 Doth rise and help Hyperion° to his horse;
And follows so the ever-running year
With profitable labor to his grave;
And but for ceremony, such a wretch,
Winding up° days with toil and nights with sleep,
285 Had the forehand° and vantage of a king.
The slave, a member of° the country's peace,
Enjoys it; but in gross° brain little wots
What watch the king keeps to maintain the peace,
Whose hours the peasant best advantages.°

Enter Erpingham.

Erpingham. My lord, your nobles, jealous° of your
290   absence,

264 **find** discover the true character of 265 **ball** orb 268 **farcèd** stuffed out with pompous phrases 270 **high shore** exalted places 275 **distressful** gained by hard toil 277 **lackey** footman who ran by the coach of his master 278 **Phoebus** sun-god 279 **Elysium** (in mythology, the abode of the blessed after death) 280 **Hyperion** sun-god (more correctly, his father) 284 **Winding up** passing 285 **forehand** upper hand 286 **member of** sharer in 287 **gross** stupid 289 **the peasant best advantages** most benefit the peasant 290 **jealous** anxious

Seek through your camp to find you.

King.   Good old knight,
Collect them all together at my tent.
I'll be before thee.

Erpingham.   I shall do't, my lord.   *Exit.*

King. O God of battles, steel my soldiers' hearts,
Possess them not with fear! Take from them now   *295*
The sense of reck'ning, or th' opposèd numbers
Pluck their hearts from them. Not today, O Lord,
O, not today, think not upon the fault°
My father made in compassing the crown!
I Richard's body have interrèd new,   *300*
And on it have bestowed more contrite tears
Than from it issued forcèd drops of blood.
Five hundred poor I have in yearly pay,
Who twice a day their withered hands hold up
Toward heaven, to pardon blood;   *305*
And I have built two chantries,
Where the sad and solemn priests sing still
For Richard's soul. More will I do:
Though all that I can do is nothing worth;
Since that my penitence comes after all,   *310*
Imploring pardon.

Enter Gloucester.

Gloucester. My liege!

King. My brother Gloucester's voice? Ay.
I know thy errand; I will go with thee.
The day, my friends, and all things stay for me.
                                        Exeunt.

---

298 **the fault** i.e., the deposition of Richard II, and the suggestion for his
subsequent murder

[Scene 2. *France. The French camp.*]

Enter the Dauphin, Orleans, Rambures,
and Beaumont.

Orleans. The sun doth gild our armor. Up, my lords!

Dauphin. Montez à cheval!° My horse! Varlet,
lacquais! Ha!

Orleans. O brave spirit!

Dauphin. Via! les eaux et la terre°—

5　*Orleans.* Rien puis? L'air et le feu.

Dauphin. Ciel, cousin Orleans.

Enter Constable.

Now, my Lord Constable?

Constable. Hark how our steeds for present service
neigh!

Dauphin. Mount them, and make incision in their
hides,

10　That their hot blood may spin° in English eyes
And dout them with superfluous courage,° ha!

Rambures. What, will you have them weep our
horses' blood?
How shall we then behold their natural tears?

Enter Messenger.

Messenger. The English are embattailed, you French
peers.

4.2.2 **Montez à cheval!** To horse!　4　**Via! les eaux et la terre** begone,
water and earth (the Dauphin is still thinking of his horse; Orleans asks if
he does not wish to ride further, to "air and fire." The Dauphin replies,
"Heaven")　10 **spin** gush forth　11 **dout them with superfluous
courage** extinguish them with overflowing blood (the supposed source of
courage)

Constable. To horse, you gallant Princes! straight to
　　　horse!　　　　　　　　　　　　　　　　　　　　　　15
　Do but behold yond poor and starvèd band,
　And your fair show° shall suck away their souls,
　Leaving them but the shales° and husks of men.
　There is not work enough for all our hands,
　Scarce blood enough in all their sickly veins　　　　20
　To give each naked curtle ax° a stain
　That our French gallants shall today draw out
　And sheathe for lack of sport. Let us but blow on
　　　them,
　The vapor of our valor will o'erturn them.
　'Tis positive 'gainst all exceptions,° lords,　　　　25
　That our superfluous lackeys and our peasants,
　Who in unnecessary action swarm
　About our squares of battle, were enow
　To purge this field of such a hilding° foe,
　Though we upon this mountain's basis by　　　　　30
　Took stand for idle speculation:°
　But that our honors must not. What's to say?
　A very little little let us do,
　And all is done. Then let the trumpets sound
　The tucket sonance° and the note to mount;　　　　35
　For our approach shall so much dare° the field
　That England shall couch° down in fear and yield.

Enter Grandpré.

Grandpré. Why do you stay so long, my lords of
　　　France?
　Yond island carrions,° desperate° of their bones,
　Ill-favoredly become the morning field.　　　　　40
　Their ragged curtains° poorly are let loose,
　And our air shakes them passing° scornfully.
　Big Mars seems bankrout° in their beggared host,

---

17 **fair show** spectacular appearance　18 **shales** shells　21 **curtle ax**
cutlass (broad-cutting sword)　25 **exceptions** objections　29 **hilding**
worthless　31 **speculation** looking on　35 **sonance** sound　36 **dare**
dazzle　37 **couch** crouch　39 **carrions** skeletons　39 **desperate** careless, without hope of saving　41 **curtains** i.e., banners　42 **passing**
extremely　43 **bankrout** bankrupt

And faintly through a rusty beaver° peeps.
45   The horsemen sit like fixèd candlesticks
With torch-staves in their hand; and their poor
    jades
Lob° down their heads, dropping the hides and
    hips,
The gum down roping° from their pale-dead eyes,
And in their pale dull mouths the gimmaled° bit
50   Lies foul with chawed grass, still and motionless;
And their executors, the knavish crows,
Fly o'er them all, impatient for their hour.
Description cannot suit itself in words
To demonstrate the life of° such a battle
55   In life so lifeless as it shows itself.

Constable. They have said their prayers, and they stay
    for death.

Dauphin. Shall we go send them dinners, and fresh
    suits,
And give their fasting horses provender,
And after fight with them?

60   *Constable.* I stay but for my guard. On to the field!
I will the banner from a trumpet° take
And use it for my haste. Come, come away!
The sun is high, and we outwear the day.   *Exeunt.*

[Scene 3. *France. The English camp.*]

*Enter Gloucester, Bedford, Exeter, Erpingham
with all his Host, Salisbury, and Westmoreland.*

Gloucester. Where is the King?

44 **beaver** face guard of a helmet   47 **Lob** droop   48 **roping** hanging
like rope   49 **gimmaled** jointed   54 **the life of** to the life   61
trumpet trumpeter

Bedford. The King himself is rode to view their
    battle.°

Westmoreland. Of fighting men they have full three-
    score thousand.

Exeter. There's five to one; besides they all are fresh.

Salisbury. God's arm strike with us! 'Tis a fearful
    odds.   5
    God bye° you, Princes all; I'll to my charge.
    If we no more meet, till we meet in heaven,
    Then joyfully, my noble Lord of Bedford,
    My dear Lord Gloucester, and my good Lord
        Exeter,
    And my kind kinsman, warriors all, adieu!   10

Bedford. Farewell, good Salisbury, and good luck go
    with thee!

Exeter. Farewell, kind lord. Fight valiantly today;
    And yet I do thee wrong to mind thee of it,
    For thou art framed of the firm truth of valor.
                                        [*Exit Salisbury.*]

Bedford. He is as full of valor as of kindness,   15
    Princely in both.

                Enter the King.

Westmoreland.   O that we now had here
    But one ten thousand of those men in England
    That do no work today!

King.   What's he that wishes so?
    My cousin Westmoreland? No, my fair cousin.
    If we are marked to die, we are enow   20
    To do our country loss; and if to live,
    The fewer men, the greater share of honor.
    God's will! I pray thee wish not one man more.
    By Jove, I am not covetous for gold,
    Nor care I who doth feed upon my cost;   25

4.3.2 **battle** battle array   6 **bye** be with

It earns° me not if men my garments wear;
Such outward things dwell not in my desires:
But if it be a sin to covet honor,
I am the most offending soul alive.
30   No, faith, my coz, wish not a man from England.
God's peace! I would not lose so great an honor
As one man more methinks would share from me
For the best hope I have. O, do not wish one more!
Rather proclaim it, Westmoreland, through my
    host,
35   That he which hath no stomach° to this fight,
Let him depart; his passport shall be made,
And crowns for convoy put into his purse;
We would not die in that man's company
That fears his fellowship° to die with us.
40   This day is called the Feast of Crispian:°
He that outlives this day, and comes safe home,
Will stand a-tiptoe when this day is named,
And rouse him at the name of Crispian.
He that shall see this day, and live old age,
45   Will yearly on the vigil feast his neighbors
And say, "Tomorrow is Saint Crispian."
Then will he strip his sleeve and show his scars,
And say, "These wounds I had on Crispin's day."
Old men forget; yet all shall be forgot,
50   But he'll remember, with advantages,°
What feats he did that day. Then shall our names,
Familiar in his mouth as household words—
Harry the King, Bedford and Exeter,
Warwick and Talbot, Salisbury and Gloucester—
55   Be in their flowing cups freshly rememb'red.
This story shall the good man teach his son;
And Crispin Crispian shall ne'er go by,
From this day to the ending of the world,
But we in it shall be rememberèd—

---

26 **earns** grieves   35 **stomach** inclination   39 **fellowship** participation   40 **Crispian** (the brothers, Crispin and Crispian [cf. line 57], fled from Rome during the persecutions of Diocletian and supported and hid themselves as humble shoemakers; they were martyred in A.D. 286)   50 **advantages** added luster

We few, we happy few, we band of brothers;   60
For he today that sheds his blood with me
Shall be my brother;° be he ne'er so vile,°
This day shall gentle his condition.°
And gentlemen in England, now abed,
Shall think themselves accursed they were not here;   65
And hold their manhoods cheap whiles any speaks
That fought with us upon Saint Crispin's day.

Enter Salisbury.

Salisbury. My sovereign lord, bestow yourself with
    speed:
The French are bravely° in their battles set
And will with all expedience° charge on us.   70

King. All things are ready, if our minds be so.

Westmoreland. Perish the man whose mind is backward now!

King. Thou dost not wish more help from England,
    coz?

Westmoreland. God's will, my liege! would you and I
    alone,
Without more help, could fight this royal battle!   75

King. Why, now thou hast unwished five thousand
    men!
Which likes me better than to wish us one.
You know your places: God be with you all!

Tucket. Enter Montjoy.

Montjoy. Once more I come to know of thee, King
    Harry,
If for thy ransom thou wilt now compound;°   80
Before thy most assurèd overthrow;
For certainly thou art so near the gulf

60–62 **brothers ... brother** (like the brother martyrs; see note, line
40) 62 **vile** low of birth 63 **gentle his condition** ennoble his
rank 69 **bravely** finely arrayed 70 **expedience** expedition, speed
80 **compound** make terms

      Thou needs must be englutted.° Besides, in mercy,
      The Constable desires thee thou wilt mind°
85   Thy followers of repentance, that their souls
      May make a peaceful and a sweet retire°
      From off these fields, where (wretches!) their poor bodies
      Must lie and fester.

King.   Who hath sent thee now?

Montjoy. The Constable of France.

90 *King.* I pray thee bear my former answer back:
      Bid them achieve° me, and then sell my bones.
      Good God, why should they mock poor fellows thus?
      The man that once did sell the lion's skin
      While the beast lived, was killed with hunting him.
95   A many of our bodies shall no doubt
      Find native graves; upon the which, I trust,
      Shall witness live in brass of this day's work.
      And those that leave their valiant bones in France,
      Dying like men, though buried in your dunghills,
      They shall be famed; for there the sun shall greet
100   them
      And draw their honors reeking° up to heaven,
      Leaving their earthly parts to choke your clime,
      The smell whereof shall breed a plague in France.
      Mark then abounding valor in our English:
105   That, being dead, like to the bullet's grazing,
      Break out into a second course of mischief,
      Killing in relapse of mortality.°
      Let me speak proudly. Tell the Constable,
      We are but warriors for the working day:°
110   Our gayness and our gilt are all besmirched
      With rainy marching in the painful° field.
      There's not a piece of feather in our host—

83 **englutted** swallowed 84 **mind** remind 86 **retire** retreat (sarcastic) 91 **achieve** kill 101 **reeking** exhaling, rising 107 **relapse of mortality** (1) renewed deadliness (2) with a deadly rebound (?) 109 **for the working day** i.e., (1) who mean business (2) who are not dressed in finery 111 **painful** arduous

Good argument, I hope, we will not fly—
And time hath worn us into slovenry.
But, by the mass, our hearts are in the trim;°   *115*
And my poor soldiers tell me, yet ere night
They'll be in fresher robes,° or they will pluck
The gay new coats o'er the French soldiers' heads
And turn them° out of service. If they do this
(As, if God please, they shall), my ransom then   *120*
Will soon be levied. Herald, save thou thy labor.
Come thou no more for ransom, gentle herald;
They shall have none, I swear, but these my joints;
Which if they have as I will leave 'em them,
Shall yield them little, tell the Constable.   *125*

Montjoy. I shall, King Harry. And so fare thee well:
Thou never shalt hear herald any more.   *Exit.*

King. I fear thou wilt once more come again for a
ransom.°

Enter York.

York. My lord, most humbly on my knee I beg   *130*
The leading of the vaward.°

King. Take it, brave York. Now, soldiers, march
away;
And how thou pleasest, God, dispose the day!
                                        Exeunt.

---

115 **in the trim** (1) in fine fettle (2) fashionably attired   117 **in fresher
robes** i.e., in heavenly robes   119 **them** i.e., the soldiers   128–29 **I
fear . . . for a ransom** (ironic)   131 **vaward** vanguard

[Scene 4. *France. The field of battle.*]

*Alarum. Excursions. Enter Pistol, French
Soldier, Boy.*

Pistol. Yield, cur!

French Soldier. Je pense que vous êtes le gentilhomme
de bonne qualité.°

Pistol. Qualtitie calmie custure me!° Art thou a gen-
5   tleman? What is thy name? Discuss.

French Soldier. O Seigneur Dieu!

Pistol. O Signieur Dew should be a gentleman.
Perpend° my words, O Signieur Dew, and mark:
O Signieur Dew, thou diest on point of fox,°
10   Except, O signieur, thou do give to me
Egregious° ransom.

French Soldier. O, prenez miséricorde, ayez pitié de
moi!°

Pistol. Moy° shall not serve; I will have forty moys,
15   Or I will fetch thy rim° out at thy throat
In drops of crimson blood.

French Soldier. Est-il impossible d'echapper la force
de ton bras?°

4.4.2–3 **Je pense ... qualité** I think you are a gentleman of high
rank   4 **Qualtitie calmie custure me** (possibly a corruption of an Irish
refrain to a popular song: *"Calen o custure me,"* for "the girl from the
[river] Suir")   8 **Perpend** consider   9 **fox** kind of sword   11 **Egregious** huge   12–13 **O, prenez ... de moi** O, have mercy, take pity on
me   14 **Moy** (no coin so called existed; possibly a reference to the measure, about a bushel)   15 **rim** lining of the stomach   17–18 **Est-il ...
bras** is there no way to escape the strength of your arm (the final "s" in
bras was still sounded before a pause in Shakespeare's time)

Pistol. Brass, cur?
  Thou damnèd and luxurious mountain goat,°   20
  Offer'st me brass?

French Soldier. O, pardonnez-moi!

Pistol. Say'st thou me so? Is that a ton of moys?
  Come hither, boy; ask me this slave in French
  What is his name.   25

Boy. Ecoutez: comment êtes-vous appelé?

French Soldier. Monsieur le Fer.

Boy. He says his name is Master Fer.

Pistol. Master Fer? I'll fer him, and firk° him, and
  ferret° him! Discuss the same in French unto him.   30

Boy. I do not know the French for "fer," and "ferret,"
  and "firk."

Pistol. Bid him prepare, for I will cut his throat.

French Soldier. Que dit-il, monsieur?

Boy. Il me commande de vous dire que vous faites   35
  vous prêt; car ce soldat ici est disposé tout à cette
  heure de couper votre gorge.°

Pistol. Owy, cuppele gorge, permafoy!
  Peasant, unless thou give me crowns, brave crowns;
  Or mangled shalt thou be by this my sword.   40

French Soldier. O, je vous supplie, pour l'amour de
  Dieu, me pardonner! Je suis gentilhomme de bonne
  maison. Gardez ma vie, et je vous donnerai deux
  cents écus.°

Pistol. What are his words?   45

---

20 **luxurious mountain goat** lustful wild lecher   29 **firk** (a euphemistic pronunciation of the common four-letter obscenity)   30 **ferret** go for, search out   34–37 **Que ... gorge** What does he say, sir? *Boy.* He bids me tell you that you must prepare yourself, for this soldier intends to cut your throat immediately   41–44 **O, je ... écus** O, I pray you, for the love of God, to pardon me. I am a gentleman of good house. Preserve my life, and I will give you two hundred écus

Boy. He prays you to save his life; he is a gentleman
of a good house, and for his ransom he will give
you two hundred crowns.

Pistol. Tell him my fury shall abate, and I
50   The crowns will take.

French Soldier. Petit monsieur, que dit-il?

Boy. Encore qu'il est contre son jurement de pardonner aucun prisonnier; néanmoins, pour les écus
que vous l'avez promis, il est content de vous
55   donner la liberté, le franchisement.

French Soldier. Sur mes genoux je vous donne mille
remercîments; et je m'estime heureux que je suis
tombé entre les mains d'un chevalier, je pense, le
plus brave, vaillant, et très distingué seigneur
60   d'Angleterre.°

Pistol. Expound unto me, boy.

Boy. He gives you, upon his knees, a thousand
thanks, and he esteems himself happy that he hath
fall'n into the hands of one (as he thinks) the most
65   brave, valorous, and thrice-worthy signieur of England.

Pistol. As I suck blood, I will some mercy show!
Follow me.

Boy. Suivez-vous le grand capitaine.
            [*Exeunt Pistol and French Soldier.*]
70   I did never know so full a voice issue from so
empty° a heart; but the saying is true, "The empty
vessel makes the greatest sound." Bardolph and
Nym had ten times more valor than this roaring
devil i' th' old play that everyone may pare his

52–60 **Encore . . . d' Angleterre** I say again that it is against his oath to
spare any prisoner; nevertheless, because of the écus you have promised
him, he is willing to give you liberty, freedom. *French Soldier.* On my
knees I give you a thousand thanks; and I count myself happy that I have
fallen into the hands of a knight, as I think, the bravest, most valiant, and
eminent gentleman in England   71 **empty** cowardly

nails° with a wooden dagger;° and they are both   75
hanged; and so would this be, if he durst steal anything adventurously. I must stay with the lackeys
with the luggage of our camp—the French might
have a good prey of us, if he knew of it, for there
is none to guard it but boys.   *Exit.*   80

[Scene 5. *France. Another part of the field.*]

*Enter Constable, Orleans, Bourbon, Dauphin,
and Rambures.*

Constable. O diable!

Orleans. O Seigneur! le jour est perdu, tout est
    perdu!°

Dauphin. Mort Dieu, ma vie! all is confounded, all!
    Reproach and everlasting shame
    Sits mocking in our plumes.   *A short alarum.*   5
    O méchante° fortune! Do not run away.

Constable. Why, all our ranks are broke.

Dauphin. O perdurable° shame! Let's stab ourselves.
    Be these the wretches that we played at dice for?

Orleans. Is this the king we sent to for his ransom?   10

Bourbon. Shame, and eternal shame, nothing but
        shame!
    Let us die in honor. Once more back again!
    And he that will not follow Bourbon now,
    Let him go hence, and with his cap in hand
    Like a base pander hold the chamber door   15

74–75 **pare his nails** clip his wings (a proverbial phrase)   75 **wooden
dagger** (weapon of the "Vice" in early Elizabethan plays)   4.5.2 **O
Seigneur . . . perdu** O sir, the day is lost, all is lost   6 **méchante** evil,
spiteful   8 **perdurable** lasting

Whilst by a slave, no gentler° than my dog,
His fairest daughter is contaminated.

Constable. Disorder, that hath spoiled° us, friend us
now!
Let us on° heaps go offer up our lives.

20 *Orleans.* We are enow yet living in the field
To smother up the English in our throngs,
If any order might be thought upon.

Bourbon. The devil take order now! I'll to the
throng;
Let life be short, else shame will be too long.
                               Exit [*with others*].

[Scene 6. *France. Another part of the field.*]

Alarum. Enter the King and his Train, [*Exeter,
and others,*] *with Prisoners.*

King. Well have we done, thrice-valiant countrymen,
But all's not done; yet keep the French the field.

Exeter. The Duke of York commends him to your
Majesty.

King. Lives he, good uncle? Thrice within this hour
5 I saw him down; thrice up again and fighting.
From helmet to the spur all blood he was.

Exeter. In which array, brave soldier, doth he lie,
Larding° the plain; and by his bloody side,
Yoke-fellow to his honor-owing° wounds,
10 The noble Earl of Suffolk also lies.
Suffolk first died; and York, all haggled° over,
Comes to him, where in gore he lay insteeped,

16 **gentler** (1) more noble (2) less rough   18 **spoiled** ruined   19 **on**
in   4.6.8 **Larding** enriching   9 **owing** owning   11 **haggled** mangled

And takes him by the beard, kisses the gashes
That bloodily did yawn upon his face.
He cries aloud, "Tarry, my cousin Suffolk!   15
My soul shall thine keep company to heaven.
Tarry, sweet soul, for mine, then fly abreast;
As in this glorious and well-foughten field
We kept together in our chivalry!"
Upon these words I came, and cheered him up;   20
He smiled me in the face, raught° me his hand,
And, with a feeble gripe, says, "Dear my lord,
Commend my service to my Sovereign."
So did he turn, and over Suffolk's neck
He threw his wounded arm, and kissed his lips;   25
And so, espoused to death, with blood he sealed
A testament of noble-ending love.
The pretty° and sweet manner of it forced
Those waters from me which I would have stopped;
But I had not so much of man in me,   30
And all my mother° came into mine eyes
And gave me up to tears.

King.   I blame you not;
For, hearing this, I must perforce compound°
With mistful eyes, or they will issue too.   *Alarum*.
But hark, what new alarum is this same?   35
The French have reinforced their scattered men.
Then every soldier kill his prisoners!
Give the word through.   *Exit [with others]*.

[Scene 7. *France. Another part of the field.*]

Enter Fluellen and Gower.

Fluellen. Kill the poys and the luggage? 'Tis expressly
    against the law of arms; 'tis as arrant a piece of

21 **raught** reached   28 **pretty** lovely   31 **mother** inherited womanly
feelings   33 **compound** come to terms

knavery, mark you now, as can be offert—in your
conscience, now, is it not?

5 *Gower.* 'Tis certain there's not a boy alive, and
the cowardly rascals that ran from the battle ha'
done this slaughter; besides, they have burned and
carried away all that was in the King's tent; wherefore the King most worthily hath caused every sol-
10 dier to cut his prisoner's throat. O, 'tis a gallant
king!

Fluellen. Ay, he was porn at Monmouth, Captain
Gower. What call you the town's name where Alexander the Pig was born?

15 *Gower.* Alexander the Great.

Fluellen. Why, I pray you, is not "pig" great? The
pig, or the great, or the mighty, or the huge, or the
magnanimous, are all one reckonings, save the
phrase is a little variations.°

20 *Gower.* I think Alexander the Great was born in
Macedon; his father was called Philip of Macedon,
as I take it.

Fluellen. I think it is in Macedon where Alexander
is porn. I tell you, Captain, if you look in the maps
25 of the orld, I warrant you sall find, in the comparisons between Macedon and Monmouth, that
the situations, look you, is both alike. There is a
river in Macedon, and there is also moreover a
river at Monmouth. It is called Wye at Monmouth;
30 but it is out of my prains what is the name of the
other river. But 'tis all one; 'tis alike as my fingers
is to my fingers, and there is salmons in both. If
you mark Alexander's life well, Harry of Monmouth's life is come after it indifferent well, for
35 there is figures° in all things. Alexander, God
knows, and you know, in his rages, and his furies,
and his wraths, and his cholers, and his moods,

4.7.19 **variations** (for "varied")   35 **figures** parallels

and his displeasures, and his indignations, and
also being a little intoxicates in his prains, did, in his
ales and his angers, look you, kill his best friend,   *40*
Cleitus.

Gower. Our King is not like him in that; he never
killed any of his friends.

Fluellen. It is not well done, mark you now, to take
the tales out of my mouth, ere it is made and   *45*
finished. I speak but in the figures and comparisons
of it: as Alexander killed his friend Cleitus, being
in his ales and his cups, so also Harry Monmouth,
being in his right wits and his good judgments,
turned away the fat knight with the great-belly°   *50*
doublet—he was full of jests, and gipes, and knav-
eries, and mocks; I have forgot his name.

Gower. Sir John Falstaff.

Fluellen. That is he: I'll tell you there is good men
porn at Monmouth.   *55*

Gower. Here comes his Majesty.

Alarum. Enter King Harry and Bourbon,
[Warwick, Gloucester, Exeter, and others],
with Prisoners. Flourish.

King. I was not angry since I came to France
Until this instant. Take a trumpet,° herald,
Ride thou unto the horsemen on yond hill:
If they will fight with us, bid them come down,   *60*
Or void the field: they do offend our sight.
If they'll do neither, we will come to them,
And make them skirr° away, as swift as stones
Enforcèd from the old Assyrian slings.
Besides, we'll cut the throats of those we have,   *65*
And not a man of them that we shall take
Shall taste our mercy. Go and tell them so.

Enter Montjoy.

50 **great-belly** (1) styled with stuffed lining (2) large-sized (appropriate
to Falstaff's girth)   58 **trumpet** trumpeter   63 **skirr** scurry

Exeter. Here comes the herald of the French, my
    liege.

Gloucester. His eyes are humbler than they used to be.

King. How now? What means this, herald? Know'st
70   thou not
    That I have fined° these bones of mine for ransom?
    Com'st thou again for ransom?

Herald.   No, great King.
    I come to thee for charitable license,
    That we may wander o'er this bloody field
75   To book° our dead, and then to bury them;
    To sort our nobles from our common men.
    For many of our princes (woe the while!)
    Lie drowned and soaked in mercenary blood;
    So do our vulgar drench their peasant limbs
80   In blood of princes, and their wounded steeds
    Fret fetlock-deep in gore, and with wild rage
    Yerk° out their armèd heels at their dead masters,
    Killing them twice. O, give us leave, great King,
    To view the field in safety, and dispose
    Of their dead bodies!

85 *King.*   I tell thee truly, herald,
    I know not if the day be ours or no,
    For yet a many of your horsemen peer°
    And gallop o'er the field.

Herald.   The day is yours.

King. Praised be God, and not our strength for it!
90   What is this castle called that stands hard by?

Herald. They call it Agincourt.

King. Then call we this the field of Agincourt,
    Fought on the day of Crispin Crispianus.

Fluellen. Your grandfather° of famous memory, an't

71 **fined** paid as a fine (he staked his bones, and having won he now
has every right to them)   75 **book** record   82 **Yerk** kick   87 **peer**
are in sight   94 **grandfather** (in fact Edward III was Henry V's great
grandfather)

please your Majesty, and your great-uncle Edward   *95*
the Plack Prince of Wales, as I have read in the
chronicles, fought a most prave pattle here in
France.

King. They did, Fluellen.

Fluellen. Your Majesty says very true. If your Maj-   *100*
esties is rememb'red of it, the Welshmen did good
service in a garden where leeks did grow, wearing
leeks in their Monmouth caps; which your Majesty
know to this hour is an honorable badge of the
service;° and I do believe your Majesty takes no   *105*
scorn to wear the leek upon Saint Tavy's day.

King. I wear it for a memorable honor;
For I am Welsh, you know, good countryman.

Fluellen. All the water in Wye cannot wash your
Majesty's Welsh plood out of your pody, I can tell   *110*
you that: God pless it, and preserve it, as long
as it pleases his Grace, and his Majesty too!

King. Thanks, good my countryman.

Fluellen. By Jeshu, I am your Majesty's countryman,
I care not who know it! I will confess it to all the   *115*
orld; I need not to be ashamed of your Majesty,
praised be God, so long as your Majesty is an honest man.

King. God keep me so!

                         Enter Williams.

                Our heralds go with him;
Bring me just notice of the numbers dead   *120*
On both our parts.

                   [*Exeunt Heralds, Montjoy, and
                            others, including Gower.*]
                   Call yonder fellow hither.

101–05 **the Welshmen . . . badge of the service** (the custom is usually
said to commemorate a British victory over the Saxons in A.D. 540)

Exeter. Soldier, you must come to the King.

King. Soldier, why wear'st thou that glove in thy cap?

Williams. And't please your Majesty, 'tis the gage of
125   one that I should fight withal, if he be alive.

King. An Englishman?

Williams. And't please your Majesty, a rascal that
swaggered with me last night; who, if alive, and
ever dare to challenge this glove, I have sworn to
130   take° him a box o' th' ear; or if I can see my glove
in his cap, which he swore, as he was a soldier, he
would wear (if alive), I will strike it out soundly.

King. What think you, Captain Fluellen, is it fit this
soldier keep his oath?

135   *Fluellen.* He is a craven and a villain else, and't please
your Majesty, in my conscience.

King. It may be his enemy is a gentleman of great
sort,° quite from the answer of his degree.°

Fluellen. Though he be as good a gentleman as the
140   devil is, as Lucifer and Belzebub himself, it is necessary, look your Grace, that he keep his vow and
his oath. If he be perjured, see you now, his reputation is as arrant a villain and a Jack-sauce° as
ever his black shoe trod upon God's ground and
145   his earth, in my conscience, law!

King. Then keep thy vow, sirrah,° when thou meet'st
the fellow.

Williams. So I will, my liege, as I live.

King. Who serv'st thou under?

150   *Williams.* Under Captain Gower, my liege.

Fluellen. Gower is a good captain, and is good knowledge and literatured in the wars.

130 **take** strike   138 **sort** rank   138 **from the answer of his degree**
above that corresponding to his own rank   143 **Jack-sauce** saucy
Jack   146 **sirrah** (term of address to an inferior)

King. Call him hither to me, soldier.

Williams. I will, my liege.   *Exit.*

King. Here, Fluellen, wear thou this favor for me,   155
and stick it in thy cap; when Alençon and myself
were down together, I plucked this glove from his
helm. If any man challenge this, he is a friend to
Alençon and an enemy to our person. If thou encounter any such, apprehend him, and° thou dost   160
me love.

Fluellen. Your Grace doo's me as great honors as
can be desired in the hearts of his subjects. I would
fain see the man, that has but two legs, that shall
find himself aggriefed at this glove; that is all. But   165
I would fain see it once, and please God of his
grace that I might see.

King. Know'st thou Gower?

Fluellen. He is my dear friend, and please you.

King. Pray thee go seek him, and bring him to my   170
tent.

Fluellen. I will fetch him.   *Exit.*

King. My Lord of Warwick, and my brother
        Gloucester,
    Follow Fluellen closely at the heels.
    The glove which I have given him for a favor   175
    May haply purchase him a box o' th' ear;
    It is the soldier's. I by bargain should
    Wear it myself. Follow, good cousin Warwick:
    If that the soldier strike him—as I judge
    By his blunt bearing, he will keep his word—   180
    Some sudden mischief may arise of it;
    For I do know Fluellen valiant,
    And, touched° with choler, hot as gunpowder,
    And quickly will return an injury.
    Follow, and see there be no harm between them.   185
    Go you with me, uncle of Exeter.   *Exeunt.*

160 **and** if   183 **touched** fired

[Scene 8. *France. Another part of the field.*]

Enter Gower and Williams.

Williams. I warrant it is to knight you, Captain.

Enter Fluellen.

Fluellen. God's will and his pleasure, Captain, I beseech you now, come apace to the King. There is
more good toward you peradventure than is in your
5   knowledge to dream of.

Williams. Sir, know you this glove?

Fluellen. Know the glove? I know the glove is a glove.

Williams. I know this, and thus I challenge it.

Strikes him.

Fluellen. 'Sblood, an arrant traitor as any's in the uni-
10   versal world, or in France, or in England!

Gower. How now, sir? You villain!

Williams. Do you think I'll be forsworn?

Fluellen. Stand away, Captain Gower. I will give treason his payment into plows, I warrant you.

15   *Williams.* I am no traitor.

Fluellen. That's a lie in thy throat. I charge you in
his Majesty's name apprehend him: he's a friend of
the Duke Alençon's.

Enter Warwick and Gloucester.

Warwick. How now, how now? What's the matter?

20   *Fluellen.* My Lord of Warwick, here is (praised be
God for it!) a most contagious treason come to

light, look you, as you shall desire in a summer's
day. Here is his Majesty.

Enter King and Exeter.

King. How now? What's the matter?

Fluellen. My liege, here is a villain and a traitor that,   25
look your Grace, has struck the glove which your
Majesty is take out of the helmet of Alençon.

Williams. My liege, this was my glove, here is the
fellow of it; and he that I gave it to in change
promised to wear it in his cap. I promised to strike   30
him if he did. I met this man with my glove in his
cap, and I have been as good as my word.

Fluellen. Your Majesty hear now, saving your Majesty's manhood, what an arrant, rascally, beggarly,
lousy knave it is! I hope your Majesty is pear me   35
testimony and witness, and will avouchment,° that
this is the glove of Alençon that your Majesty is give
me, in your conscience, now.

King. Give me thy glove, soldier. Look, here is the
fellow of it.   40
'Twas I indeed thou promisèd'st to strike;
And thou hast given me most bitter terms.

Fluellen. And please your Majesty, let his neck answer for it, if there is any martial law in the world.

King. How canst thou make me satisfaction?   45

Williams. All offenses, my lord, come from the heart:
never came any from mine that might offend your
Majesty.

King. It was ourself thou didst abuse.

Williams. Your Majesty came not like yourself: you   50
appeared to me but as a common man; witness the
night, your garments, your lowliness. And what
your Highness suffered under that shape, I be-

4.8.36 **avouchment** i.e., acknowledge

55   seech you take it for your own fault, and not mine;
      for had you been as I took you for, I made no
      offense. Therefore I beseech your Highness pardon
      me.

      King. Here, uncle Exeter, fill this glove with crowns,
      And give it to this fellow. Keep it, fellow,
60   And wear it for an honor in thy cap,
      Till I do challenge it. Give him the crowns;
      And, Captain, you must needs be friends with him.

      Fluellen. By this day and this light, the fellow has
      mettle enough in his belly. Hold, there is twelve
65   pence for you; and I pray you to serve God, and
      keep you out of prawls and prabbles, and quarrels
      and dissensions, and, I warrant you, it is the better
      for you.

      Williams. I will none of your money.

70   *Fluellen.* It is with a good will, I can tell you; it will
      serve you to mend your shoes. Come, wherefore
      should you be so pashful? Your shoes is not so
      good. 'Tis a good silling, I warrant you, or I will
      change it.

                Enter [an English] Herald.

75   *King.* Now, herald, are the dead numb'red?

      Herald. Here is the number of the slaught'red French.

                        [Gives a paper.]

      King. What prisoners of good sort° are taken, uncle?

      Exeter. Charles Duke of Orleans, nephew to the King;
      John Duke of Bourbon and Lord Bouciqualt:
80   Of other lords and barons, knights and squires,
      Full fifteen hundred, besides common men.

      King. This note doth tell me of ten thousand French
      That in the field lie slain. Of princes, in this num-
      ber,

      77 **sort** rank

And nobles bearing banners,° there lie dead
One hundred twenty-six; added to these,   85
Of knights, esquires, and gallant gentlemen,
Eight thousand and four hundred; of the which,
Five hundred were but yesterday dubbed knights.
So that in these ten thousand they have lost
There are but sixteen hundred mercenaries;   90
The rest are princes, barons, lords, knights, squires,
And gentlemen of blood and quality.
The names of those their nobles that lie dead:
Charles Delabreth, High Constable of France;
Jacques of Chatillon, Admiral of France;   95
The master of the crossbows, Lord Rambures;
Great Master of France, the brave Sir Guichard
    Dauphin;
John Duke of Alençon; Anthony Duke of Brabant,
The brother to the Duke of Burgundy;
And Edward Duke of Bar; of lusty earls,
Grandpré and Roussi, Faulconbridge and Foix,   100
Beaumont and Marle, Vaudemont and Lestrale.
Here was a royal fellowship of death!
Where is the number of our English dead?
                    [*Herald gives another paper.*]
Edward the Duke of York, the Earl of Suffolk,   105
Sir Richard Ketly, Davy Gam, esquire;
None else of name; and of all other men
But five-and-twenty. O God, thy arm was here!
And not to us, but to thy arm alone,
Ascribe we all! When, without stratagem,   110
But in plain shock and even play of battle,
Was ever known so great and little loss
On one part and on th' other? Take it, God,
For it is none but thine!

Exeter.   'Tis wonderful!

King. Come, go we in procession to the village;   115
    And be it death proclaimèd through our host
    To boast of this, or take that praise from God
    Which is His only.

84 **bearing banners** i.e., with coats of arms

108 LIFE OF HENRY THE FIFTH 4.8.

Fluellen. Is it not lawful, and please your Majesty,
120   to tell how many is killed?

King. Yes, Captain; but with this acknowledgment,
  That God fought for us.

Fluellen. Yes, my conscience, he did us great good.

King. Do we all holy rites:
125   Let there be sung "Non nobis" and "Te Deum,"
  The dead with charity° enclosed in clay,
  And then to Calais; and to England then;
  Where ne'er from France arrived more happy men.
                                Exeunt.

126 **charity** pious concern

ACT 5

Enter Chorus.

Vouchsafe to those that have not read the story
That I may prompt them; and of such as have,
I humbly pray them to admit th' excuse°
Of time, of numbers, and due course of things
Which cannot in their huge and proper life   5
Be here presented. Now we bear the King
Toward Calais. Grant him there. There seen,
Heave him away upon your wingèd thoughts
Athwart the sea. Behold the English beach
Pales in° the flood, with men, wives, and boys,   10
Whose shouts and claps outvoice the deep-mouthed
    sea,
Which, like a mighty whiffler° fore the King,
Seems to prepare his way. So let him land,
And solemnly see him set on to London.
So swift a pace hath thought that even now   15
You may imagine him upon Blackheath;
Where that his lords desire him to have borne
His bruisèd helmet and his bended sword
Before him through the city. He forbids it,
Being free from vainness and self-glorious pride;   20
Giving full trophy, signal, and ostent°
Quite from himself, to God. But now behold,
In the quick forge and working house of thought,
How London doth pour out her citizens!

5 Prologue 3 **th' excuse** i.e., the reasons why the actors rely on the
chorus rather than full stage enactment 10 **Pales in** encloses 12 **whif-
fler** officer who clears the way for a procession 21 **trophy, signal, and
ostent** token, sign, and show (of victory)

25   The mayor and all his brethren in best sort°—
    Like to the senators of th' antique Rome,
    With the plebeians swarming at their heels—
    Go forth and fetch their conqu'ring Caesar in;
    As, by a lower but by loving° likelihood,
30   Were now the general° of our gracious Empress
    (As in good time he may) from Ireland coming,
    Bringing rebellion broachèd° on his sword,
    How many would the peaceful city quit
    To welcome him! Much more, and much more cause,
35   Did they this Harry. Now in London place him;
    As yet the lamentation of the French
    Invites° the King of England's stay at home;
    The Emperor's coming° in behalf of France
    To order peace between them; and omit
40   All the occurrences, whatever chanced,
    Till Harry's back-return again to France.
    There must we bring him; and myself have played°
    The interim, by rememb'ring you 'tis past.
    Then brook° abridgment; and your eyes advance,
45   After your thoughts, straight back again to France.
                               Exit.

[Scene 1. *France. The English camp.*]

Enter Fluellen and Gower.

Gower. Nay, that's right. But why wear you your leek today? Saint Davy's day is past.

25 **sort** array   29 **loving** lovingly anticipated   30 **general** i.e., the Earl of Essex, who left to suppress rebellion in Ireland on March 27, 1599 (by the end of June 1599 Essex's failure became obvious)   32 **broachèd** impaled   37 **Invites** i.e., gives excuse and safety for   38 **The Emperor's coming** (the Holy Roman Emperor came to England, May 1, 1416)   42 **played** filled up, represented   44 **brook** tolerate

Fluellen. There is occasions and causes why and
wherefore in all things. I will tell you ass my friend,
Captain Gower: the rascally, scauld,° beggarly,   5
lousy, pragging knave, Pistol—which you and yourself, and all the world, know to be no petter than
a fellow, look you now, of no merits—he is come
to me, and prings me pread and salt yesterday, look
you, and bid me eat my leek. It was in a place   10
where I could not breed no contention with him;
but I will be so bold as to wear it in my cap till
I see him once again, and then I will tell him a
little piece of my desires.

Enter Pistol.

Gower. Why, here he comes, swelling like a turkey   15
cock.

Fluellen. 'Tis no matter for his swellings nor his turkey cocks. God pless you, Aunchient Pistol! You
scurvy, lousy knave, God pless you!

Pistol. Ha, art thou bedlam?° Dost thou thirst, base
Trojan,°   20
To have me fold up Parca's° fatal web?
Hence! I am qualmish at the smell of leek.

Fluellen. I peseech you heartily, scurvy, lousy knave,
at my desires, and my requests, and my petitions,
to eat, look you, this leek. Because, look you, you   25
do not love it, nor your affections, and your ap-
petites and your disgestions doo's not agree with
it, I would desire you to eat it.

Pistol. Not for Cadwallader° and all his goats.°

Fluellen. There is one goat for you.   (*Strikes him.*)   30
Will you be so good, scauld knave, as eat it?

5.1.5 **scauld** scurvy   20 **bedlam** mad   20 **Trojan** boon companion,
dissolute adventurer (slang)   21 **Parca** i.e., Parcae, the three Fates, said
to spin the web of man's destiny (they cut the thread when the pattern
was completed, so ending a life)   29 **Cadwallader** the last British
king   29 **goats** (inhabitants of the Welsh mountains and, hence, used
contemptuously of Welshmen)

Pistol. Base Trojan, thou shalt die!

Fluellen. You say very true, scauld knave, when
God's will is. I will desire you to live in the mean-
35   time and eat your victuals. Come, there is sauce
for it. [Strikes him.] You called me yesterday
mountain-squire;° but I will make you today a
squire of low degree.° I pray you fall to; if you
can mock a leek, you can eat a leek.

40 *Gower.* Enough, Captain, you have astonished° him.

Fluellen. I say I will make him eat some part of my
leek, or I will peat his pate four days.—Bite, I pray
you; it is good for your green° wound, and your
ploody coxcomb.°

45 *Pistol.* Must I bite?

Fluellen. Yes, certainly, and out of doubt, and out of
question too, and ambiguities.

Pistol. By this leek, I will most horribly revenge—I
eat and eat—I swear°—

50 *Fluellen.* Eat, I pray you. Will you have some more
sauce to your leek? There is not enough leek to
swear by.

Pistol. Quiet thy cudgel, thou dost see I eat.

Fluellen. Much good do° you, scauld knave, heartily.
55   Nay, pray you throw none away, the skin is good
for your broken coxcomb. When you take occasions to see leeks hereafter, I pray you mock at
'em; that is all.

Pistol. Good.

37 **mountain-squire** owner of worthless land (term of contempt)
38 **squire of low degree** (reference to the title of a medieval metrical
romance; also a quibble on "low," as opposed to "mountain," line
37) 40 **astonished** stunned, dismayed 43 **green** raw 44 **coxcomb**
(1) cap worn by a fool (2) head (ludicrously) 48–49 **By this leek . . . I
swear** (Pistol changes his tune as his view of the situation changes;
Fluellen probably cudgels him on "revenge" and "swear" and is placated
while he is actually eating) 54 **do** i.e., may it do you

Fluellen. Ay, leeks is good. Hold you, there is a groat　60
to heal your pate.

Pistol. Me a groat?

Fluellen. Yes verily, and in truth you shall take it,
or I have another leek in my pocket which you
shall eat.　65

Pistol. I take thy groat in earnest° of revenge.

Fluellen. If I owe you anything, I will pay you in
cudgels; you shall be a woodmonger, and buy
nothing of me but cudgels. God bye° you, and keep
you, and heal your pate.　　　　　　　　*Exit.*　70

Pistol. All hell shall stir for this!

Gower. Go, go; you are a counterfeit cowardly knave.
Will you mock at an ancient tradition, begun upon
an honorable respect,° and worn as a memorable
trophy of predeceased valor, and dare not avouch　75
in your deeds any of your words? I have seen you
gleeking and galling° at this gentleman twice or
thrice. You thought, because he could not speak
English in the native garb, he could not therefore
handle an English cudgel. You find it otherwise,　80
and henceforth let a Welsh correction teach you a
good English condition. Fare ye well.　　　*Exit.*

Pistol. Doth Fortune play the huswife° with me now?
　　News have I, that my Doll° is dead i' th' spital
　　Of malady of France;°　85
　　And there my rendezvous° is quite cut off.
　　Old I do wax, and from my weary limbs
　　Honor is cudgeled. Well, bawd I'll turn,

---

66 **in earnest** as a token　69 **bye** be with　74 **respect** regard, consideration　77 **gleeking and galling** gibing and annoying　83 **huswife** hussy　84 **my Doll** i.e., Doll Tearsheet (said to be in the spital—i.e., hospital—in 2.1.77–80; a change or confusion in Shakespeare's mind must have been involved here, for Pistol's wife was Nell Quickly; or, perhaps, for "Doll" the text should read "Nell"—other proper names are confused in the Folio)　85 **malady of France** venereal disease　86 **rendezvous** refuge, retreat

And something lean to° cutpurse of quick hand.
90 To England will I steal, and there I'll steal;
And patches will I get unto these cudgeled scars,
And swear I got them in the Gallia wars.   *Exit.*

[Scene 2. *France. An apartment in the French
King's palace.*]

*Enter, at one door, King Henry, Exeter, Bedford,
[Gloucester,] Warwick, [Westmoreland,] and
other Lords; at another, Queen Isabel, the
[French] King, the Duke of Burgundy, [the
Princess Katherine, Alice,] and other French.*

King Henry. Peace to this meeting, wherefore we are
    met!°
Unto our brother France and to our sister
Health and fair time of day; joy and good wishes
To our most fair and princely cousin Katherine;
5 And as a branch and member of this royalty,
By whom this great assembly is contrived,
We do salute you, Duke of Burgundy;
And, princes French, and peers, health to you all!

France. Right joyous are we to behold your face,
10 Most worthy brother England; fairly met;
So are you, princes English, every one.

Queen. So happy be the issue, brother England,
Of this good day and of this gracious meeting
As we are now glad to behold your eyes—
15 Your eyes which hitherto have borne in them,
Against the French that met them in their bent,°

89 **something lean to** have a leaning towards the profession
of 5.2.1 **Peace to this meeting, wherefore we are met** peace, for
which we are here met, be to this meeting 16 **bent** direction

The fatal balls of murdering basilisks.°
The venom of such looks, we fairly hope,
Have lost their quality, and that this day
Shall change all griefs and quarrels into love.   20

King Henry. To cry amen to that, thus we appear.

Queen. You English princes all, I do salute you.

Burgundy. My duty to you both, on° equal love,
   Great Kings of France and England! That I have
      labored
   With all my wits, my pains, and strong endeavors   25
   To bring your most imperial Majesties
   Unto this bar° and royal interview,
   Your Mightiness on both parts best can witness.
   Since, then, my office hath so far prevailed
   That, face to face and royal eye to eye,   30
   You have congreeted,° let it not disgrace me
   If I demand before this royal view,
   What rub,° or what impediment there is
   Why that the naked, poor, and mangled Peace,
   Dear nurse of arts, plenties, and joyful births,   35
   Should not, in this best garden of the world,
   Our fertile France, put up her lovely visage.
   Alas, she hath from France too long been chased!
   And all her husbandry doth lie on heaps,°
   Corrupting in it° own fertility.   40
   Her vine, the merry cheerer of the heart,
   Unprunèd dies; her hedges even-pleached,°
   Like prisoners wildly overgrown with hair,
   Put forth disordered twigs; her fallow leas°
   The darnel,° hemlock, and rank fumitory   45
   Doth root upon, while that the coulter° rusts
   That should deracinate° such savagery;
   The even mead, that erst brought sweetly forth

17 **basilisks** (1) fabulous reptiles, said to kill with their breath and look
(2) large cannon   23 **on** of   27 **bar** place for judgment   31 **congreeted** exchanged greetings   33 **rub** obstacle   39 **on heaps** fallen in
ruin   40 **it** its   42 **even-pleached** neatly interwoven and trimmed
44 **fallow leas** unsown arable land   45 **darnel** ryegrass (injurious to
growing grain)   46 **coulter** knife that precedes the ploughshare
47 **deracinate** root up

The freckled cowslip, burnet, and green clover,
50   Wanting the scythe, all uncorrected, rank,
Conceives by idleness,° and nothing teems°
But hateful docks, rough thistles, kecksies,° burrs,
Losing both beauty and utility.
And all our vineyards, fallows, meads, and hedges,
55   Defective in their natures, grow to wildness,
Even so our houses, and ourselves, and children,
Have lost, or do not learn for want of time,
The sciences that should become our country;
But grow like savages—as soldiers will,
60   That nothing do but meditate on blood—
To swearing, and stern looks, diffused° attire,
And everything that seems unnatural.
Which to reduce° into our former favor°
You are assembled; and my speech entreats
65   That I may know the let° why gentle Peace
Should not expel these inconveniences,
And bless us with her former qualities.

King Henry. If, Duke of Burgundy, you would° the
       peace,
Whose want gives growth to th' imperfections
70   Which you have cited, you must buy that peace
With full accord to all our just demands;
Whose tenors and particular effects
You have, enscheduled briefly, in your hands.

Burgundy. The King hath heard them; to the which
       as yet
There is no answer made.

75 *King Henry.*   Well then, the peace,
Which you before so urged, lies in his answer.

France. I have but with a cursitory° eye

---

51 **Conceives by idleness** (cf. proverb, "Idleness is the mother of vice") 51 **teems** is brought forth 52 **kecksies** umbelliferous plants (e.g., cow parsley) 61 **diffused** disorderly 63 **reduce** restore 63 **favor** appearance 65 **let** hindrance 68 **would** desire 77 **cursitory** cursory

O'erglanced the articles. Pleaseth your Grace
To appoint some of your Council presently
To sit with us once more, with better heed   80
To resurvey them, we will suddenly
Pass our accept and peremptory answer.°

King Henry. Brother, we shall. Go, uncle Exeter,
And brother Clarence, and you, brother Gloucester,
Warwick, and Huntingdon—go with the King,   85
And take with you free power to ratify,
Augment, or alter, as your wisdoms best
Shall see advantageable for our dignity,
Anything in or out of our demands,
And we'll consign° thereto. Will you, fair sister,   90
Go with the princes or stay here with us?

Queen. Our gracious brother, I will go with them;
Haply a woman's voice may do some good
When articles too nicely° urged be stood° on.

King Henry. Yet leave our cousin Katherine here
  with us.   95
She is our capital demand, comprised
Within the fore-rank of our articles.

Queen. She hath good leave.
          *Exeunt omnes. Manet° King [Henry] and
          Katherine [with the Gentlewoman Alice].*

King Henry.   Fair Katherine, and most fair!
Will you vouchsafe to teach a soldier terms
Such as will enter at a lady's ear,   100
And plead his love suit to her gentle heart?

Katherine. Your Majesty shall mock at me; I cannot
  speak your England.

King Henry. O fair Katherine, if you will love me

81–82 **suddenly/Pass our accept and peremptory answer** in very
short time deliver our accepted and conclusive answer   90 **consign**
agree   94 **nicely** minutely, scrupulously   94 **stood** insisted   98s.d.
Manet remains (in Elizabethan stage directions the Latin third person
singular commonly occurs with a plural subject)

105 soundly with your French heart, I will be glad to
hear you confess it brokenly with your English
tongue. Do you like me, Kate?

Katherine. Pardonnez-moi, I cannot tell wat is "like
me."

110 *King Henry.* An angel is like you, Kate, and you are
·like an angel.

Katherine. Que dit-il? Que je suis semblable à les
anges?

Alice. Oui, vraiment, sauf votre Grace, ainsi dit-il.°

115 *King Henry.* I said so, dear Katherine, and I must not
blush to affirm it.

Katherine. O bon Dieu! les langues des hommes sont
pleines de tromperies.

King Henry. What says she, fair one? That the
120 tongues of men are full of deceits?

Alice. Oui, dat de tongues of de mans is be full of
deceits:—dat is de Princesse.°

King Henry. The Princess is the better Englishwoman.° I' faith, Kate, my wooing is fit for thy
125 understanding; I am glad thou canst speak no better
English, for if thou couldst, thou wouldst find me
such a plain king that thou wouldst think I had sold
my farm to buy my crown. I know no ways to
mince it° in love, but directly to say, "I love you."
130 Then, if you urge me farther than to say, "Do you
in faith?" I wear out my suit.° Give me your answer, i' faith, do; and so clap hands,° and a bargain. How say you, lady?

Katherine. Sauf votre honneur, me understand well.

112–14 **Que ... dit-il** what does he say? That I am like the angels?
Alice. Yes, truly, save your Grace, he says so   122 **dat is de Princesse**
that is what the Princess says   123–24 **is the better Englishwoman**
(because she sees through flattery)   129 **mince it** speak prettily
131 **wear out my suit** spend all my courtship   132 **clap hands** shake
hands (in token of a bargain)

King Henry. Marry, if you would put me to verses, or *135*
to dance for your sake, Kate, why, you undid me.
For the one I have neither words nor measure;°
and for the other, I have no strength in measure,°
yet a reasonable measure in strength. If I could
win a lady at leapfrog, or by vaulting into my sad- *140*
dle with my armor on my back, under the correction of bragging be it spoken, I should quickly leap
into a wife.° Or if I might buffet for my love, or
bound my horse for her favors, I could lay on like
a butcher, and sit like a jackanapes,° never off. *145*
But, before God, Kate, I cannot look greenly,° nor
gasp out my eloquence, nor I have no cunning in
protestation: only downright oaths, which I never
use till urged, nor never break for urging. If thou
canst love a fellow of this temper, Kate, whose face *150*
is not worth sunburning,° that never looks in his
glass for love of anything he sees there, let thine
eye be thy cook.° I speak to thee plain soldier: if
thou canst love me for this, take me; if not, to say
to thee that I shall die, is true—but for thy love, *155*
by the Lord, no; yet I love thee too. And while
thou liv'st, dear Kate, take a fellow of plain and
uncoined° constancy, for he perforce must do thee
right, because he hath not the gift to woo in other
places; for these fellows of infinite tongue, that can *160*
rhyme themselves into ladies' favors, they do always reason themselves out again. What! A speaker
is but a prater; a rhyme is but a ballad;° a good
leg will fall, a straight back will stoop, a black
beard will turn white, a curled pate will grow bald, *165*
a fair face will wither, a full eye will wax hollow:
but a good heart, Kate, is the sun and the moon,

137 **measure** meter   138 **strength in measure** ability for dancing
140–43 **win a lady at leapfrog ... leap into a wife** (to "leap" and
"vault" were common in bawdy senses, and clearly used so by Shakespeare in other plays)   145 **jackanapes** ape   146 **greenly** foolishly,
sheepishly   151 **not worth sunburning** so ugly that the sun cannot
make it more so   152–53 **thine eye be thy cook** your eye present me
more attractively than I would be without its help   158 **uncoined** (1)
not yet current (2) unalloyed   163 **ballad** (the most popular and unso-
phisticated verse form)

or rather, the sun, and not the moon, for it shines
bright and never changes, but keeps his course
170   truly. If thou would have such a one, take me; and
take me, take a soldier; take a soldier, take a king.
And what say'st thou then to my love? Speak, my
fair—and fairly, I pray thee.

Katherine. Is it possible dat I sould love de ennemie
175   of France?

King Henry. No, it is not possible you should love
the enemy of France, Kate; but in loving me you
should love the friend of France: for I love France
so well, that I will not part with a village of it—I
180   will have it all mine. And, Kate, when France is
mine and I am yours, then yours is France, and
you are mine.

Katherine. I cannot tell wat is dat.

King Henry. No, Kate? I will tell thee in French,
185   which I am sure will hang upon my tongue like a
new-married wife about her husband's neck, hardly
to be shook off. Je quand sur le possession de
France, et quand vous avez le possession de moi
(let me see, what then? Saint Denis° be my
190   speed!) donc votre est France, et vous êtes
mienne.° It is as easy for me, Kate, to conquer the
kingdom as to speak so much more French; I shall
never move thee in French, unless it be to laugh
at me.

195 · *Katherine.* Sauf votre honneur, le Français que vous
parlez, il est meilleur que l'Anglais lequel je parle.°

King Henry. No, faith, is't not, Kate. But thy speaking
of my tongue, and I thine, most truly-falsely,° must
needs be granted to be much at one.° But, Kate,

189 **Saint Denis** patron saint of France   187–91 **Je quand . . . mienne**
when I have possession of France, and when you have possession of me
. . . then France is yours, and you are mine   195–96 **Sauf . . . parle** save
your honor, the French that you speak is better than the English that I
speak   198 **truly-falsely** in good faith but bad French and English   199 **at one** (1) alike (2) in sympathy

dost thou understand thus much English? Canst 200
thou love me?

Katherine. I cannot tell.°

King Henry. Can any of your neighbors tell, Kate?
I'll ask them. Come, I know thou lovest me; and
at night, when you come into your closet,° you'll 205
question this gentlewoman about me; and I know,
Kate, you will to her dispraise those parts in me
that you love with your heart; but, good Kate,
mock me mercifully, the rather, gentle Princess,
because I love thee cruelly. If ever thou beest mine, 210
Kate—as I have a saving faith within me tells me
thou shalt—I get thee with scambling,° and thou
must therefore needs prove a good soldier-breeder.
Shall not thou and I, between Saint Denis and Saint
George, compound a boy, half French, half Eng- 215
lish, that shall go to Constantinople,° and take the
Turk by the beard? Shall we not? What say'st thou,
my fair flower-de-luce?

Katherine. I do not know dat.

King Henry. No; 'tis hereafter to know, but now to 220
promise. Do but now promise, Kate, you will endeavor for your French part of such a boy; and for my
English moiety take the word of a king, and a
bachelor. How answer you, la plus belle Katherine du
monde, mon très cher et devin déesse?°   225

Katherine. Your majestee ave fausse French enough to
deceive de most sage demoiselle dat is en France.

King Henry. Now, fie upon my false French! By mine
honor in true English, I love thee, Kate; by which
honor I dare not swear thou lovest me, yet my 230
blood begins to flatter me that thou dost, notwith-

---

202 **I cannot tell** (1) I don't know (2) I cannot speak   205 **closet** private chamber   212 **scambling** scrimmaging   216 **Constantinople**
(taken by the Turks in 1453, thirty-one years after Henry's death;
throughout the sixteenth century Christian princes aspired to crusade
against the Turks)   224–25 **la plus ... déesse** the fairest Katherine in
the world, my dearest and divine goddess

standing the poor and untempering° effect of my
visage. Now beshrew my father's ambition! He was
thinking of civil wars when he got me, therefore
235   was I created with a stubborn outside, with an
aspect of iron, that when I come to woo ladies, I
fright them. But in faith, Kate, the elder I wax the
better I shall appear. My comfort is that old age,
that ill layer-up° of beauty, can do no more spoil
240   upon my face. Thou hast me, if thou hast me, at
the worst; and thou shalt wear me, if thou wear
me,° better and better; and therefore tell me, most
fair Katherine, will you have me? Put off your
maiden blushes; avouch the thoughts of your heart
245   with the looks of an empress; take me by the hand,
and say, "Harry of England, I am thine!" which
word thou shalt no sooner bless mine ear withal, but
I will tell thee aloud, "England is thine, Ireland is
thine, France is thine, and Henry Plantagenet is
250   thine"; who, though I speak it before his face, if
he be not fellow with the best king, thou shalt find
the best king of good fellows. Come, your answer
in broken° music; for thy voice is music, and thy
English broken; therefore, Queen of all, Katherine,
255   break thy mind to me in broken English: Wilt thou
have me?

Katherine. Dat is as it shall please de Roi mon père.

King Henry. Nay, it will please him well, Kate; it
shall please him, Kate.

260   *Katherine.* Den it sall also content me.

King Henry. Upon that I kiss your hand, and I call
you my queen.

Katherine. Laissez, mon seigneur, laissez, laissez! Ma
foi, je ne veux point que vous abaissiez votre
265   grandeur en baisant la main d'une de votre sei-

232 **untempering** without softening influence   239 **ill layer-up** ill
preserver, wrinkler   241–42 **if thou wear me** if you possess me
253 **broken** arranged for parts

gneurie indigne serviteur. Excusez-moi, je vous
supplie, mon très puissant seigneur.°

King Henry. Then I will kiss your lips, Kate.

Katherine. Les dames et demoiselles pour être baisées
devant leur noces, il n'est pas la coutume de　270
France.°

King Henry. Madam my interpreter, what says she?

Alice. Dat it is not be de fashon pour le ladies of
France—I cannot tell wat is "baiser" en Anglish.

King Henry. To kiss.　　275

Alice. Your Majestee entendre bettre que moi.

King Henry. It is not a fashion for the maids in
France to kiss before they are married, would she
say?

Alice. Oui, vraiment.　　280

King Henry. O Kate, nice° customs cursy° to great
kings. Dear Kate, you and I cannot be confined
within the weak list° of a country's fashion: we
are the makers of manners, Kate; and the liberty
that follows our places° stops the mouth of all find-　285
faults, as I will do yours for upholding the nice
fashion of your country in denying me a kiss.
Therefore patiently, and yielding. [*Kisses her.*] You
have witchcraft in your lips, Kate: there is more
eloquence in a sugar touch of them than in the　290
tongues of the French Council; and they should
sooner persuade Harry of England than a general
petition of monarchs. Here comes your father.

Enter the French Power and the English Lords.

263–67 **Laissez . . . seigneur** stop, my lord, stop, stop! Indeed, I do not
wish to lower your greatness by kissing the hand of your unworthy servant. Excuse me, I beg you, my most powerful lord　269–71 **Les
dames . . . France** it is not customary in France for ladies and young
girls to be kissed before their marriage　281 **nice** fastidious　281 **cursy**
curtsy, bow　283 **list** limit, bound　285 **follows our places** is the consequence of our royal status

Burgundy. God save your Majesty! My royal cousin,
295   Teach you our princess English?

King Henry. I would have her learn, my fair cousin,
how perfectly I love her, and that is good English.

Burgundy. Is she not apt?

King Henry. Our tongue is rough, coz, and my con-
300   dition° is not smooth; so that, having neither the
voice nor the heart of flattery about me, I cannot
so conjure up the spirit of love in her that he will
appear in his true likeness.

Burgundy. Pardon the frankness of my mirth if I an-
305   swer you for that. If you would conjure in her, you
must make a circle; if conjure up love in her in his
true likeness, he must appear naked and blind. Can
you blame her then, being a maid yet rosed over
with the virgin crimson of modesty, if she deny the
310   appearance of a naked blind boy in her naked°
seeing self? It were, my lord, a hard condition° for
a maid to consign° to.

King Henry. Yet they do wink° and yield, as love is
blind and enforces.

315 *Burgundy.* They are then excused, my lord, when
they see not what they do.

King Henry. Then, good my lord, teach your cousin
to consent winking.

Burgundy. I will wink° on her to consent, my lord,
320   if you will teach her to know my meaning; for
maids well summered, and warm kept, are like flies
at Bartholomew-tide,° blind, though they have their
eyes; and then they will endure handling which
before would not abide looking on.

299–300 **condition** temperament   310 **naked** unprotected   311 **condition** (1) stipulation (2) state of being   312 **consign** agree   313 **wink**
shut their eyes   319 **wink** give a significant look   322 **Bartholomew-
tide** (St. Bartholomew's day is August 24th; by this time flies have
become torpid)

King Henry. This moral ties me over° to time and a *325*
  hot summer; and so I shall catch the fly, your
  cousin, in the latter end, and she must be blind too.

Burgundy. As love is, my lord, before it loves.

King Henry. It is so; and you may, some of you,
  thank love for my blindness, who cannot see many *330*
  a fair French city for one fair French maid that
  stands in my way.

France. Yes, my lord, you see them perspectively,°
  the cities turned into a maid; for they are all girdled
  with maiden walls that war hath never ent'red. *335*

King Henry. Shall Kate be my wife?

France. So please you.

King Henry. I am content, so the maiden cities you talk
  of may wait on her; so the maid that stood in
  the way for my wish shall show me the way to my *340*
  will.°

France. We have consented to all terms of reason.

King Henry. Is't so, my lords of England?

Westmoreland. The King hath granted every article:
  His daughter first; and in sequel, all, *345*
  According to their firm proposèd natures.

Exeter. Only he hath not yet subscribed this: Where
  your Majesty demands that the King of France,
  having any occasion to write for matter of grant,°
  shall name your Highness in this form, and with *350*
  this addition in French, "Notre très cher fils Henri,
  Roi d'Angleterre, Héritier de France"; and thus in
  Latin, "Praeclarissimus filius noster Henricus, Rex
  Angliae, et Haeres Franciae."

---

325 **ties me over** restricts me   333 **perspectively** as through an optical
glass giving strange, displaced or broken images   341 **will** (1) desire (2)
sexual desire   349 **grant** granting lands or titles.

355 *France.* Nor this I have not, brother, so denied
    But your request shall make me let it pass.

King Henry. I pray you then, in love and dear alliance,
    Let that one article rank with the rest,
    And thereupon give me your daughter.

France. Take her, fair son, and from her blood raise
360   up
    Issue to me, that the contending kingdoms
    Of France and England, whose very shores look
    pale°
    With envy of each other's happiness,
    May cease their hatred, and this dear° conjunction
365   Plant neighborhood° and Christian-like accord
    In their sweet bosoms; that never war advance
    His bleeding sword 'twixt England and fair France.

Lords. Amen!

King Henry. Now, welcome, Kate; and bear me witness all,
370   That here I kiss her as my sovereign Queen.

                              Flourish.

Queen. God, the best maker of all marriages,
    Combine your hearts in one, your realms in one!
    As man and wife, being two, are one in love,
    So be there 'twixt your kingdoms such a spousal
375   That never may ill office,° or fell jealousy,
    Which troubles oft the bed of blessed marriage,
    Thrust in between the paction° of these kingdoms
    To make divorce of their incorporate° league;
    That English may as French, French Englishmen,
380   Receive each other! God speak this Amen!

All. Amen!

362 **pale** (an allusion to the white cliffs bordering the English Channel)   364 **dear** (1) significant (2) loving (3) dearly bought (?)   365 **neighborhood** neighborliness   375 **office** performance of a function or duty   377 **paction** compact   378 **incorporate** united in one body (appropriate to both marriage and peace settlement)

King Henry. Prepare we for our marriage; on which
    day,
  My Lord of Burgundy, we'll take your oath,
  And all the peers', for surety of our leagues.
  Then shall I swear to Kate, and you to me,   *385*
  And may our oaths well kept and prosp'rous be!
                            Sennet.° Exeunt.

[EPILOGUE]

Enter Chorus.

Thus far with rough, and all-unable pen,
  Our bending° author hath pursued the story,
In little room confining mighty men,
  Mangling by starts° the full course of their glory.
Small time: but in that small, most greatly lived   *5*
  This star of England. Fortune made his sword;
By which, the world's best garden° he achieved;
  And of it left his son imperial lord.
Henry the Sixth, in infant bands crowned King
  Of France and England, did this king succeed;   *10*
Whose state so many had the managing,
  That they lost France, and made his England
    bleed:
Which oft our stage hath shown;° and for their sake,
In your fair minds let this acceptance take.°

FINIS

386s.d. **Sennet** trumpet call for the departure of a procession   Epilogue
2 **bending** (1) bending under the weight of his task (2) "stooping to your
clemency" (*Hamlet*, 3.2.155)   4 **starts** fits and starts   7 **world's best
garden** i.e., France (cf. 5.2.36)   13 **oft our stage hath shown** (a reference to *1, 2* and *3 Henry VI*)   14 **this acceptance take** this play find
favor

Textual Note

The first edition of *Henry the Fifth* was a quarto published in 1600 with a title page reading:

THE
CRONICLE
History of Henry the fift,
With his battell fought at *Agin Court* in
France. Togither with *Auntient*
Pistoll.

*As it hath bene sundry times playd by the Right honorable
the Lord Chamberlaine his seruants.*

This was a shortened version and a "bad" text; probably some actors had pieced together their own text, which was subsequently cut and rearranged a little for the convenience of a touring company.

Two more quarto editions followed in 1602 and 1619 (its title page, however, being dated 1608); both were reprints from the first edition.

The first, and only, authoritative edition appeared in the collected folio of Shakespeare's *Comedies, Histories and Tragedies* that was published in 1623. Spellings, punctuation, variations in nomenclature, the nature of some of the stage directions and of some of the errors all suggest that this was printed either from Shakespeare's autograph working-manuscript (or "foul papers" as bibliographers usually term this, despite its general clarity and uniformity), or else from a good copy of Shakespeare's manuscript. A few directions for noises and a duplicate entry suggest that the manuscript may have been annotated lightly by a bookkeeper (or stage manager).

This Folio text is divided into five unequal acts by the occurrence of entries for the Chorus to speak appropriate prologues, but another division, running the first two acts together and dividing Act 4 into two after its sixth scene, is marked with Act-Headings. Both arrangements involve difficulties: that of the printed headings disregards the Chorus' prologues that clearly belong to the original composition of the play; that of the Chorus suggests that the play was partly rewritten at some state of composition. This rewriting must have involved the early Pistol and Mrs. Quickly episodes: the prologue before Act 2 announces that the scene

> Is now transported, gentles, to Southampton.
> There is the playhouse now, there must you sit,
> And thence to France . . .

but in 2.1 the scene is still London, in Eastcheap, and then, after one scene at Southampton, 2.3 is again London for the account of Falstaff's death. These confusions are partly covered up by two concluding lines to 2 Prologue:

> But, till the King come forth, and not till then,
> Unto Southampton do we shift our scene.

Probably 2.1 and 2.3 were both invented and inserted after the composition of the first two acts had been completed, or nearly completed, in a form that is now lost. If so, it seems likely that Shakespeare began the play intending to fulfill his promise in the Epilogue to *Part Two, Henry the Fourth* and take Falstaff to France—and that he then decided to omit Falstaff and so had to effect some cutting, rewriting and patching. Such a decision may have affected later parts of the play as well: some editors believe that Pistol has inherited some of the business originally designed for Falstaff (but not his idiom); others that Henry's talk with Pistol and the soldiers before Agincourt is a late addition. There can, of course, be no certain knowledge of such processes of composition; what is undoubted is that the Folio text is a good, authoritative version of the play as Shakespeare wrote or rewrote it.

Obviously the Folio must be the basis for any modern text. This present edition reproduced it wherever possible, modernizing spelling, and altering punctuation and verse lineations where the editor's sense of literary and dramatic fitness dictated. Abbreviations have been expanded and speech prefixes regularized. Stage directions have been amplified where necessary, such additions being printed within square brackets. Obvious typographical errors have been corrected and eccentric spellings regularized where appropriate without notice, but all significant emendations are noted below. In this list the adopted reading is given in italics and is followed by the rejected Folio reading in roman type or a note of the Folio's omission within square brackets. If the adopted reading occurs in the first quarto edition it is followed by "Q" within square brackets.

1.2.74 *heir* [Q] th'Heire   131 *blood* Bloods   163 *her* their   197 *majesty* [Q] Maiesties   212 *End* [Q] And

2.1.26 *mare* name   44,45 *Iceland* Island   75 *thee defy* [Q] defie thee   82 *enough* [Q] enough to   108–09 *Nym. I shall . . . betting?* [Q; F omits]   119 *that's* that   121 *Ah* A

2.2.87 *him with* with   107 *a* an   139 *mark the* make thee   148 *Henry* [Q] Thomas   159 *I in* in   176 *have sought* [Q] sought   181 s.d. *Exeunt* Exit

2.3.17 *'a babbled* a Table   26 *so upward* [Q] so vp-peer'd   50 *word* [Q] world

2.4.107 *pining* [Q] priuy

3.Chorus 4 *Hampton* Douer   6 *fanning* fayning

3.1.7 *conjure* commune   17 *noble* Noblish   24 *men* me   32 *Straining* Stráying

3.3.32 *heady* headly   35 *Defile* Desire

3.4.1 *été* este   1–2 *parles bien* bien parlas   8–13 *Et les doigts . . . écolier* [F assigns "*Et les doigts*" to Alice, lines 9–11 to Katherine, and "*La main . . . écolier*" (in lines 12–13) to Alice]   10 *souviendrai* souemeray   16 *Nous* [F omits]   41 *pas déjà* y desia   43 *Non* Nome   47 *Sauf* Sans

3.5.11 *Dieu* du   45 *Foix* Loys   46 *knights* Kings

3.6.31 *her* [Q] his   109 *o' fire* a fire   117 *lenity* [Q] Leuitie

3.7.12 *pasterns* postures   13 *Ça, ha!* ch' ha: 62 *lief* liue   68 *et la truie est la leuye*

4.Chorus   27 *Presenteth* Presented

4.1.3 *Good* God   35 *Qui va là?* Che vous la?   95 *Thomas* Iohn   184 *mote* Moth   234s.d. *Exeunt Soldiers* Exit Souldiers [after line 229]   250 *What* What?   250 *adoration* Odoration   296 *or* of   315 *friends* [Q] friend

4.2.2 *Montez à* Monte   2 *Varlet* Verlot   4 *eaux et la terre* ewes & terre   5 *le feu* feu   6 *Ciel* Cein   25 *'gainst* against   49 *gimmaled* Iymold

4.3.13–14 *Exeter. And yet . . . truth of valor* [F gives after lines 11 and 12, spoken by Bedford]   26 *earns* yernes   48 *And say . . . Crispin's day.* [Q; F omits]   105 *grazing* crazing

4.4.15 *Or* for   36–37 *à cette heure* asture   37 *couper* couppes   54 *l'avez promis* layt a promets   57 *remercîments* remercious   57–58 *suis tombé* intombe   59 *distingué* distinie   69 *Suivez* Saaue

4.5.2 *perdu . . . perdu* perdia . . . perdie   3 *Mort* Mor   12 *in honor* in   16 *by a* [Q] a base

4.6.34 *mistful* mixtfull

4.7.17 *great* grear   80 *their* with   113 *countryman* [Q] countrymen   119 *God* [Q] Good

4.8.44 *martial* Marshall   115 *we* me

5.1.73 *begun* began   85 *Of* of a   92 *swear* swore

5.2.12 *England* Ireland   50 *all* withall   72 *tenors* Tenures   77 *cursitory* curselarie   93 *Haply* Happily   118 *pleines* plein   196 *est meilleur* & melieus   264 *abaissez* abbaisse   265 *d'une de votre* d'une nostre   269 *baisées* baisee   270 *coutume* costume   274 *baiser* buisse   335 *never ent'red* entred   377 *paction* Pation

The Sources of *Henry V*

Shakespeare's main source for this play was Holinshed's *Chronicles*. He simplified the King's continual wars in France by concentrating on the siege of Harfleur, the battle of Agincourt and the Treaty of Troyes; in his play the successful negotiations for peace immediately follow victory, without the abortive discussions and further years of fighting recounted by Holinshed. Shakespeare also omitted all but one early reference to the Scots and every incident concerned with the dissenting Lollards in England and the execution of Sir John Oldcastle. The most relevant passages from Holinshed are reprinted after this note.

In this source Shakespeare would have found no doubt about the greatness of Henry the Fifth: the character sketch included in the account of his death speaks, in terms similar to the Chorus of the play, of "a pattern in princehood, a lodestar in honor, and mirror of magnificence," and marginal notes highlight his various wise decisions and valiant acts. Yet at the same time the terrible effects of Henry's wars are considered by Holinshed with sympathy for their victims and something of Shakespeare's complexity of view may have been suggested by the chronicler; accounts of the sieges of Harfleur and Rouen are particularly relevant here (pages 149–50 and 163–65 below) and comments on the killing of prisoners (pages 158–59). The Duke of Burgundy's affecting introduction to the peace talks at the beginning of 5.2. may owe something to Holinshed's account of French opinion after Agincourt (pages 160–61). Henry's prayer for pardon that details his penance for his father's "fault . . . in compassing the crown" (4.1.297ff.) obviously owes something to Holinshed's description of Richard II's burial at the beginning of the reign (page 137) and possibly to his comment on the Earl of Cambridge's motive for treason (pages 146–47), which Shakespeare did not use at that place; Holinshed, like Shakespeare, recognized the weakness of Henry's claim to the English throne while he was claiming the French in the name of justice and right.

A further source for the play was the anonymous history-play, *The Famous Victories of Henry the Fifth,* published in 1598. Some resemblances may well be accidental, but the handling of the English claims to the French crown, the tennis ball challenge, the Treaty of Troyes and the royal wooing suggests a direct indebtedness. Some of Pistol's episodes may derive from low comedy scenes in *The Famous Victories.* This source may be read in full in the Signet Shakespeare edition of *Henry IV, Part I.*

Even while following Holinshed in story and occasionally in words, Shakespeare also referred to Hall's *The Union of the Noble and Illustre Famelies of Lancastre and York* (1542). This earlier version of the chronicle seems to have influenced the first act especially, and perhaps Exeter's speech on the calamities of war in 2.4 and the French view of the English in 3.5 and 7.

For various small details in the narrative and for discussions of military discipline and the rights of war and government, Shakespeare echoed numerous Elizabethan books. Among these are John Lyly's *Euphues and his England* (1580) for the Archbishop's account of the kingdom of the bees in 1.2, Tacitus' *Annals* (translated 1598) for Henry's talk with common soldiers before battle and *A Brief Discourse of War* (1590) written by the Welsh knight Sir Roger Williams for some parts of Fluellen's disquisitions.

RAPHAEL HOLINSHED

From Chronicles of England, Scotland, and Ireland* (1587) edition)

Henry Prince of Wales, son and heir to King Henry the Fourth, born in Wales at Monmouth on the river of Wye, after his father was departed took upon him the regiment of this realm of England, the twentieth of March; the morrow after proclaimed king, by the name of Henry the Fifth, in the year of the world 5375, after the birth of our Savior, by our account 1413. . . .

(*Homage done to King Henry before his coronation.*) Such great hope and good expectation was had of this man's fortunate success to follow that, within three days after his father's decease, diverse noblemen and honorable personages did to him homage, and sware to him due obedience, which had not been seen done to any of his predecessors, kings of this realm, till they had been possessed of the crown. (*The day of King Henry's coronation a very tempestuous day.*) He was crowned the ninth of April being Passion Sunday, which was a sore, ruggy and tempestuous day, with wind, snow and sleet, that men greatly marveled thereat, making diverse interpretations what the same might signify. (*A notable example of a worthy prince.*) But this king even at first appointing with himself, to show that in his person princely honors should change public manners, he determined to put on him the shape of a new man. For whereas aforetime he had made himself a companion unto misruly

* Marginal glosses, other than references to authorities, are given here in italics and in parentheses.

mates of dissolute order and life, he now banished them all from his presence (but not unrewarded, or else unpreferred) inhibiting them upon a great pain, not once to approach, lodge or sojourn within ten miles of his court or presence; and in their places he chose men of gravity, wit and high policy, by whose wise counsel he might at all times rule to his honor and dignity; calling to mind how once, to high offense of the King his father, he had with his fist stricken the Chief Justice for sending one of his minions (upon desert) to prison, when the Justice stoutly commanded himself also strait to ward, and he (then Prince) obeyed. The King after expelled him out of his Privy Council, banished him the court and made the Duke of Clarence (his younger brother) President of Council in his stead. This reformation in the new king Christopher Ockland hath reported, fully consenting with this. For saith he:

> *Ille inter juvenes paulo lascivior ante,*
> *Defuncto genitore gravis constansque repente,*
> *Moribus ablegat corruptis regis ab aula*
> *Assuetos socios, & nugatoribus acrem*
> *Poenam (siquisquam sua tecta reviserit) addit,*
> *Atque ita mutatus facit omnia principe digna,*
> *Ingenio magno post consultoribus usus, &c.*

[Previously he has been somewhat wanton among the young men, but on the death of his father immediately becoming grave and reliable he sent away from the royal court his accustomed companions with their corrupt manners and also laid down bitter punishments for these triflers should they return to his dwellings. And, thus changed, he does all things worthy of a prince, and with noble mind makes use of wise counselors.]

But now that the King was once placed in the royal seat of the realm, he virtuously considering in his mind that all goodness cometh of God, determined to begin with something acceptable to his divine majesty, and therefore commanded the clergy sincerely and truly to preach the word of God, and to live accordingly, that they might be the lanterns of light to the temporalty, as their profession required. The laymen he willed to serve God, and obey their prince, prohibiting them above all things breach of matrimony, custom in swearing and, namely, wilfull perjury. Beside this, he elected the best learned men in the laws of the realm to the offices of justice; and men of good living, he preferred to high degrees and authority. (*A parliament.*) Immediately after Easter he called a parliament, in which diverse good statutes and wholesome ordinances, for the preservation and advancement of the commonwealth were devised and established. (*The funerals of King Henry the Fourth kept at Canterbury.*) On Trinity Sunday were the solemn exequies done at Canterbury for his father, the King himself being present thereat.

(*St. George's day made a double feast.*) About the same time, at the special instance of the King, in a convocation of the clergy holden at Paul's in London, it was ordained that St. George his day should be celebrate and kept as a double feast. The Archbishop of Canterbury meant to have honored St. Dunstan's day with like reverence, but it took not effect. When the King had settled things much to his purpose, he caused the body of King Richard to be removed with all funeral dignity convenient for his estate, from Langley to Westminster, where he was honorably interred with Queen Anne, his first wife, in a solemn tomb erected and set up at the charges of this king. Polichronicon saith that after the body of the dead king was taken up out of the earth, this new king (happily tendering the magnificence of a prince, and abhoring obscure burial) caused the same to be conveyed to Westminster in a royal seat (or chair of estate) covered all over with black velvet, and adorned with banners of diverse arms round about. All the horses likewise (saith this author) were appareled with black, and bare sundry suits of arms. Many other solemnities were had at his interment, according to the quality of the age wherein he lived and died. . . .

(*A disdainful embassage.*) Whilst in the Lent season the King lay at Kennilworth, there came to him from Charles Dauphin of France certain ambassadors, that brought with them a barrel of Paris balls, which from their master they presented to him for a token that was taken in very ill part, as sent in scorn to signify that it was more meet for the King to pass the time with such childish exercise than to attempt any worthy exploit. Wherefore the King wrote to him that ere aught long, he would toss him some London balls that perchance should shake the walls of the best court in France. . . .

(*Anno Reg. 2; 1414.*) In the second year of his reign, King Henry called his high court of parliament, the last day of April in the town of Leicester, in which parliament many profitable laws were concluded, and many petitions moved were for that time deferred. Amongst which, one was that a bill exhibited in the parliament holden at Westminster in the eleventh year of King Henry the Fourth (which by reason the King was then troubled with civil discord, came to none effect) might now with good deliberation be pondered, and brought to some good conclusion. (*A bill exhibited to the parliament against the clergy.*) The effect of which supplication was that the temporal lands devoutly given, and disordinately spent by religious and other spiritual persons, should be seized into the King's hands, sith the same might suffice to maintain, to the honor of the King and defense of the realm, fifteen earls, fifteen hundred knights, six thousand and two hundred esquires, and a hundred almshouses for relief only of the poor, impotent and needy persons, and the King to have clearly to his coffers twenty thousand pounds, with many other provisions and values of religious houses, which I pass over.

This bill was much noted, and more feared among the religious sort, whom surely it touched very near, and therefore, to find remedy against it, they determined to assay all ways to put by and overthrow this bill; wherein they thought, best to try if they might move the King's mood with some sharp invention, that he should not regard the importunate petitions of the commons. (*The Archbishop of Canterbury's oration in the Parliament House.*) Whereupon, on a day in the parliament, Henry Chichely, Archbishop of Canterbury, made a pithy oration, wherein he declared how, not only the Duchies of Normandy and Aquitaine, with the Counties of Anjou and Maine, and the country of Gascoigne, were by undoubted title appertaining to the King, as to the lawful and only heir of the same, but also the whole realm of France, as heir to his great-grandfather, King Edward the Third.

(*The Salic Law.*) Herein did he much inveigh against the surmised and false feigned law Salic, which the Frenchmen allege ever against the kings of England in bar of their just title to the crown of France. The very words of that supposed law are these, *In terram Salicam mulieres ne succedant,* that is to say, "Into the Salic land let not women succeed." Which the French glossers expound to be the realm of France, and that this law was made by King Pharamond; whereas yet their own authors affirm that the land Salic is in Germany, between the rivers of Elbe and Sala, and that when Charles the Great had overcome the Saxons, he placed there certain Frenchmen, which having in disdain the dishonest manners of the German women, made a law that the females should not succeed to any inheritance within that land, which at this day is called Meisen, (*Meisen.*) so that, if this be true, this law was not made for the realm of France, nor the Frenchmen possessed the land Salic, till four hundred and one and twenty years after the death of Pharamond, the supposed maker of this Salic law, for this Pharamond deceased in the year 426, and Charles the Great subdued the Saxons and placed the Frenchmen in those parts beyond the river of Sala in the year 805.

Moreover, it appeareth by their own writers, that King Pepin, which deposed Childeric, claimed the crown of France, as heir general, for that he was descended of Blithild, daughter to King Clothair the First. Hugh Capet also, who usurped the crown upon Charles Duke of Lorraine, the sole heir male of the line and stock of Charles the Great, to make his title seem true and appear good, though indeed it was stark naught, conveyed himself as heir to the Lady Lingard, daughter to King Charlemain, son to Lewis the Emperor, that was son to Charles the Great. King Lewis also, the Tenth, otherwise called St. Lewis, being very heir to the said usurper Hugh Capet, could never be satisfied in his conscience how he might justly keep and possess the crown of France till he was persuaded and fully instructed that Queen Isabel his grandmother was lineally descended of the Lady Ermengard, daughter and heir to the above-named Charles Duke of Lorraine, by the which marriage the blood and line of Charles the Great was again united and restored to the crown and scepter of France, so that more clear than the sun it openly appeareth that the title of King Pepin, the claim of Hugh Capet, the possession of Lewis, yea and the French kings to this day, are derived and conveyed from the heir female, though they would under the color of such a feigned law bar the kings and princes of this realm of England of their right and lawful inheritance.

The Archbishop further alleged out of the Book of Numbers this saying: "When a man dyeth without a son, having said sufficiently for the proof of the King's just and let the inheritance descend to his daughter." At length, his inheritance, to spare neither blood, sword, nor fire, lawful title to the crown of France, he exhorted him to advance forth his banner to fight for his right, to conquer sith his war was just, his cause good, and his claim true. And to the intent his loving chaplains and obedient subjects of the spirituality might show themselves willing and desirous to aid his Majesty, for the recovery of his ancient right and true inheritance, the Archbishop declared that, in their spiritual Convocation, they had granted to his Highness such a sum of money as never by no spiritual persons was to any prince before those days given or advanced.

(*The Earl of Westmoreland persuadeth the King to the conquest of Scotland.*) When the Archbishop had ended his prepared tale, Ralph Nevill, Earl of Westmoreland, and as then Lord Warden of the Marches against Scotland, understanding that the King, upon a courageous desire to recover his right in France, would surely take the wars in hand, thought good to move the King to begin first with Scotland, and thereupon declared how easy a matter it should be to make a conquest there, and how greatly the same should further his wished purpose for the subduing of the Frenchmen, concluding the sum of his tale with this old saying: that *"Whoso will France win, must with Scotland first begin."* Many matters he touched, as well to show how necessary the conquest of Scotland should be as also to prove how just a cause the King had to attempt it, trusting to persuade the King and all other to be of his opinion.

(*The Duke of Exeter his wise and pithy answer to the Earl of Westmoreland's saying.*) But after he had made an end, the Duke of Exeter, uncle to the King, a man well learned and wise (who had been sent into Italy by his father, intending that he should have been a priest), replied against the Earl of Westmoreland's oration, affirming rather that he which would Scotland win, he with France must first begin. (*A true saying.*) "For if the King might once compass the conquest of France, Scotland could not long resist; so that conquer France, and Scotland would soon obey. For where should the Scots learn policy and skill to defend themselves, if they had not their bringing up and training in France? If the French pensions maintained not the Scottish nobility, in what case should they be? Then take away France, and the Scots will soon be tamed; France being to Scotland the same that the sap is to the tree, which being taken away, the tree must needs die and wither."

To be brief, the Duke of Exeter used such earnest and pithy persuasions to induce the King and the whole assembly of the parliament to credit his words that immediately after he had made an end, all the company began to cry, "War! War! France! France!" Hereby the bill for dissolving of religious houses was clearly set aside, and nothing thought on but only the recovering of France, according as the Archbishop had moved. And upon this point, after a few acts besides for the wealth of the realm established, the parliament was prorogued unto Westminster. . . . [During this parliament King Henry made his brother John the Duke of Bedford, and his brother Humphrey the Duke of Gloucester. He received ambassadors from France and Burgundy, and sent ambassadors in return.]

. . . the English ambassadors, having a time appointed them to declare their message, admitted to the French King's presence, required of him to deliver unto the King of England the realm and crown of France, with the entire duchies of Aquitaine, Normandy and Anjou, with the countries of Poitiou and Maine. Many other requests they made, and this offered withal: that if the French King would, without war and effusion of Christian blood, render to the King their master his very right and lawful inheritance, that he would be content to take in marriage the Lady Katherine, daughter to the French King, and to endow her with all the duchies and countries before rehearsed; and if he would not so do, then the King of England did express and signify to him that, with the aid of God and help of his people, he would recover his right and inheritance wrongfully withholden from him, with mortal war and dint of sword. This in effect doth our

English poet comprise in his report of the occasion, which Henry the Fifth took to arrear battle against the French King, putting into the mouths of the said King of England's ambassadors an imagined speech, the conclusion whereof he maketh to be either restitution of that which the French had taken and detained from the English, or else fire and sword. His words are these,

> . . . *raptum nobis aut redde Britannis,*
> *Aut ferrum expectes, ultrices insuper ignes.*

The Frenchmen, being not a little abashed at these demands, thought not to make any absolute answer in so weighty a cause till they had further breathed, and therefore prayed the English ambassadors to say to the King their master that they now having no opportunity to conclude in so high a matter, would shortly send ambassadors into England, which should certify and declare to the King their whole mind, purpose and intent. The English ambassadors returned with this answer, making relation of everything that was said or done. King Henry, after the return of his ambassadors, determined fully to make war in France, conceiving a good and perfect hope to have fortunate success, sith victory for the most part followeth where right leadeth, being advanced forward by justice and set forth by equity. . . .

[Preparations were made for the invasion of France.]

The Frenchmen having knowledge hereof, the Dauphin, who had the governance of the realm because his father was fallen into his old disease of frenzy, sent for the Dukes of Berri and Alençon, and all the other lords of the council of France, by whose advice it was determined that they should not only prepare a sufficient army to resist the King of England whensoever he arrived to invade France, but also to stuff and furnish the towns on the frontiers and seacoasts with convenient garrisons of men; and further to send to the King of England a solemn embassage to make to him some offers according to the demands before rehearsed. The charge of this embassage was committed to the Earl of Vendome, to Master William Bouratier, Archbishop of Bourges,

and to Master Peter Fremell, Bishop of Lisieux, to the Lords
of Yvry and Braquemont, and to Master Gaultier Cole, the
King's secretary, and diverse others.

(*Anno Reg. 3. Ambassadors out of France.*) These ambassadors, accompanied with three hundred fifty horses, passed
the sea at Calais and landed at Dover, before whose arrival
the King was departed from Windsor to Winchester, intending to have gone to Hampton, there to have surveyed his
navy. But hearing of the ambassadors approaching, he tar-
ried still at Winchester, where the said French lords showed
themselves very honorably before the King and his nobility.
At time prefixed, before the King's presence, sitting in his
throne imperial, the Archbishop of Bourges made an eloquent and a long oration, dissuading war and praising peace;
offering to the King of England a great sum of money, with
diverse countries, being in very deed but base and poor, as a
dowry with the Lady Katherine in marriage, so that he would
dissolve his army and dismiss his soldiers, which he had
gathered and put in a readiness.

When his oration was ended, the King caused the ambassadors to be highly feasted, and set them at his own table.
And after a day assigned in the foresaid hall, the Archbishop
of Canterbury to their oration made a notable answer, the
effect whereof was, that if the French King would not give
with his daughter in marriage the duchies of Aquitaine,
Anjou and all other seignories and dominions sometimes
appertaining to the noble progenitors of the King of England, he would in no wise retire his army nor break his
journey, but would with all diligence enter into France and
destroy the people, waste the country and subvert the towns
with blood, sword and fire, and never cease till he had recov-
ered his ancient right and lawful patrimony. The King
avowed the Archbishop's saying, and in the word of a prince
promised to perform it to the uttermost.

(*A proud presumptuous prelate.*) The Archbishop of
Bourges, much grieved that his embassage was no more
regarded, after certain brags blustered out with impatience,
as more presuming upon his prelacy, than respecting his
duty of considerance to whom he spake and what became
him to say, he prayed safe conduct to depart. (*The wise answer of the King to the Bishop.*) Which the King gently

granted, and added withal to this effect: "I little esteem your French brags, and less set by your power and strength; I know perfectly my right to my region, which you usurp; and except you deny the apparent truth, so do yourselves also. If you neither do nor will know it, yet God and the world knoweth it. The power of your master you see, but my puissance ye have not yet tasted. If he have loving subjects, I am (I thank God) not unstored of the same; and I say this unto you, that before one year pass, I trust to make the highest crown of your country to stoop, and the proudest miter to learn his humiliatedo. In the meantime, tell this to the usurper your master, that within three months I will enter into France, as into mine own true and lawful patrimony, appointing to acquire the same, not with brag of words, but with deeds of men and dint of sword, by the aid of God, in whom is my whole trust and confidence. Further matter at this present I impart not unto you, saving that with warrant you may depart surely and safely into your country, where I trust sooner to visit you than you shall have cause to bid me welcome." With this answer the ambassadors sore displeased in their minds (although they were highly entertained and liberally rewarded) departed into their country, reporting to the Dauphin how they had sped. . . .

[The King takes defensive measures against the Scots.]

(*The Queen-Mother governor of the realm.*) When the King had all provisions ready, and ordered all things for the defense of his realm, he leaving behind him, for governor of the realm, the Queen his mother-in-law, departed to Southampton to take ship into France. And first princely appointing to advertise the French King of his coming, therefore dispatched Antelope, his Pursuivant-at-Arms, with letters to him for restitution of that which he wrongfully withheld, contrary to the laws of God and man; the King further declaring how sorry he was that he should be thus compelled, for repeating of his right and just title of inheritance, to make war to the destruction of Christian people, but sithence he had offered peace which could not be received, now for fault of justice, he was forced to take arms. Nevertheless exhorted the French King, in the bowels of Jesu Christ, to render him that which was his own, whereby effusion of Christian blood might be avoided. These letters chiefly to this effect and purpose were written and dated from Hampton the fifth of August. When the same were presented to the French King, and by his council well perused, answer was made that he would take advice, and provide therein as time and place should be convenient, so the messenger licensed to depart at his pleasure.

When King Henry had fully furnished his navy with men, munition and other provisions, perceiving that his captains misliked nothing so much as delay, determined his soldiers to go a shipboard and away. (*The Earl of Cambridge and other lords apprehended for treason.*) But see the hap, the night before the day appointed for their departure he was credibly informed that Richard Earl of Cambridge, brother to Edward Duke of York, and Henry Lord Scroop of Masham, Lord Treasurer, with Thomas Grey, a knight of Northumberland, being confederate together, had conspired his death. Wherefore he caused them to be apprehended. The said Lord Scroop was in such favor with the King that he admitted him sometime to be his bedfellow, in whose fidelity the King reposed such trust that when any private or public council was in hand, this lord had much in the determination of it. For he represented so great gravity in his countenance, such modesty in behavior and so virtuous zeal to all godliness in his talk that whatsoever he said was thought for the most part necessary to be done and followed. Also the said Sir Thomas Grey (as some write) was of the King's Privy Council.

These prisoners upon their examination, confessed that for a great sum of money which they had received of the French King, they intended verily either to have delivered the King alive into the hands of his enemies, or else to have murdered him before he should arrive in the Duchy of Normandy. (*King Henry's words to the traitors.*) When King Henry had heard all things opened which he desired to know, he caused all his nobility to come before his presence, before whom he caused to be brought the offenders also, and to them said, "Having thus conspired the death and destruction of me, which am the head of the realm and governor of the people, it may be (no doubt) but that you likewise have sworn the confusion of all that are here with me, and also the desolation of your own country. To what horror (O Lord) for any true English heart to consider that such an execrable iniquity should ever so bewrap you, as for pleasing of a foreign enemy to imbrue your hands in your blood and to ruin your own native soil. Revenge herein touching my person, though I seek not, yet for the safeguard of you my dear friends and for due preservation of all sorts, I am by office to cause example to be showed. Get ye hence therefore ye poor miserable wretches to the receiving of your just reward, wherein God's majesty give you grace of his mercy and repentance of your heinous offenses." (*The Earl of Cambridge and the other traitors executed.*) And so immediately they were had to execution.

This done, the King calling his lords again afore him, said in words few and with good grace: of his enterprises he recounted the honor and glory, whereof they with him were to be partakers; the great confidence he had in their noble minds, which could not but remember them of the famous feats that their ancestors aforetime in France had achieved, whereof the due report forever recorded remained yet in register; the great mercy of God that had so graciously revealed unto him the treason at hand, whereby the true hearts of those afore him made so eminent and apparent in his eye as they might be right sure he would never forget it; the doubt of danger to be nothing in respect of the certainty of honor that they should acquire, wherein himself (as they saw) in person would be lord and leader through God's grace; to whose majesty, as chiefly was known the equity of his demand, even so to His mercy did he only recommend the success of his travels. When the King had said, all the noblemen kneeled down and promised faithfully to serve him, duly to obey him, and rather to die than to suffer him to fall into the hands of his enemies.

This done, the King thought that surely all treason and conspiracy had been utterly extinct—not suspecting the fire which was newly kindled and ceased not to increase till at length it burst out into such a flame that, catching the beams of his house and family, his line and stock was clean consumed to ashes. Diverse write that Richard Earl of Cambridge did not conspire with the Lord Scroop and Thomas

Grey for the murdering of King Henry to please the French King withal, but only to the intent to exalt to the crown his brother-in-law, Edmund Earl of March, as heir to Lionel Duke of Clarence; after the death of which Earl of March, for diverse secret impediments not able to have issue, the Earl of Cambridge was sure that the crown should come to him by his wife, and to his children, of her begotten. And therefore (as was thought) he rather confessed himself for need of money to be corrupted by the French King than he would declare his inward mind and open his very intent and secret purpose which, if it were espied, he saw plainly that the Earl of March should have tasted of the same cup that he had drunken, and what should have come to his own children he much doubted. Therefore destitute of comfort and in despair of life to save his children, he feigned that tale, desiring rather to save his succession than himself, which he did indeed, for his son Richard Duke of York not privily but openly claimed the crown, and Edward his son both claimed it and gained it, as after it shall appear. . . .

But now to proceed with King Henry's doings. (*The King saileth over into France with his host.*) After this, when the wind came about prosperous to his purpose, he caused the mariners to weigh up anchors and hoist up sails, and to set forward with a thousand ships, on the vigil of Our Lady Day the Assumption, and took land at Caux, commonly called Criquetot[?], where the river of Seine runneth into the sea, without resistance. (*A charitable proclamation.*) At his first coming on land, he caused proclamation to be made that no person should be so hardy on pain of death, either to take anything out of any church that belonged to the same, or to hurt or do any violence either to priests, women or any such as should be found without weapon or armor and not ready to make resistance; (*Princely and wisely.*) also that no man should renew any quarrel or strife, whereby any fray might arise to the disquieting of the army.

The next day after his landing, he marched toward the town of Harfleur, standing on the river of Seine between two hills. He besieged it on every side, raising bulwarks and a bastille in which the two Earls of Kent and Huntington were placed, with Cornwall, Grey, Steward and Porter. On that side towards the sea, the King lodged with his field, and the

Duke of Clarence on the further side towards Rouen. There were within the town the Lords de Estoueville and Gaucourt, with diverse other that valiantly defended the siege, doing what damage they could to their adversaries; and, damming up the river that hath his course through the town, the water rose so high betwixt the King's camp and the Duke of Clarence' camp (divided by the same river) that the Englishmen were constrained to withdraw their artillery from one side, where they had planted the same.

The French King being advertised that King Henry was arrived on that coast, sent in all haste the Lord Delabreth, Constable of France, the Seneschal of France, the Lord Bouciqualt Marshal of France, the Seneschal of Hainault, the Lord Ligny with other, which fortified towns with men, victuals and artillery on all those frontiers towards the sea. (*The King besieged Harfleur.*) And hearing that Harfleur was besieged, they came to the castle of Candebec being not far from Harfleur, to the intent they might succor their friends which were besieged, by some policy or means. But the Englishmen, notwithstanding all the damage that the Frenchmen could work against them forayed the country, spoiled the villages, bringing many a rich prey to the camp before Harfleur. And daily was the town assaulted, for the Duke of Gloucester, to whom the order of the siege was committed, made three mines under the ground and, approaching to the walls with his engines and ordinance, would not suffer them within to take any rest.

For although they with their countermining somewhat disappointed the Englishmen, and came to fight with them hand to hand within the mines so that they went no further forward with that work, yet they were so enclosed on each side, as well by water as land, that succor they saw could none come to them. . . .

The Captains within the town, perceiving that they were not able long to resist the continual assaults of the Englishmen, knowing that their walls were undermined and like to be overthrown . . . at the first requested a truce until Sunday next following the feast of St. Michael, in which meantime, if no succor came to remove the siege, they would undertake to deliver the town into the King's hands, their lives and goods saved.

The King advertised hereof, sent them word that except they would surrender the town to him the morrow next ensuing, without any condition, they should spend no more time in talk about the matter. (*A five days' respite.*) But yet at length through the earnest suit of the French lords, the King was contented to grant them truce until nine of the clock the next Sunday, being the two and twentieth of September, with condition that, if in the meantime no rescue came, they should yield the town at that hour, with their bodies and goods to stand at the King's pleasure. And for assurance thereof, they delivered into the King's hands thirty of their best captains and merchants within that town as pledges. But other write that it was convenanted that they should deliver but only twelve pledges, and that if the siege were not raised by the French King's power within six days next following, then should they deliver the town into the King of England['s] hands, and thirty of the chiefest personages within the same, to stand for life or death at his will and pleasure: and as for the residue of the men of war and townsmen, they should depart whither they would, without carrying forth either armor, weapon or goods.

The King nevertheless was after content to grant a respite upon certain conditions, that the captains within might have time to send to the French King for succor (as before ye have heard) lest he, intending greater exploits, might lose time in such small matters. When this composition was agreed upon, the Lord Bacqueville was sent unto the French King, to declare in what point the town stood. To whom the Dauphin answered that the King's power was not yet assembled in such number as was convenient to raise so great a siege. (*Harfleur yielded and sacked.*) This answer being brought unto the captains within the town, they rendered it up to the King of England, after that the third day was expired, which was on the day of St. Maurice, being the seven and thirtieth day after the siege was first laid. The soldiers were ransomed, and the town sacked, to the great gain of the Englishmen. Some writing of this yielding up of Harfleur, do in like sort make mention of the distress whereto the people, then expelled out of their habitations, were driven; insomuch as parents with their children, young maids and old folk went out of the town gates with heavy hearts (God wot) as put to their present shifts to seek them a new abode. . . .

All this done, the King ordained captain to the town his uncle the Duke of Exeter, who established his lieutenant there, one Sir John Falstaff, with fifteen hundred men, or (as some have) two thousand and thirty-six knights, whereof the Baron of Carew and Sir Hugh Lutterell were two councilors. . . .

King Henry, after the winning of Harfleur, determined to have proceeded further in the winning of other towns and fortresses; but because the dead time of the winter approached, it was determined by the advice of his council that he should in all convenient speed set forward, and march through the country towards Calais by land, lest his return as then homewards should of slanderous tongues be named a running away; (*Great death in the host by the flux.*) and yet that journey was adjudged perilous, by reason that the number of his people was much minished by the flux and other fevers, which sore vexed and brought to death above fifteen hundred persons of the army; and this was the cause that his return was the sooner appointed and concluded. . . .

[Henry refortified Harfleur and, in spite of the gathering of French troops and the laying waste of the country before him, pressed forward.] (*The King's army but of 15,000.*) [He] determined to make haste towards Calais and not to seek for battle, except he were thereto constrained, because that his army by sickness was sore diminished, in so much that he had but only two thousand horsemen and thirteen thousand archers, billmen, and of all sorts of other footmen.

(*The English army sore afflicted.*) The Englishmen were brought into some distress in this journey, by reason of their victuals in manner spent, and no hope to get more; for the enemies had destroyed all the corn before they came. Rest could they none take, for their enemies with alarms did ever so infest them. Daily it rained and nightly it froze; of fuel there was great scarcity, of fluxes plenty; money enough, but wares for their relief to bestow it on had they none. (*Justice in war.*) Yet in this great necessity, the poor people of the country were not spoiled, nor anything taken of them without payment nor any outrage or offense done by the Englishmen, except one which was that a soldier took a pax out of a church, for which he was apprehended and the King not once removed till the box was restored and the offender strangled. (*Note the force of justice.*) The people of the countries thereabouts hearing of such zeal in him to the maintenance of justice, ministered to his army victuals and other necessaries, although by open proclamation so to do they were prohibited.

(*The French King consulteth how to deal with the Englishmen.*) The French King being at Rouen, and hearing that King Henry was passed the river of Somme, was much displeased therewith and assembling his council to the number of five and thirty, asked their advice what was to be done. (*Dauphin, King of Sicily.*) There was amongst these five and thirty, his son the Dauphin, calling himself King of Sicily; the Dukes of Berri and Bretagne, the Earl of Ponthieu, the King's youngest son, and other high estates. At length thirty of them agreed that the Englishmen should not depart unfought withal, and five were of a contrary opinion; but the greater number ruled the matter. (*The French King sendeth defiance to King Henry.*) And so Montjoy, King-at-Arms, was sent to the King of England to defy him as the enemy of France, and to tell him that he should shortly have battle. (*King Henry's answer to the defiance.*) King Henry advisedly answered: "Mine intent is to do as it pleaseth God; I will not seek your master at this time, but if he or his seek me, I will meet with them God willing. If any of your nation attempt once to stop me in my journey now towards Calais, at their jeopardy be it; and yet wish I not any of you so unadvised as to be the occasion that I dye your tawny ground with your red blood."

When he had thus answered the herald, he gave him a princely reward and license to depart. Upon whose return, with this answer, it was incontinently on the French side proclaimed that all men of war should resort to the Constable to fight with the King of England. Whereupon, all men apt for armor and desirous of honor drew them toward the field. The Dauphin sore desired to have been at the battle, but he was prohibited by his father; likewise Philip, Earl of Charolois, would gladly have been there, if his father, the Duke of Burgundy, would have suffered him—many of his men stole away and went to the Frenchmen. The King of England hearing that the Frenchmen approached, and that there was another river for him to pass with his army by a bridge, and doubting lest if the same bridge should be broken, it would be greatly to his hinderance, appointed certain captains with their bands to go thither with all speed before him and to take possession thereof, and so to keep it till his coming thither.

Those that were sent, finding the Frenchmen busy to break down their bridge, assailed them so vigorously that they discomfited them, and took and slew them; and so the bridge was preserved till the King came and passed the river by the same with his whole army. This was on the two and twentieth day of October.

(*King Henry rideth forth to take view of the French Army.*) [The Duke of York found out that a great French army was at hand and] declared to the King what he had heard, and the King thereupon, without all fear or trouble of mind, caused the battle which he led himself to stay, and incontinently rode forth to view his adversaries, and that done, returned to his people and with cheerful countenance caused them to be put in order of battle, assigning to every captain such room and place as he thought convenient, and so kept them still in that order till night was come, and then determined to seek a place to encamp and lodge his army in for that night.

There was not one amongst them that knew any certain place whither to go in that unknown country, but by chance they happened upon a beaten way, white in sight, by the which they were brought into a little village, where they were refreshed with meat and drink somewhat more plenteously than they had been diverse days before. Order was taken by commandment from the King, after the army was first set in battle array, that no noise or clamor should be made in the host, so that in marching forth to this village every man kept himself quiet. But at their coming into the village fires were made to give light on every side, as there likewise were in the French host which was encamped not past two hundred and fifty paces distant from the English. (*The number of the French men three score thousand.*) The chief leaders of the French host were these: the Constable of France, the Marshall, the Admiral, the Lord Rambures Master of the Crossbows and other of the French nobility, which came and pitched down their standards and banners in the county of St. Paul, within the territory of Agincourt, having in their army (as some write) to the number of three score thousand horsemen, besides footmen, wagoners and other.

(*The battle of Agincourt, the 25 of October, 1415.*) They were lodged even in the way by the which the Englishmen must needs pass towards Calais, and all that night after their coming thither made great cheer and were very merry, pleasant and full of game. The Englishmen also for their parts were of good comfort and nothing abashed of the matter, and yet they were both hungry, weary, sore traveled and vexed with many cold diseases. Howbeit reconciling themselves with God by housel and shrift, requiring assistance at his hands that is the only giver of victory, they determined rather to die than to yield or flee. The day following was the five and twentieth of October in the year 1415, being then Friday and the feast of Crispin and Crispinian, a day fair and fortunate to the English but most sorrowful and unlucky to the French. . . . [The French order of battle is described.]

(*The French esteemed six to one English.*) Thus the Frenchmen, being ordered under their standards and banners, made a great show; for surely they were esteemed in number six times as many, or more, than was the whole company of the Englishmen, with wagoners, pages and all. They rested themselves, waiting for the bloody blast of the terrible trumpet, till the hour between nine and ten of the clock of the same day, during which season, the Constable made unto the captains and other men of war a pithy oration, exhorting and encouraging them to do valiantly, with many comfortable words and sensible reasons. King Henry also, like a leader and not as one led, like a sovereign and not an inferior, perceiving a plot of ground very strong and meet for his purpose, which on the back half was fenced with the village wherein he had lodged the night before, and on both sides defended with hedges and bushes, thought good there to embattle his host, and so ordered his men in the same place as he saw occasion, and as stood for his most advantage.

(*The order of the English army and archers.*) First, he sent privily two hundred archers into a low meadow, which was near to the vanguard of his enemies but separated with a great ditch, commanding them there to keep themselves close till they had a token to them given to let drive at their adversaries. (*The vanward all of archers.*) Beside this, he appointed a vanward, of the which he made captain Edward Duke of York, who of an haughty courage had desired that office, and with him were the Lords Beaumont, Willoughby and Fanhope, and this battle was all of archers. The middle ward was governed by the King himself, with his brother, the Duke of Gloucester, and the Earls of Marshall, Oxford and Suffolk, in the which were all the strong billmen. The Duke of Exeter, uncle to the King, led the rearward, which was mixed both with billmen and archers. The horsemen like wings went on every side of the battle.

(*Archers the greatest force of the English army.*) Thus the King having ordered his battles, feared not the puissance of his enemies, but (*A politic invention.*) yet to provide that they should not with the multitude of horsemen break the order of his archers, in whom the force of his army consisted (for in those days the yeomen had their limbs at liberty, sith their hose were then fastened with one point, and their jacks long and easy to shoot in, so that they might draw bows of great strength and shoot arrows of a yard long, beside the head), he caused stakes bound with iron sharp at both ends, of the length of five or six foot, to be pitched before the archers and of each side the footmen like an hedge, to the intent that if the barded horses ran rashly upon them, they might shortly be gored and destroyed. Certain persons also were appointed to remove the stakes, as by the moving of the archers occasion and time should require, so that the footmen were hedged about with stakes and the horsemen stood like a bulwark between them and their enemies, without the stakes. . . .

King Henry, by reason of his small number of people to fill up his battles, placed his vanguard so on the right hand of the main battle, which himself led, that the distance betwixt them might scarce be perceived, and so in like case was the rearward joined on the left hand, that the one might the more readily succor another in time of need. (*King Henry's oration to his men.*) When he had thus ordered his battles, he left a small company to keep his camp and carriage, which remained still in the village, and then, calling his captains and soldiers about him, he made to them a right grave oration, moving them to play the men, whereby to obtain a glorious victory, as there was hope certain they should, the rather if they would but remember the just cause for which they fought, and whom they should encounter—such faint-hearted people as their ancestors had so often overcome. To conclude, many words of courage he uttered, to stir them to do manfully, assuring them that England should never be charged with his ransom, nor any Frenchman triumph over him as a captive, for either by famous death or glorious victory would he (by God's grace) win honor and fame.

(*A wish.*) It is said that as he heard one of the host utter his wish to another thus: "I would to God there were with us now so many good soldiers as are at this hour within England!" the King answered: "I would not wish a man more here than I have; we are indeed in comparison to the enemies but a few, but if God of his clemency do favor us and our just cause (as I trust He will) we shall speed well enough. (*A noble courage of a valiant prince.*) But let no man ascribe victory to our own strength and might, but only to God's assistance, to whom I have no doubt we shall worthily have cause to give thanks therefore. And if so be that for our offenses' sakes we shall be delivered into the hands of our enemies, the less number we be, the less damage shall the realm of England sustain; but if we should fight in trust of multitude of men and so get the victory (our minds being prone to pride) we should thereupon peradventure ascribe the victory not so much to the gift of God, as to our own puissance, and thereby provoke his high indignation and displeasure against us; and if the enemy get the upper hand, then should our realm and country suffer more damage and stand in further danger. But be you of good comfort, and show yourselves valiant, God and our just quarrel shall defend us, and deliver these our proud adversaries with all the multitude of them which you see (or at the least the most of them) into our hands." Whilst the King was yet thus in speech, either army so maligned the other, being as then in open sight, that every man cried: "Forward, forward!" The Dukes of Clarence, Gloucester and York were of the same opinion, yet the King stayed a while, lest any jeopardy were not foreseen or any hazard not prevented. The Frenchmen in the meanwhile, as though they had been sure of victory, made great triumph, for the captains had determined before how to divide the spoil, and the soldiers the night before had played the Englishmen at dice. The noblemen had devised a chariot, wherein they might triumphantly convey the King captive to the city of Paris, crying to their soldiers: "Haste you to the spoil, glory and honor!"—little weening (God wot) how soon their brags should be blown away.

Here we may not forget how the French, thus in their jollity, sent an herald to King Henry to inquire what ransom he would offer. Whereunto he answered that within two or three hours he hoped it would so happen that the Frenchmen should be glad to common rather with the Englishmen for their ransoms, than the English to take thought for their deliverance, promising for his own part that his dead carcass should rather be a prize to the Frenchmen than that his living body should pay any ransom. When the messenger was come back to the French host, the men of war put on their helmets and caused their trumpets to blow to the battle. They thought themselves so sure of victory that diverse of the noblemen made such haste towards the battle that they left many of their servants and men of war behind them, and some of them would not once stay for their standards: as amongst other the Duke of Brabant, when his standard was not come, caused a banner to be taken from a trumpet and fastened to a spear, the which he commanded to be borne before him instead of his standard.

But when both these armies coming within danger either of other, set in full order of battle on both sides, they stood still at the first, beholding either other's demeanor, being not distant in sunder past three bow shots. And when they had on both parts thus stayed a good while without doing anything (except that certain of the French horsemen advancing forwards, betwixt both the hosts, were by the English archers constrained to return back) advice was taken amongst the Englishmen what was best for them to do. Thereupon all things considered, it was determined that, sith the Frenchmen would not come forward, the King with his army embattled (as ye have heard) should march towards them and, so leaving their truss and baggage in the village where they lodged the night before, only with their weapons, armor and stakes prepared for the purpose, as ye have heard.

These made somewhat forward, before whom there went an old knight, Sir Thomas Erpingham (a man of great experience in the war) with a warder in his hand; and when he cast up his warder, all the army shouted. (*The English gave the onset.*) But that was a sign to the archers in the meadow, which therewith shot wholly altogether at the vanward of the Frenchmen, who when they perceived the archers in the meadow, and saw they could not come at them for a ditch that was betwixt them, with all haste set upon the forward of King Henry, (*The two armies join battle.*) but, ere they could join, the archers in the forefront and the archers on that side which stood in the meadow, so wounded the footmen, galled the horses and cumbered the men of arms, that the footmen durst not go forward, the horsemen ran together upon plumps without order, some overthrew such as were next them, and the horses overthrew their masters; and so at the first joining, the Frenchmen were foully discomforted and the Englishmen highly encouraged.

(*The vanward of the French discomforted.*) When the French vanward was thus brought to confusion, the English archers cast away their bows and took into their hands axes, mauls, swords, bills and other hand-weapons, and with the same slew the Frenchmen until they came to the middle ward. (*Their battle beaten.*) Then approached the King and so encouraged his people that shortly the second battle of the Frenchmen was overthrown and dispersed, not without great slaughter of men; howbeit, diverse were relieved by their varlets and conveyed out of the field. The Englishmen were so busied in fighting and taking of the prisoners at hand, that they followed not in chase of their enemies, nor would once break out of their array of battle. Yet sundry of the Frenchmen strongly withstood the fierceness of the English, when they came to handy strokes, so that the fight sometime was doubtful and perilous. Yet as part of the French horsemen set their course to have entered upon the King's battle, with the stakes overthrown, they were either taken or slain. Thus this battle continued three long hours.

(*A valiant king.*) The King that day showed himself a valiant knight, albeit almost felled by the Duke of Alençon;

yet with plain strength he slew two of the Duke's company, and felled the Duke himself, whom when he would have yielded, the King's guard (contrary to his mind) slew out of hand. In conclusion, the King minding to make an end of that day's journey, caused his horsemen to fetch a compass about and to join with him against the rearward of the Frenchmen, in the which was the greatest number of people. (*The French rearward discomforted.*) When the Frenchmen perceived his intent, they were suddenly amazed and ran away like sheep, without order or array. Which when the King perceived, he encouraged his men and followed so quickly upon the enemies that they ran hither and thither, casting away their armor; many on their knees desired to have their lives saved.

(*The King's camp robbed.*) In the mean season, while the battle thus continued and that the Englishmen had taken a great number of prisoners, certain Frenchmen on horseback ... to the number of six hundred horsemen, which were the first that fled, hearing that the English tents and pavilions were a good way distant from the army, without any sufficient guard to defend the same, either upon a covetous meaning to gain by the spoil or upon a desire to be revenged, entered upon the King's camp and there spoiled the hales [i.e., temporary shelters], robbed the tents, brake up chests and carried away caskets, and slew such servants as they found to make any resistance. For which treason and haskardy in thus leaving their camp at the very point of fight, for winning of spoil where none to defend it, very many were after committed to prison, and had lost their lives if the Dauphin had longer lived.

But when the outcry of the lackeys and boys, which ran away for fear of the Frenchmen thus spoiling the camp, came to the King's ears, he doubting lest his enemies should gather together again and begin a new field, and mistrusting further that the prisoners would be an aid to his enemies, or the very enemies to their takers indeed, if they were suffered to live, contrary to his accustomed gentleness, commanded by sound of trumpet that every man (upon pain of death) should incontinently slay his prisoner. (*All the prisoners slain.*) When this dolorous decree and pitiful proclamation was pronounced, pity it was to see how some Frenchmen were suddenly sticked with daggers, some were brained with poleaxes, some slain with mauls, other had their throats cut, and some their bellies paunched, so that in effect, having respect to the great number, few prisoners were saved.

When this lamentable slaughter was ended, the Englishmen disposed themselves in order of battle, ready to abide a new field and also to invade and newly set on their enemies. (*A fresh onset.*) With great force they assailed the Earls of Marle and Faulconbridge, and the Lords of Louvail and of Thine, with six hundred men of arms, who had all that day kept together, but now slain and beaten down out of hand. (*A right wise and valiant challenge of the King.*) Some write, that the King perceiving his enemies in one part to assemble together, as though they meant to give a new battle for preservation of the prisoners, sent to them an herald, commanding them either to depart out of his sight or else to come forward at once and give battle, promising herewith that if they did offer to fight again, not only those prisoners which his people already had taken but also so many of them as in this new conflict which they thus attempted should fall into his hands, should die the death without redemption.

The Frenchmen fearing the sentence of so terrible a decree, without further delay parted out of the field. (*Thanks given to God for the victory.*) And so about four of the clock in the afternoon, the King when he saw no appearance of enemies, caused the retreat to be blown; and gathering his army together, gave thanks to almighty God for so happy a victory, causing his prelates and chaplains to sing this psalm: *"In exitu Israel de Aegypto,"* and commanded every man to kneel down on the ground at this verse: *"Non nobis Domine, non nobis, sed nomini tuo da gloriam."* (*A worthy example of a godly prince.*) Which done, he caused *"Te Deum,"* with certain anthems to be sung, giving laud and praise to God, without boasting of his own force or any human power. That night he and his people took rest, and refreshed themselves with such victuals as they found in the French camp, but lodged in the same village where he lay the night before.

In the morning, Montjoy, King-at-Arms, and four other French heralds came to the King to know the number of prisoners, and to desire burial for the dead. Before he made them answer (to understand what they would say) he demanded of them why they made to him that request, considering that he knew not whether the victory was his or theirs. When Mont-joy by true and just confession had cleared that doubt to the high praise of the King, he desired of Montjoy to understand the name of the castle near adjoining. (*The battle of Agin-court.*) When they had told him that it was called Agincourt, he said, "Then shall this conflict be called the battle of Agin-court." He feasted the French officers of arms that day, and granted them their request, which busily sought through the field for such as were slain. But the Englishmen suffered them not to go alone, for they searched with them and found many hurt, but not in jeopardy of their lives, whom they took prisoners, and brought them to their tents. When the King of England had well refreshed himself and his soldiers that had taken the spoil of such as were slain, he with his prisoners in good order returned to his town of Calais.

(*The same day that the new Mayor went to Westminster to receive his oath, the advertisement of this noble victory came to the city in the morning betimes ere men were up from their beds.*) When the tidings of this great victory was blown into England, solemn processions and other praisings to almighty God with bonfires and joyful triumphs were ordained in every town, city and borough, and the Mayor and citizens of London went the morrow after the day of St. Simon and Jude from the church of St. Paul to the church of St. Peter at Westminster in devout manner, rendering to God hearty thanks for such fortunate luck sent to the King and his army. (*Three graves that held five thousand and eight hun-dred corpses.*) The same Sunday that the King removed from the camp at Agincourt towards Calais, diverse French-men came to the field to view again the dead bodies . . . [whereof] were buried by account five thousand and eight hundred persons, beside them that were carried away by their friends and servants, and others which, being wounded, died in hospitals and other places.

After this their dolorous journey and pitiful slaughter, diverse clerks of Paris made many a lamentable verse, com-plaining that the King reigned by will and that councilors were partial; affirming that the noblemen fled against nature, and that the commons were destroyed by their prodigality;

declaring also that the clergy were dumb and durst not say the truth and that the humble commons duly obeyed and yet ever suffered punishment: for which cause by divine persecution the less number vanquished the greater. Wherefore they concluded that all things went out of order, and yet was there no man that studied to bring the unruly to frame. It was no marvel though this battle was lamentable to the French nation, for in it were taken and slain the flower of all the nobility of France.

(*Noblemen prisoners.*) There were taken prisoners, Charles Duke of Orleans nephew to the French King, John Duke of Bourbon, the Lord Bouciqualt, one of the Marshals of France (he after died in England), with a number of other lords, knights and esquires, at the least fifteen hundred, besides the common people. (*The number slain on the French part.*) There were slain in all of the French part to the number of ten thousand men, whereof were princes and noblemen bearing banners one hundred twenty and six; to these, of knights, esquires and gentlemen, so many as made up the number of eight thousand and four hundred (of the which five hundred were dubbed knights the night before the battle) so as of the meaner sort, not past sixteen hundred. Amongst those of the nobility that were slain, these were the chiefest, Charles Lord Delabreth, High Constable of France; Jacques of Chatillon, Lord of Dampierre, Admiral of France; the Lord Rambures, Master of the Crossbows; Sir Guichard Dauphin, Great Master of France; John Duke of Alençon; Anthony Duke of Brabant, brother to the Duke of Burgundy; Edward Duke of Bar; the Earl of Nevers, another brother to the Duke of Burgundy; with the Earls of Marle, Vaudemont, Beaumont, Grandpré, Roussi, Fauconbridge, Foix and Lestrake, beside a great number of lords and barons of name.

(*Englishmen slain.*) Of Englishmen, there died at this battle, Edward Duke of York, the Earl of Suffolk, Sir Richard Ketly and Davy Gam, Esquire, and of all other not above five and twenty persons, as some do report; but other writers of greater credit affirm that there were slain above five or six hundred persons. Titus Livius saith that there were slain of Englishmen, beside the Duke of York and the Earl of Suffolk, a hundred persons at the first encounter. The

Duke of Gloucester, the King's brother, was sore wounded about the hips, and borne down to the ground so that he fell backwards, with his feet towards his enemies, whom the King bestrid and like a brother valiantly rescued from his enemies and, so saving his life, caused him to be conveyed out of the fight into a place of more safety. The whole order of this conflict, which cost many a man's life and procured great bloodshed before it was ended, is lively described in *Anglorum Praeliis*. . . .

After that the King of England had refreshed himself and his people at Calais, and that such prisoners as he had left at Harfleur (as ye have heard) were come to Calais unto him, the sixth day of November he with all his prisoners took shipping, and the same day landed at Dover, having with him the dead bodies of the Duke of York and the Earl of Suffolk, and caused the Duke to be buried at his college of Fotheringay and the Earl at New Elm. In this passage, the seas were so rough and troublous that two ships belonging to Sir John Cornwall, Lord Fanhope, were driven into Zeeland; howbeit, nothing was lost nor any person perished. The Mayor of London and the aldermen, appareled in orient grained scarlet, and four hundred commoners clad in beautiful murrey, well mounted and trimly horsed, with rich collars and great chains, met the King on Blackheath, rejoicing at his return. And the clergy of London, with rich crosses, sumptuous copes and massy censers, received him at St. Thomas of Waterings with solemn processing.

(*The great modesty of the King.*) The King, like a grave and sober personage, and as one remembering from whom all victories are sent, seemed little to regard such vain pomp and shows as were in triumphant sort devised for his welcoming home from so prosperous a journey, in so much that he would not suffer his helmet to be carried with him, whereby might have appeared to the people the blows and dints that were to be seen in the same; neither would he suffer any ditties to be made and sung by minstrels of his glorious victory, for that he would wholly have the praise and thanks altogether given to God. The news of this bloody battle being reported to the French King as then sojourning at Rouen filled the court full of sorrow. . . .

[Shortly after Agincourt the Dauphin died "either for

melancholy that he had for the loss of Agincourt, or by some
sudden disease." In the following year the English made further inroads in France, and Henry made a league with the
Emperor, who came to England as a "mediator for peace";
Henry also made a truce with the Duke of Burgundy.

In 1417, Henry again invaded France, capturing Caen; at
home the Scots were repelled. In 1418, Cherbourg was taken
and Rouen besieged.]

(*King Henry his justice.*) Now as it chanced, the King in
going about the camp to survey and view the warders, he
espied two soldiers that were walking abroad without the
limits assigned, whom he caused straightways to be apprehended and hanged upon a tree of great height, for a terror to
others, that none should be so hardy to break such orders as
he commanded them to observe. . . .

[In Rouen] victuals began sore to fail them. . . . (*Extreme
famine within Rouen.*) If I should rehearse (according to the
report of diverse writers) how dearly dogs, rats, mice and
cats were sold within the town, and how greedily they were
by the poor people eaten and devoured, and how the people
daily died for fault of food, and young infants lay sucking in
the streets on their mothers' breasts, lying dead, starved for
hunger, the reader might lament their extreme miseries. A
great number of poor silly creatures were put out at the gates,
which were by the Englishmen that kept the trenches beaten
and driven back again to the same gates, which they found
closed and shut against them. And so they lay between the
walls of the city and the trenches of the enemies, still crying
for help and relief, for lack whereof great numbers of them
daily died.

(*A virtuous and charitable prince.*) Howbeit, King Henry
moved with pity, upon Christmas day, in the honor of
Christ's nativity, refreshed all the poor people with victuals,
to their great comfort and his high praise. . . .

[Messengers come to the King in the New Year request-
ing a parley.] (*A presumptuous orator.*) One of them . . . who
showing himself more rash than wise, more arrogant than
learned, first took upon him to show wherein the glory of
victory consisted, advising the King not to show his manhood in famishing a multitude of poor, simple and innocent
people, but rather suffer such miserable wretches as lay

betwixt the walls of the city and the trenches of his siege to pass through the camp, that they might get their living in other places, and then if he durst manfully assault the city and by force subdue it, he should win both worldly fame and merit great meed at the hands of almighty God for having compassion of the poor, needy and indigent people.

(*The King's answer to this proud message.*) When this orator had said, the King who no request less suspected than that which was thus desired, began awhile to muse; and after he had well considered the crafty cautel of his enemies, with a fierce countenance and bold spirit he reproved them, both for their subtle dealing with him and their malapert presumption, in that they should seem to go about to teach him what belonged to the duty of a conqueror. And therefore since it appeared that the same was unknown unto them, he declared that the goddess of battle, called Bellona, had three handmaidens, ever of necessity attending upon her, as blood, fire and famine. And whereas it lay in his choice to use them all three—yea, two or one of them at his pleasure— he had appointed only the meekest maid of those three damsels to punish them of that city, till they were brought to reason.

And whereas the gain of a captain attained by any of the said three handmaidens was both glorious, honorable and worthy of triumph; yet of all the three, the youngest maid, which he meant to use at that time was most profitable and commodious. . . . And as to assault the town, he told them that he would they should know, he was both able and willing thereto, as he should see occasion; but the choice was in his hand, to tame them either with blood, fire or famine, or with them all, whereof he would take the choice at his pleasure, and not at theirs.

This answer put the French ambassadors in a great study, musing much at his excellent wit and haughtiness of courage. . . . (*A truce for eight days.*) They upon consultation had together required once again to have access to his royal presence, which being granted, they humbling themselves on their knees, besought him to take a truce for eight days. . . . The King like a merciful prince granted to them their asking. . . .

[Rouen surrendered and, then after further fighting, the Duke of Burgundy sought peace-talks.]

(*Either part was appointed to bring with them not past two thousand and five hundred men of war.*) . . . the place of interview and meeting was appointed to be beside Meulan on the river of Seine, where in a fair place every part was by commissioners appointed to their ground. When the day of appointment approached, which was the last day of May, the King of England accompanied with the Dukes of Clarence and Gloucester, his brethren, the Duke of Exeter his uncle, and Henry Beaufort clerk, his other uncle, which after was Bishop of Winchester and Cardinal, with the Earls of March, Salisbury and others, to the number of a thousand men of war, entered into his ground, which was barred about and ported, wherein his tents were pight in a princely manner.

(*A treaty of peace.*) Likewise for the French part came Isabel the French Queen, because her husband was fallen into his old frantic disease, having in her company the Duke of Burgundy and the Earl of St. Paul, and she had attending upon her the fair Lady Katherine her daughter, with six and twenty ladies and damosels; and had also for her furniture a thousand men of war. The said Lady Katherine was brought by her mother, only to the intent that the King of England, beholding her excellent beauty, should be so inflamed and rapt in her love that he, to obtain her to his wife, should the sooner agree to a gentle peace and loving concord. (*Seven times, the last being on the last day of June.*) But though many words were spent in this treaty, and that they met at eight several times, yet no effect ensued, nor any conclusion was taken by this friendly consultation, so that both parties after a princely fashion took leave each of other, and departed; the Englishmen to Mantes, and the Frenchmen to Pontoise. . . .

[Henry came to an eighth meeting but the French representatives did not.]

By reason whereof no conclusion sorted to effect of all this communication, save only that a certain spark of burning love was kindled in the King's heart by the sight of the Lady Katherine.

The King without doubt was highly displeased in his mind that this communication came to no better pass. Wherefore he mistrusting that the Duke of Burgundy was the very let and stop of his desires, said unto him before his departure: "Cousin, we will have your King's daughter and all things that we demand with her, or we will drive your King and you out of his realm." "Well," said the Duke of Burgundy, "before you drive the King and me out of his realm, you shall be well wearied, and thereof we doubt little." . . .

[Warfare again broke out, Pontoise and Gisors falling to Henry, and then the whole of Normandy. The Duke of Burgundy was murdered by the Dauphin's men and then his son, Duke Philip, sought for peace.]

(*King Henry condescendeth to a treaty of peace.*) Whilst these victorious exploits were thus happily achieved by the Englishmen, and that the King lay still at Rouen in giving thanks to almighty God for the same, there came to him eftsoons ambassadors from the French King and the Duke of Burgundy to move him to peace. The King minding not to be reputed for a destroyer of the country which he coveted to preserve, or for a causer of Christian blood still to be spilt in his quarrel, began so to incline and give ear unto their suit and humble request that at length (after often sending to and fro) and that the Bishop of Arras and other men of honor had been with him, and likewise the Earl of Warwick and the Bishop of Rochester had been with the Duke of Burgundy, they both finally agreed upon certain articles, so that the French King and his commons would thereto assent.

Now was the French King and the Queen with their daughter, Katherine, at Troyes in Champagne governed and ordered by them, which so much favored the Duke of Burgundy that they would not, for any earthly good, once hinder or pull back one jot of such articles as the same Duke should seek to prefer. (*A truce tripartite.*) And therefore what needeth many words?—a truce tripartite was accorded between the two Kings and the Duke, and their countries, and order taken that the King of England should send, in the company of the Duke of Burgundy, his ambassadors unto Troyes in Champagne, sufficiently authorized to treat and conclude of so great matter. (*Ambassadors from King Henry to the French King.*) The King of England, being in good hope that all his affairs should take good success as he could wish or desire, sent to the Duke of Burgundy his uncle, the Duke of

Exeter, the Earl of Salisbury, the Bishop of Ely, the Lord Fanhope, the Lord Fitz Hugh, Sir John Robsert and Sir Philip Hall, with diverse doctors to the number of five hundred horse, which in the company of the Duke of Burgundy came to the city of Troyes the eleventh of March. The King, the Queen and the Lady Katherine them received, and heartily welcomed, showing great signs and tokens of love and amity.

(*The articles of the peace concluded between King Henry and the French King.*) After a few days they fell to council, in which at length it was concluded that King Henry of England should come to Troyes, and marry the Lady Katherine; and the King her father after his death should make him heir of his realm, crown and dignity. It was also agreed, that King Henry, during his father-in-law's life, should in his stead have the whole government of the realm of France, as regent thereof, with many other covenants and articles, as after shall appear. To the performance whereof, it was accorded that all the nobles and estates of the realm of France, as well spiritual as temporal, and also the cities and commonalties, citizens and burgesses of towns, that were obeisant at that time to the French King, should take a corporal oath. These articles were not at the first in all points brought to a perfect conclusion. But after the effect and meaning of them was agreed upon by the commissioners, the Englishmen departed towards the King their master, and left Sir John Robsert behind to give his attendance on the Lady Katherine.

King Henry, being informed by them of that which they had done, was well content with the agreement and with all diligence prepared to go unto Troyes. . . .

The Duke of Burgundy, accompanied with many noblemen, received him two leagues without the town and conveyed him to his lodging. . . . (*King Henry cometh to Troyes to the French King.*) And after that he had reposed himself a little, he went to visit the French King, the Queen and the Lady Katherine, whom he found in St. Peter's church, where was a very joyous meeting betwixt them (and this was on the twentieth day of May), and (*King Henry affieth the French King's daughter.*) there the King of England and the Lady Katherine were affianced. After this, the two kings and their council assembled together diverse days, wherein the first concluded agreement was in diverse points altered and brought to a certainty, according to the effect above mentioned. . . .

[The articles of peace included:]

1. First, it is accorded between our father and us that forsomuch as by the bond of matrimony made for the good of the peace between us and our most dear beloved Katherine, daughter of our said father and of our most dear mother Isabel, his wife, and the same Charles and Isabel been made our father and mother; therefore them as our father and mother we shall have and worship, as it fitteth and seemeth so worthy a prince and princess to be worshipped, principally before all other temporal persons of the world.

25. Also that our said father, during his life, shall name, call, and write us in French in this manner: *"Notre très cher fils, Henri, Roi d'Angleterre, Héritier de France,"* and in Latin in this manner: *Praeclarissimus filius noster Henricus, Rex Angliae et Haeres Franciae."*

28. Also that thenceforward, perpetually, shall be still rest, and that in all manner of wise, dissensions, hates, rancors, envies and wars, between the same realms of France and England, and the people of the same realms, drawing to accord of the same peace, may cease and be broken. . . .

[The marriage took place on 2 June 1420. The Dauphin held the south and fought against Henry and the peace. In 1422 Henry fell sick on campaign and died in August.]

[The Character of Henry V.]

This Henry was a king, of life without spot; a prince whom all men loved, and of none disdained; a captain against whom fortune never frowned, nor mischance once spurned, whose people him (so severe a justicer) both loved and obeyed (and so humane withal that he left no offense unpunished nor friendship unrewarded); a terror to rebels, and suppressor of sedition; his virtues notable, his qualities most praiseworthy.

In strength and nimbleness of body from his youth few to him comparable, for in wrestling, leaping and running no man well able to compare. In casting of great iron bars and heavy stones he excelled commonly all men, never shrinking at cold, nor slothful for heat; and when he most labored, his head commonly uncovered; no more weary of harness than a light cloak; very valiantly abiding at needs both hunger and thirst; so manful of mind as never seen to quinch at a wound or to smart at the pain, not to turn his nose from evil savor nor close his eyes from smoke or dust; no man more moderate in eating and drinking, with diet not delicate but rather more meet for men of war than for princes or tender stomachs. Every honest person was permitted to come to him, sitting at meal, where either secretly or openly to declare his mind. High and weighty causes as well between men of war and other he would gladly hear, and either determined them himself, or else for end committed them to others. He slept very little, but that very soundly, in so much that when his soldiers sung at nights or minstrels played, he then slept fastest; courage invincible; of purpose unmutable; so wisehardy always, as fear was banished from him; at every alarum he first in armor and foremost in ordering. In time of war such was his providence, bounty and hap, as he had true intelligence not only what his enemies did but what they said and intended; of his devises and purposes few, before the thing was at the point to be done, should be made privy.

He had such knowledge in ordering and guiding an army, with such a gift to encourage his people, that the Frenchmen had constant opinion he could never be vanquished in battle. Such wit, such prudence, and such policy withal, that he never enterprised anything before he had fully debated and forecast all the main chances that might happen, which done, with all diligence and courage, he set his purpose forward. What policy he had in finding present remedies for sudden mischiefs and what engines in saving himself and his people in sharp distresses, were it not that by his acts they did plainly appear, hard were it by words to make them credible. Wantonness of life and thirst in avarice had he quite quenched in him; virtues indeed in such an estate of sovereignty, youth and power, as very rare, so right commendable

Commentaries

WILLIAM HAZLITT

From Characters of Shakespear's Plays

Henry V is a very favorite monarch with the English nation, and he appears to have been also a favorite with Shakespear, who labors hard to apologize for the actions of the king, by showing us the character of the man, as "the king of good fellows." He scarcely deserves this honor. He was fond of war and low company:—we know little else of him. He was careless, dissolute, and ambitious;—idle, or doing mischief. In private, he seemed to have no idea of the common decencies of life, which he subjected to a kind of regal license; in public affairs, he seemed to have no idea of any rule of right or wrong, but brute force, glossed over with a little religious hypocrisy and archiepiscopal advice. His principles did not change with his situation and professions. His adventure on Gadshill was a prelude to the affair of Agincourt, only a bloodless one; Falstaff was a puny prompter of violence and outrage compared with the pious and politic Archbishop of Canterbury, who gave the king carte blanche, in a genealogical tree of his family, to rob and murder in circles of latitude and longitude abroad—to save the possessions of the church at home. This appears in the speeches in Shakespear, where the hidden motives that actuate princes and their advisers in war and policy are better laid open than in speeches from the throne or woolsack.

From *Characters of Shakespear's Plays* by William Hazlitt, 2nd ed (London: Taylor & Hessey, 1818).

Henry, because he did not know how to govern his own kingdom, determined to make war upon his neighbors. Because his own title to the crown was doubtful, he laid claim to that of France. Because he did not know how to exercise the enormous power, which had just dropped into his hands, to any one good purpose, he immediately undertook (a cheap and obvious resource of sovereignty) to do all the mischief he could. Even if absolute monarchs had the wit to find out objects of laudable ambition, they could only "plume up their wills" in adhering to the more sacred formula of the royal prerogative, "the right divine of kings to govern wrong," because will is only then triumphant when it is opposed to the will of others, because the pride of power is only then shown, not when it consults the rights and interests of others, but when it insults and tramples on all justice and all humanity. Henry declares his resolution "when France is his, to bend it to his awe, or break it all to pieces"— a resolution worthy of a conqueror, to destroy all that he cannot enslave; and what adds to the joke, he lays all the blame of the consequences of his ambition on those who will not submit tamely to his tyranny. Such is the history of kingly power, from the beginning to the end of the world— with this difference, that the object of war formerly, when the people adhered to their allegiance, was to depose kings; the object latterly, since the people swerved from their allegiance, has been to restore kings, and to make common cause against mankind. The object of our late invasion and conquest of France was to restore the legitimate monarch, the descendant of Hugh Capet, to the throne: Henry V in his time made war on and deposed the descendant of this very Hugh Capet, on the plea that he was a usurper and illegitimate. What would the great modern catspaw of legitimacy and restorer of divine right have said to the claim of Henry and the title of the descendants of Hugh Capet? Henry V it is true, was a hero, a King of England, and the conqueror of the king of France. Yet we feel little love or admiration for him. He was a hero, that is, he was ready to sacrifice his own life for the pleasure of destroying thousands of other lives: he was a king of England, but not a constitutional one, and we only like kings according to the law; lastly, he was a conqueror of the French king, and for this we dislike him less than if he had conquered the French people. How then do we like him? We like him in the play. There he is a very amiable monster, a very splendid pageant. As we like to gaze at a panther or a young lion in their cages in the Tower, and catch a pleasing horror from their glistening eyes, their velvet paws, and dreadless roar, so we take a very romantic, heroic, patriotic, and poetical delight in the boasts and feats of our younger Harry, as they appear on the stage and are confined to lines of ten syllables; where no blood follows the stroke that wounds our ears, where no harvest bends beneath horses' hoofs, no city flames, no little child is butchered, no dead men's bodies are found piled on heaps and festering the next morning—in the orchestra!

So much for the politics of this play; now for the poetry. Perhaps one of the most striking images in all Shakespear is that given of war in the first lines of the Prologue.

> O for a Muse of fire, that would ascend
> The brightest heaven of invention:
> A kingdom for a stage, princes to act,
> And monarchs to behold the swelling scene!
> Then should the warlike Harry, like himself,
> Assume the port of Mars, and *at his heels*
> (*Leash'd in like hounds*) *should famine, sword, and fire*
> *Crouch for employment.*

Rubens, if he had painted it, would not have improved upon this simile.

The conversation between the Archbishop of Canterbury and the Bishop of Ely, relating to the sudden change in the manners of Henry V, is among the well-known *Beauties* of Shakespear. It is indeed admirable both for strength and grace. It has sometime occurred to us that Shakespear, in describing "the reformation" of the Prince, might have had an eye to himself—

> Which is a wonder how his Grace should glean it,
> Since his addiction was to courses vain,
> His companies unlettered, rude, and shallow,
> His hours filled up with riots, banquets, sports;
> And never noted in him any study,

> Any retirement, any sequestration
> From open haunts and popularity.
>   *Ely.* The strawberry grows underneath the nettle,
> And wholesome berries thrive and ripen best
> Neighbor'd by fruit of baser quality:
> And so the Prince obscur'd his contemplation
> Under the veil of wilderness, which no doubt
> Grew like the summer grass, fastest by night,
> Unseen, yet crescive in his faculty.

This at least is as probable an account of the progress of the poet's mind as we have met with in any of the Essays on the Learning of Shakespear.

Nothing can be better managed than the caution which the king gives the meddling Archbishop not to advise him rashly to engage in the war with France, his scrupulous dread of the consequences of that advice, and his eager desire to hear and follow it. [Hazlitt quotes 1.2.13–32]

Another characteristic instance of the blindness of human nature to everything but its own interests is the complaint made by the king of "the ill neighborhood" of the Scot in attacking England when she was attacking France.

> For once the eagle (England) being in prey,
> To her unguarded nest the weazel (Scot)
> Comes sneaking, and so sucks her princely eggs.

It is worth observing that in all these plays, which give an admirable picture of the spirit of the "good old times," the moral inference does not at all depend upon the nature of the actions, but on the dignity or meanness of the persons committing them. "The eagle England" has a right "to be in prey," but "the weazel Scot" has none "to come sneaking to her nest," which she has left to pounce upon others. Might was right, without equivocation or disguise, in that heroic and chivalrous age. The substitution of right for might, even in theory, is among the refinements and abuses of modern philosophy.

A more beautiful rhetorical delineation of the effects of

subordination in a commonwealth can hardly be conceived than the following:— [Hazlitt quotes 1.2.180–213].

Henry V is but one of Shakespear's second-rate plays. Yet by quoting passages, like this, from his second-rate plays alone, we might make a volume "rich with his praise,"

> As is the oozy bottom of the sea
> With sunken wrack and sumless treasures.

Of this sort art the king's remonstrance to Scroop, Grey, and Cambridge, on the detection of their treason, his address to the soldiers at the siege of Harfleur, and the still finer one before the battle of Agincourt, the description of the night before the battle, and the reflections on ceremony put into the mouth of the king. [Hazlitt quotes 4.1.238–89]

Most of these passages are well known: there is one, which we do not remember to have seen noticed, and yet it is no whit inferior to the rest in heroic beauty. It is the account of the deaths of York and Suffolk. [Hazlitt quotes 4.6.3–27]

But we must have done with splendid quotations. The behavior of the king, in the difficult and doubtful circumstances in which he is placed, is as patient and modest as it is spirited and lofty in his prosperous fortune. The character of the French nobles is also very admirably depicted; and the Dauphin's praise of his horse shows the vanity of that class of persons in a very striking point of view. Shakespear always accompanies a foolish prince with a satirical courtier, as we see in this instance. The comic parts of *Henry V* are very inferior to those of *Henry IV*. Falstaff is dead, and without him, Pistol, Nym, and Bardolph are satellites without a sun. Fluellen the Welshman is the most entertaining character in the piece. He is good-natured, brave, choleric, and pedantic. His parallel between Alexander and Harry of Monmouth, and his desire to have "some disputations" with Captain Macmorris on the discipline of the Roman wars, in the heat of the battle, are never to be forgotten. His treatment of Pistol is as good as Pistol's treatment of his French prisoner. There are two other remarkable prose passages in this play: the conversation of Henry in disguise with the three

W. B. YEATS

From Ideas of Good and Evil

In *La Peau de chagrin* Balzac spends many pages in describing a coquette, who seems the image of heartlessness, and then invents an improbable incident that her chief victim may discover how beautifully she can sing. Nobody had ever heard her sing, and yet in her singing, and in her chatter with her maid, Balzac tells us, was her true self. He would have us understand that behind the momentary self, which acts and lives in the world, and is subject to the judgment of the world, there is that which cannot be called before any mortal judgment seat, even though a great poet, or novelist, or philosopher be sitting upon it. Great literature has always been written in a like spirit, and is, indeed, the Forgiveness of Sin, and when we find it becoming the Accusation of Sin, as in George Eliot, who plucks her Tito in pieces with as much assurance as if he had been clockwork, literature has begun to change into something else. George Eliot had a fierceness hardly to be found but in a woman turned argumentative, but the habit of mind her fierceness gave its life to was characteristic of her century, and is the habit of mind of the Shakespearian critics. They and she gave up in a century of utilitarianism, when nothing about a man seemed important except his utility to the State, and nothing so useful to the State as the actions whose effect can be weighed by reason. The deeds of Coriolanus, Hamlet, Timon, Richard II had no obvious use, were, indeed, no

From *Essays and Introductions* by W. B. Yeats (New York and London: The Macmillan Co., Publishers, 1961). Reprinted by permission of the Macmillan Co.

more than the expression of their personalities, and so it was thought Shakespeare was accusing them, and telling us to be careful lest we deserve the like accusations. It did not occur to the critics that you cannot know a man from his actions because you cannot watch him in every kind of circumstance, and that men are made useless to the State as often by abundance as by emptiness, and that a man's business may at times be revelation, and not reformation. Fortinbras was, it is likely enough, a better king than Hamlet would have been, Aufidius was a more reasonable man than Coriolanus, Henry V was a better man-at-arms than Richard II, but, after all, were not those others who changed nothing for the better and many things for the worse greater in the Divine Hierarchies? Blake has said that "the roaring of lions, the howling of wolves, the raging of the stormy sea, and the destructive sword are portions of Eternity, too great for the eye of man," but Blake belonged by right to the ages of Faith, and thought the State of less moment than the Divine Hierarchies. Because reason can only discover completely the use of those obvious actions which everybody admires, and because every character was to be judged by efficiency in action, Shakespearian criticism became a vulgar worshipper of success. I have turned over many books in the library at Stratford-on-Avon, and I have found in nearly all an antithesis, which grew in clearness and violence as the century grew older, between two types, whose representatives were Richard II, "sentimental," "weak," "selfish," "insincere," and Henry V, "Shakespeare's only hero." These books took the same delight in abasing Richard II that schoolboys do in persecuting some boy of fine temperament, who has weak muscles and a distaste for school games. And they had the admiration for Henry V that schoolboys have for the sailor or soldier hero of a romance in some boys' paper. I cannot claim any minute knowledge of these books, but I think that these emotions began among the German critics, who perhaps saw something French and Latin in Richard II, and I know that Professor Dowden, whose book I once read carefully, first made these emotions eloquent and plausible. He lived in Ireland, where everything has failed, and he meditated frequently upon the perfection of character which had, he thought, made England successful, for, as we say, "cows beyond the water have long horns." He forgot that England, as Gordon has said, was made by her adventurers, by her people of wildness and imagination and eccentricity; and thought that Henry V, who only seemed to be these things because he had some commonplace vices, was not only the typical Anglo-Saxon, but the model Shakespeare held up before England; and he even thought it worthwhile pointing out that Shakespeare himself was making a large fortune while he was writing about Henry's victories. In Professor Dowden's successors this apotheosis went further; and it reached its height at a moment of imperialistic enthusiasm, of ever-deepening conviction that the commonplace shall inherit the earth, when somebody of reputation, whose name I cannot remember, wrote that Shakespeare admired this one character alone out of all his characters. The Accusation of Sin produced its necessary fruit, hatred of all that was abundant, extravagant, exuberant, of all that sets a sail for shipwreck, and flattery of the commonplace emotions and conventional ideals of the mob, the chief Paymaster of accusation.

I cannot believe that Shakespeare looked on his Richard II with any but sympathetic eyes, understanding indeed how ill-fitted he was to be king, at a certain moment of history, but understanding that he was lovable and full of capricious fancy, "a wild creature" as Pater has called him. The man on whom Shakespeare modeled him had been full of French elegances as he knew from Holinshed, and had given life a new luxury, a new splendor, and been "too friendly" to his friends, "too favorable" to his enemies. And certainly Shakespeare had these things in his head when he made his king fail, a little because he lacked some qualities that were doubtless common among his scullions, but more because he had certain qualities that are uncommon in all ages. To suppose that Shakespeare preferred the men who deposed his king is to suppose that Shakespeare judged men with the eyes of a Municipal Councilor weighing the merits of a Town Clerk; and that had he been by when Verlaine cried out from his bed, "Sir, you have been made by the stroke of a pen, but I have been made by the breath of God," he would have thought the Hospital Superintendent the better man. He saw indeed, as I think, in Richard II the defeat that awaits all, whether they be artist or saint, who find themselves where men ask of them a rough energy and have nothing to give but some contemplative virtue, whether lyrical fantasy, or sweetness of temper, or dreamy dignity, or love of God, or love of His creatures. He saw that such a man through sheer bewilderment and impatience can become as unjust or as violent as any common man, any Bolingbroke or Prince John, and yet remain "that sweet lovely rose." The courtly and saintly ideals of the Middle Ages were fading, and the practical ideals of the modern age had begun to threaten the unuseful dome of the sky; Merry England was fading, and yet it was not so faded that the poets could not watch the procession of the world with that untroubled sympathy for men as they are, as apart from all they do and seem, which is the substance of tragic irony.

Shakespeare cared little for the State, the source of all our judgments, apart from its shows and splendors, its turmoils and battles, its flamings-out of the uncivilized heart. He did indeed think it wrong to overturn a king, and thereby to swamp peace in civil war, and the historical plays from *Henry IV* to *Richard III*, that monstrous birth and last sign of the wrath of Heaven, are a fulfillment of the prophecy of the Bishop of Carlisle, who was "raised up by God" to make it; but he had no nice sense of utilities, no ready balance to measure deeds, like that fine instrument, with all the latest improvements, Gervinus and Professor Dowden handle so skillfully. He meditated as Solomon, not as Bentham meditated, upon blind ambitions, untoward accidents, and capricious passions, and the world was almost as empty in his eyes as it must be in the eyes of God.

> Tired with all these, for restful death I cry;—
>   As, to behold desert a beggar born,
> And needy nothing trimm'd in jollity,
>   And purest faith unhappily forsworn,
> And gilded honor shamefully misplaced,
>   And maiden virtue rudely strumpeted,
> And right perfection wrongfully disgraced,
>   And strength by limping sway disabled,
> And art made tongue-tied by authority,
>   And folly, doctorlike, controlling skill,

And simple truth miscall'd simplicity,
     And captive good attending captain ill:
Tired with all these, from these would I be gone,
Save that, to die, I leave my love alone.

   The Greeks, a certain scholar has told me, considered that
myths are the activities of the Daimons, and that the Daimons shape our characters and our lives. I have often had the
fancy that there is some one myth for every man, which, if
we but knew it, would make us understand all he did and
thought. Shakespeare's myth, it may be, describes a wise
man who was blind from very wisdom, and an empty man
who thrust him from his place, and saw all that could be seen
from very emptiness. It is in the story of Hamlet, who saw
too great issues everywhere to play the trivial game of life,
and of Fortinbras, who came from fighting battles about "a
little patch of ground" so poor that one of his captains would
not give "six ducats" to "farm it," and who was yet ac-
claimed by Hamlet and by all as the only befitting king. And
it is in the story of Richard II, that unripened Hamlet, and of
Henry V, that ripened Fortinbras. To pose character against
character was an element in Shakespeare's art, and scarcely
a play is lacking in characters that are the complement of
one another, and so, having made the vessel of porcelain,
Richard II, he had to make the vessel of clay, Henry V. He
makes him the reverse of all that Richard was. He has the
gross vices, the coarse nerves, of one who is to rule among
violent people, and he is so little "too friendly" to his friends
that he bundles them out of doors when their time is over. He
is as remorseless and undistinguished as some natural force,
and the finest thing in his play is the way his old companions
fall out of it brokenhearted or on their way to the gallows;
and instead of that lyricism which rose out of Richard's
mind like the jet of a fountain to fall again where it had risen,
instead of that fantasy too enfolded in its own sincerity to
make any thought the hour had need of, Shakespeare has
given him a resounding rhetoric that moves men as a leading
article does today. His purposes are so intelligible to everybody that everybody talks of him as if he succeeded, although he fails in the end, as all men great and little fail in
Shakespeare. His conquests abroad are made nothing by a

woman turned warrior. That boy he and Katherine were to "compound," "half French, half English," "that" was to "go to Constantinople and take the Turk by the beard," turns out a saint and loses all his father had built up at home and his own life.

Shakespeare watched Henry V not indeed as he watched the greater souls in the visionary procession, but cheerfully, as one watches some handsome spirited horse, and he spoke his tale, as he spoke all tales, with tragic irony.   [1901]

E. M. W. TILLYARD

From Shakespeare's History Plays

I have conjectured that Hall's chronicle caught Shakespeare's youthful imagination and impelled him to dramatize the whole stretch of English history from the prosperity of Edward III, through the disasters that succeeded, to the establishment of civil peace under the Tudors. In all the History Plays so far written (*King John* excepted, which is outside the sequence) he had fulfilled his obligation. But in the last three plays he had quite exceeded it by giving, concurrently with the strict historical theme, his epic picture of medieval and of contemporary England. But this excess could not cancel the residue of his obligation. He had created his picture of the great traditional villain king; he had still to create his picture of the great hero king. Richard III had figured in *2* and *3 Henry VI* and had declared his character. But that was not enough. Hall, by incorporating More's life of Richard III, dwells on that king with a special emphasis. Shakespeare fulfills his obligation to Hall by giving Richard a play to himself, in which his monstrosity is done full justice to. Hall, following the tradition established by Polydore Vergil, makes Henry V the second exceptional figure in his chronicle: the copybook paragon of kingly virtue, to balance Richard the monstrous pattern of concentrated vice. If Shakespeare was to carry his work through he was obliged to treat Henry like Richard: to allow him a play to himself. There was a personal reason why Shakespeare should now

From *Shakespeare's History Plays* by E. M. W. Tillyard (London: Chatto and Windus, 1944; New York: The Macmillan Co., 1946). Reprinted by permission of Chatto and Windus, Ltd.

acquiesce in the precedent of Hall: he had finished the theme of England or Respublica and was almost forced to allow a concrete hero to dominate his next History Play.

But Shakespeare also had his duty to the expectations of an Elizabethan audience. Having achieved popularity in showing Henry's youthful dissipation he could not, without scandal, refuse to show Henry in his traditional part of perfect king. And this traditional part contained factors not found in Hall: namely his sudden miraculous conversion when he came to the throne and his preeminence among English kings as the bluff hearty man and the good mixer. The legend of his conversion was powerful and of long standing. It began with the chronicler Walsingham, who said that Henry on coming to the throne was turned suddenly into another man, and persisted in the *Famous Victories of Henry V*, where only a miracle can account for the abrupt transition from waster to serious monarch. The tradition of good mixer finds typical expression in the king's dealing with Simon Eyre in Dekker's *Shoemaker's Holiday*.

Here then were two obligations; and they were both impossible of worthy fulfillment. In creating his epic of England Shakespeare had set himself an exacting standard. His political hero, to be worthy of the standard just set, must be the symbol of some great political principle. And there was no principle he could symbolize. The preeminently successful political hero in great literature is Aeneas; and it was Virgil's powerful and steady belief in the missionary and civilizing destiny of Rome that animated him. England had not yet reached the stage of Virgil's Rome. She had preserved herself, had achieved union, had "rested true" to herself, but she did not yet stand consciously for any wide political idea. The Tudors were successful by personal astuteness rather than by exemplifying any principle. They were not for export, not ecumenical. Thus Henry V, who could at best stand for Elizabethan political principle, could only fail when great weight was put on him. In other words Shakespeare for his hero was obliged ultimately to choose *homo* not *rex*. It is interesting that Milton did precisely the same when he rejected his political hero Arthur for his universal hero Adam. A further difficulty was that the sophisticated, eminently courtly, and not at all exclusively English character whom Shakespeare had created in Prince Hall had no connection at all with the inhuman copybook hero of Polydore Vergil.

To fulfill the second obligation in a manner worthy of the plays he had just written was also impossible. The whole point of the Prince's character was that his conversion was not sudden, that he had been preparing with much deliberation for the coming burden. And as for being the hearty man and the good mixer, the Prince may indeed have charmed his audience by the mere fact of his presence at Eastcheap; but his fundamental detachment and persistent irony are quite at odds with the popular conception of a simple forthright energetic man, transparent in character and separated from simple humble souls only by the accident of his exalted position. It would have been too risky to allow him to remain the ironist after he had come to the throne.

Shakespeare came to terms with this hopeless situation by jettisoning the character he had created and substituting one which, though lacking all consistency, satisfied the requirements both of the chroniclers and of popular tradition. No wonder if the play constructed round him shows a great falling off in quality.

Not that Shakespeare jettisoned his old creation without a struggle. He would hardly have begun his play with

> O for a Muse of fire, that would ascend
> The brightest heaven of invention:

if he had felt quite hopeless of his genius soaring into the empyrean, and thus achieving a miraculous solution of the seemingly impossible. And in the first scene where Henry appears (1.2) and once or twice later Shakespeare does try to invest his hero with a glamour that shall by its sheer blinding power make us insensible to any inconsistencies. The prelates and nobles who incite Henry to great deeds in France speak splendidly:

> Gracious lord,
> Stand for your own, unwind your bloody flag,
> Look back into your mighty ancestors;
> Go, my dread lord, to your great-grandsire's tomb,

> From whom you claim; invoke his warlike spirit,
> And your great-uncle's, Edward the Black Prince,
> Who on the French ground played a tragedy,
> Making defeat on the full power of France,
> Whiles his most mighty father on a hill
> Stood smiling, to behold his lion's whelp
> Forage in blood of French nobility.   (1.2.100–10)

Ely reinforces these words of Canterbury with

> Awake remembrance of these valiant dead
> And with your puissant arm renew their feats.
> You are their heir; you sit upon their throne;
> The blood and courage that renownèd them
> Runs in your veins: and my thrice-puissant liege
> Is in the very May-morn of his youth,
> Ripe for exploits and mighty enterprises.   (115–21)

These lines not only dazzle us with their brilliance but they place Henry in the grand context of English history and make us forget the subtle personal touches of his previous character. And they do even more. They refer back to a specific passage in *Henry IV*, the reference to May suggesting the description of Henry and his companions before Shrewsbury,

> As full of spirit as the month of May.   (4.1.100)

It looks as if Shakespeare was trying desperately, by creating casual links between Prince Hal and Henry V, to mask their fundamental discrepancy. Anyhow we cannot but be appeased for the moment; and when Exeter continues with

> Your brother kings and monarchs of the earth
> Do all expect that you should rouse yourself,
> As did the former lions of your blood,   (1.2.122–24)

we are still more appeased, for Exeter here takes up Henry's promise, made at the end of the last play, that he will accept his due place among the other monarchs in the ocean of

royalty, that his vanity will no longer beat idly on the rocks
but that

> Now doth it turn and ebb back to the sea,
> Where it shall mingle with the state of floods
> And flow henceforth in formal majesty.   (5.3.131–33)

Further questionings about Henry's character are held off by
Exeter's noble commonplace on the order of government
being like music:

> While that the armèd hand doth fight abroad,
> Th' advisèd head defends itself at home;
> For government, though high, and low, and lower,
> Put into parts, doth keep in one consent,
> Congreeing in a full and natural close,
> Like music.   (1.2.178–83)

and by Canterbury's splendid comparison of the state to the
beehive. But the truth cannot be withheld forever and out it
comes in Henry's speech to the French ambassador about
the tennis balls: a speech whose heavy irony and orotundity
compare poorly with the Prince's light ironies and truly
Olympian grandeur in *Henry IV*. It is not the same man
speaking. Later efforts to inflate Henry to greatness are no
more successful. His reproof of the traitor, Lord Scroop, at
Southampton, is wonderful poetry, possibly the finest thing
in the play; yet it is queerly ineffective in its context. The
Henry we knew was an unerring judge of human nature and
never gave himself away. When he says of Scroop

> Thou that didst bear the key of all my counsels,
> That knew'st the very bottom of my soul,
> That (almost) mightst have coined me into gold.
> (2.2.96–98)

he speaks gloriously, he may charm us for the moment, but
he ultimately bewilders us. He is utterly inconsistent with
his old self and with any of the pieces of self that make
up his patchwork character in the present play. Nor can one

plead that his words are a sententious passage spoken out of character: they are too emotional. One is tempted to suppose (as nowhere else in all Shakespeare's History Plays) that the poet, defeated in the real business of his drama, is drawing on personal experience and filling up the gap with an account of how someone at some time let him, Shakespeare, down. Once again Shakespeare tried to save his play in the scenes before Agincourt. Of Henry's conversation with Bates and Williams, Johnson wrote that "the whole argument is well followed, and properly concluded." This is a just comment, but the conversation does not get beyond the sober and the rational. It has the chill of Brutus's speech over Caesar's body rather than the warmth of the prose of the previous plays. Henry's following soliloquy "Upon the king!" is splendid poetry and yet somehow extrinsic to the play, a piece of detached eloquence on a subject on which Shakespeare had long meditated with interest and fervor.

Finally, there is a curious reference back to *Henry IV* near the end of the play, as if even then, when the game was lost, Shakespeare was still hankering after continuity with his late masterpiece. It is where Henry, courting Katherine, mentions his skill in vaulting onto his horse fully armed.

> If I could win a lady at leapfrog, or by vaulting into my saddle with my armor on my back, under correction of bragging be it spoken, I should quickly leap into a wife.   (5.2.139–43)

Here is a clear reminiscence of the gay description in *1 Henry IV* of Prince Hal mounting his horse. But how alien the two passages are: the earlier a brilliant piece of Renaissance painting; the other, with its stalely indecent double meaning, a piece of sheer writing down to the populace. In spite of these efforts to manufacture connections and of the closeness with which its plot follows on, *Henry V* is as truly separated from the two parts of *Henry IV* as *Richard II* is allied to them.

But I need not deal exhaustively with the play's shortcomings, when they have been set forth in such masterly fashion by Mark Van Doren in his *Shakespeare*. I will rather point out how conscientiously Shakespeare fulfilled his double obligation: to the chroniclers and to his public. If his muse failed to ascend the brightest heaven of invention at least it tried to pay the debts it owed below the sphere of the moon.

First, Shakespeare through the mouth of the Archbishop prolongs the chronicle story of Henry's sudden conversion:

> Never was such a sudden scholar made;
> Never came reformation in a flood
> With such a heady currance scouring faults;
> Nor never Hydra-headed willfulness
> So soon did lose his seat—and all at once—
> As in this king.   (1.1.32–37)

To suppose that Shakespeare meant the Archbishop here to be wrong, just as Poins had been wrong, about Henry's true character is to introduce a subtlety quite alien to the rest of the play. Shakespeare is submitting to the popular tradition of the chronicles and going back on his own earlier creation. Another legacy of the chronicle tradition, Henry's rejection of his old companions, had been done justice to in the previous play. Yet Shakespeare is careful to bring it in again when he makes Fluellen say,

> So also Harry Monmouth, being in his right wits and his good judgments, turned away the fat knight with the great-belly doublet.   (4.7.48–51)

With this rejection was coupled the election of grave counselors and the heed Henry gave them. And here Shakespeare pays his debt in full, and once again at his own expense. His Prince Hal had been an eminently self-reliant and self-sufficient young man, one who would never accept the advice of others without subjecting it to the closest scrutiny. In the debate in 1.2 on the French war Henry is a different person. He hardly interposes, much less argues. As a thinker he is quite passive, leaving the business to others. When these have pronounced their verdict, he accepts it without a word of comment but initiates action with

> Call in the messengers sent from the Dauphin.   (221)

The perfect courtier in whom intellect and activity was finely balanced has given way to the pure man of action, whose thinking is done for him by his counselors. His subsequent pedestrian thoughtfulness when he argues with Bates and Williams is inconsistent alike with Prince Hal's brilliant intellect and with the narrow activity he shows both in the scene with his counselors and his courtship of Katherine. Then the chroniclers (Polydore Vergil and Hall) tell us that Henry was able to learn wisdom by historical precedent. Shakespeare makes his Henry refer to the past history of his country:

> For you shall read that my great-grandfather
> Never went with his forces into France
> But that the Scot on his unfurnished kingdom
> Came pouring. (1.2.146–49)

Finally, the chroniclers make much of Henry's piety, and Shakespeare follows them very conscientiously. He pays his debt; but at what a cost. We have only to compare Henry's pious comments on the miraculously low number of English casualties at Agincourt (twenty-five) and his orders for the *Non Nobis* and the *Te Deum* to be sung, with the last scenes of *Richard III* and certain parts of *Hamlet* to recognize how chilly they are. The platitudes of piety can become ultimate statements of overwhelming power if they issue from a worthy context. Occurring as they do here in a play which is constructed without intensity, they can only depress.

Other debts to the chroniclers concern not Henry's character but ideas about history. Before dealing with these I will speak of Shakespeare's fulfilling his debt to his audience by making Henry the hearty king, the good mixer. It was probably his sense of this debt that made him depress Henry's intellectual power in the debate about the French war referred to above. He fulfills it in Henry's familiarity with his "kinsman" Fluellen and his exchange of gages with Williams. But it is in his courtship of Katherine that Henry reaches his full degree of bluffness and heartiness. "I know not," says Johnson, "why Shakespeare now gives the king nearly such a character as he made him formerly ridicule in Percy." Johnson may well ask; for the whole distance between the poles divides the lubberly wooer with his coarse complexion, who "could lay on like a butcher," from the "king of courtesy" of the earlier play.

To revert to the chroniclers, Shakespeare does in *Henry V* keep alive the theme of civil war, but more faintly than in any other of his History Plays. He clearly intended the play to be a splendid interlude, when the ancestral curse was for the moment suspended, figuring in some sort the golden age of Elizabeth. But the curse is not forgotten, for Henry prays before Agincourt that the death of Richard II should not be visited on him then, and he even remembers it when he courts Katherine:

> Now, beshrew my father's ambition! He was thinking of civil wars when he got me, therefore was I created with a stubborn outside, with an aspect of iron.   (5.2.233–36)

And the conspiracy of Richard Earl of Cambridge actually reenacts the theme.

In one historical matter *Henry V* is unique in Shakespeare: its partiality to things Welsh refers obliquely to that side of the Tudor myth which Spenser and Warner, among the poets, developed.

> *Fluellen.* All the water in Wye cannot wash your majesty's Welsh plood out of your pody, I can tell you that: God pless it, and pre-serve it, as long as it pleases his Grace, and his Majesty too!
> *Henry.* Thanks, good my countryman.   (4.7.109–130)

I fancy too that Shakespeare spares the French king the ridicule he heaps on the Dauphin, because he was father of Katherine, who, widowed of Henry V, married Owen Tudor and became the ancestress of Henry VII. The French king always speaks with dignity.

I wrote above that *Henry V* was constructed without inten-sity. It is worth mentioning one or two points in which this is true. After the Archbishop's fable of the bees there is little of the cosmic lore that marks the other History Plays. When Shakespeare's mind was working intensely it was aware of the whole range of the universe: events were not isolated but took place concurrently with other events on all the planes of existence. But the settings of the different scenes in this play are simple and confined. Even the battle of Agincourt evokes no correspondences in the heavens or elsewhere. A second sign of slack construction is the unevenness of the verse. There are passages of flatness among the rhetoric. The rhetoric has been better remembered than the flatness. But take the opening of 2.4 (the first scene showing the French court) up to the arrival of Exeter: it is written in the flattest verse, a relapse into the style of the more primitive parts of *1 Henry VI*; and, though Exeter proceeds to liven things a little, the verse remains lethargic. Nor is there much energy in the verse portions of the play's last scene. A third sign of weak construction is the casualness of the comic scenes. Whereas in *Henry IV* these were linked in all sorts of ways with the serious action, in *Henry V* they are mainly detached scenes introduced for mere variety. The farewell scene of Pistol and the Hostess in London is good enough in itself, but it is quite episodic. It would be unfair, however, not to mention the redeeming brilliance of Fluellen. For sheer original invention Shakespeare never made a better character. Had the rest of the play backed him up, he would (as his creator probably meant him to do) have filled the place of Falstaff not unworthily.

I fancy, too, that Fluellen helps us to understand Shakespeare's state of mind when he wrote *Henry V*. Fluellen is an entire innovation, like nobody else in Shakespeare before (though many years after he may have begotten the Baron of Bradwardine); and he suggests that Shakespeare was now wanting to do something fresh. Whenever Fluellen, the new character, is on the stage, Shakespeare's spirits seem to rise and he ceases to flog himself into wit or rhetoric. There are other things in the play that suggest Shakespeare's longing for a change. The coarseness of Henry's courtship of Katherine is curiously exaggerated; one can almost say hectic: as if Shakespeare took a perverse delight in writing up something he had begun to hate. Henry's reproof of Scroop, already noted as alien in tone to the norm of the play, has a quality as new as the character of Fluellen; for it is tragic and looks forward to Shakespeare's future bent of mind—

May it be possible that foreign hire
Could out of thee extract one spark of evil
That might annoy my finger? 'Tis so strange
That, though the truth of it stands off as gross
As black and white, my eye will scarcely see it.

(2.2.100–04)

That is one of the tragic themes: the unbelievable contradiction of appearance and reality; felt by Troilus about Cressida, by Hamlet about his mother, and by Othello about Desdemona. It has nothing to do with the matters that have most been the concern of this book: with politics, with patterns of history, with ancestral curses, with England's destiny and all the order of her society. It is a personal and not a public theme.

That Shakespeare was wanting to do something new is not at all to be wondered at. He had written his epic of England and had no more to say on the matter. In writing it he had developed characters of uncommon subtlety and in Prince Hal he had pictured a man, having indeed settled a conflict, but one in whom a genuine conflict had taken place. No wonder if Henry V, traditionally the man who knew exactly what he wanted and went for it with utter singleness of heart, was the very reverse of what Shakespeare was growing truly interested in. And no wonder if in his next great public character, Brutus, Shakespeare pictured a man like Prince Hal in being subjected to a conflict but unlike him in being torn asunder by its operations.[1]

---

[1] These last sentences make suggestions rather like those of Granville-Barker in his essay "*From* Henry V *to* Hamlet" in *Aspects of Shakespeare*, Oxford 1933. I refer the reader to this excellent essay. But I differ in thinking Prince Hal a much subtler character than Granville-Barker apparently does and look on Brutus as a development from the Prince as well as a reaction from Henry V.

JONATHAN DOLLIMORE AND
ALAN SINFIELD

History and Ideology:
The Instance of *Henry V*

> Behind the disorder of history Shakespeare assumed some kind
> of order or degree on earth having its counterpart in heaven. Fur-
> ther, . . . in so assuming he was using the thought-idiom of his age
> and could have avoided doing so only by not thinking at all.
>
> (Tillyard, *Shakespeare's History Plays*,
> 1944 (1962) p. 21)

The objections are familiar enough: the "Elizabethan World
Picture" simplifies the Elizabethans and, still more, Shakespeare. Yet if we look again at what Tillyard was oppos-
ing, his historicism seems less objectionable—assertions,
for example, that Shakespeare does not "seem to call for
explanations beyond those which a whole heart and a free
mind abundantly supply"; that "he betrays no bias in affairs
of church or state"; that "No period of English literature has
less to do with politics than that during which English letters
reached their zenith" (Campbell 1964, pp. 3–4). All these
quotations are taken by Lily B. Campbell from critics influential between the wars. She and Tillyard demonstrate
unquestionably that there was an ideological position, something like "the Elizabethan World Picture," and that it is
a significant presence in Shakespeare's plays. Unfortunate-
ly inadequacies in their theorizing of ideology have set the

From *Alternative Shakespeare*, ed. John Drakakis (Methuen, 1985),
pp. 206–15. We reprint the first part of an essay divided into two parts.

agenda for most subsequent work. We shall argue initially that even that criticism which has sought to oppose the idea that Shakespeare believed in and expresses a political hier-archy whose rightness is guaranteed by its reflection of a divine hierarchy, is trapped nevertheless in a problematic of order, one which stems from a long tradition of idealist philosophy.

Tillyard makes little of the fact that the writers he dis-cusses were members of the class fraction of which the gov-ernment of the country was constituted, or were sponsored by the government, or aspired to be. He seems not to notice that the *Homily Against Disobedience and Wilful Rebellion* is designed to preserve an oppressive regime—he admires the "dramatic touch" at the start, "a splendid picture of orig-inal obedience and order in the Garden of Eden" (Tillyard 1944 (1962), p. 69). His skills of critical analysis do not show him that the projection of an alleged human order onto an alleged divine order affords, in effect even if not inten-tion, a mystifying confirmation of the *status quo*. On the contrary, he claims to show that Shakespeare was "the voice of his own age first and only through being that, the voice of humanity" (ibid., p. 237). In similar fashion, Campbell speaks of "the political philosophy of [Shakespeare's] age" as "universal truth":

> If, however, he is not merely a poet but a great poet, the particu-lars of his experience are linked in meaning to the universal of which they are a representative part . . . a passion for universal truth . . . takes his hatred and his love out of the realm of the petty and into the realm of the significant.   (Campbell 1964, p. 6)

Of course, much critical energy has been spent on oppos-ing Tillyard and Campbell; they were writing during the Second World War, and the idea that the great English writer propounded attitudes which tended to encourage acquies-cence in government policy has come to seem less attractive subsequently. One point of view argues that Shakespeare saw through the Tudor Myth and, with it, all human aspira-tions and especially political aspirations. Shakespeare's plays are thus made to speak an absurdist or nihilist idea of the "human condition"—a precise reversal of the divinely guaranteed harmony proclaimed by Tillyard. A second point of view again argues the limitations of the Tudor Myth and the futility of politics, but asserts over against these the possibility of individual integrity. This inhibits even more effectively specific consideration of how power works and how it may be challenged, since integrity may be exercised within—or, even better, over and against—any sociopolitical arrangements.

Anguish at the failure of the idea of order is represented most importantly by Jan Kott's *Shakespeare Our Contemporary* (1967). Kott sees that the Tudor Myth was always a political device, and he argues that the history plays disclose this. He sees also that the legitimacy or illegitimacy, the goodness or badness of the monarch, is not the real issue: "there are no bad kings, or good kings; kings are only kings. Or let us put it in modern terms: there is only the king's situation, and the system" (p. 14). Kott has here the basis for a materialist analysis of power and ideology, but then takes the argument towards an inevitable, all-encompassing inversion of cosmic order: "The implacable roller of history crushes everybody and everything. Man is determined by his situation, by the step of the grand staircase on which he happens to find himself" (p. 39). There seems to be no play in such a system—no scope for intervention, subversion, negotiation; analysis of specific historical process, with the enabling as well as the limiting possibilities within an ideological conjuncture, seems futile—the point being, precisely, that everything is pointless.

Kott does little more than invert the Elizabethan World Picture: the terms of the debate are not changed. As Derrida insists, a metaphysic of order is not radically undermined by invoking disorder; the two terms are necessary to each other, within the one problematic.[1] Order is predicated on the undesirability of disorder, and vice versa. "Theatre of the Absurd," which Kott invokes in his chapter comparing *King Lear* to Beckett's *Endgame*, takes its whole structure from the absence of God, and therefore cannot but affirm the importance and desirability of God. Kott's approach has been influential, especially in the theatre, for it has chimed in with attention to modernist and existentialist writings

which offer as profound studies of the human condition a
critique of progressive ideals and an invocation of "spiritual" alienation.[2]

The limitations of the Tudor Myth are pressed also by
Wilbur Sanders in *The Dramatist and the Received Idea*
(1968). Here the switch is not towards the futility of existence generally but towards the priority of personal integrity. Like Kott, he sees the plays as showing political
action to be essentially futile, and that there is an in-
evitability in historical process before which "even the best
type of conservatism is ultimately powerless" (p. 157). But
Sanders' next move is not into the absurd, but into a coun-
tervailing ideal order of individual integrity: the issue is how
far any character "has been able to find a mature, responsible, fully human way of preserving his integrity in face of
the threatening realities of political life" (p. 166; cf. also p.
190). The selfish and inconsequential nature of this project,
especially in so far as it is assigned to those who actually
exercise power over others in their society, seems not to
strike Sanders. Moreover, by refusing to discuss the political
conditions within which integrity is to be exercised, he
deprives his characters of knowledge which they would
need to make meaningful choices; for instance, the decision
York has to make between Richard II and Bolingbroke is
structured by contradictions in the concept of monarchy
and the position of regent, and York's integrity cannot be
analysed sensibly without discussing those contradictions
(cf. Sanders 1968, pp. 183–85).

Sanders' position approaches the point where historical
sequence, with all its injustice and suffering, may be regarded merely as a testing ground for the individual to
mature upon. He seeks to fend off such anarchistic implications by declaring that "In Shakespeare's imagination the
ideal social order, the mutuality of fulfilled human society,
is inseparably bound up with the sacredness of the individual" (p. 332). Literary critics have tended to place much
stress on the sacredness, the redemptive power of the individual, especially in discussions of the tragedies. G. K.
Hunter summarizes what he calls the "modern" view of *King
Lear*:

[It] is seen as the greatest of tragedies because it not only strips and reduces and assaults human dignity, but because it also shows . . . the process of restoration by which humanity can recover from degradation. . . . [Lear's] retreat into the isolated darkness of his own mind is also a descent into the seed-bed of a new life; for the individual mind is seen here as a place from which a man's most important qualities and relationships draw the whole of their potential.   (Hunter 1978, pp. 251–52)

Sanders' recourse to the individual is less confident than this; in fact in places he remains poised uneasily between Kott and Tillyard, unable entirely to admit or repudiate the position of either. The characters he considers prove "seriously defective" and he is driven to acknowledge the possibility that Shakespeare is expressing "tragic cynicism" (p. 185). Thus he veers towards Kott. To protect himself from this, and to posit some final ground for the integrity he demands, he swerves back towards something very like Tillyard's Christian humanism, wondering even "whether we can receive [the Elizabethans'] humane wisdom without their belief in absolutes" (p. 333). The entrapment of the Shakespearean characters is thus reproduced for the modern reader, who is required similarly to quest for an elusive wholeness within conditions whose determinants are to be neither comprehended nor challenged.

Perhaps the most fundamental error in all these accounts of the role of ideology is falsely to unify history and/or the individual human subject. In one, history is unified by a teleological principle conferring meaningful order (Tillyard), in another by the inverse of this—Kott's "implacable roller." And Sanders' emphasis on moral or subjective integrity implies a different though related notion of unity: an experience of subjective autonomy, of an essential self uncontaminated by the corruption of worldly process; "individual integrity" implies in the etymology of both words an ideal unity: the undivided, the integral.

Theories of the ultimate unity of both history and the human subject derive of course from a Western philosophical tradition where, moreover, they have usually implied each other: the universal being seen as manifested through individual essences which in turn presuppose universals.

Often unawares, idealist literary criticism has worked within or in the shadow of this tradition, as can be seen for example in its insistence that the universal truths of great literature are embodied in coherent and consistent "characters."[3]

The alternative to this is not to become fixated on its negation—universal chaos and subjective fragmentation—but rather to understand history and the human subject in terms of social and political process. Crucial for such an understanding is a materialist account of ideology.

Ideology is composed of those beliefs, practices and institutions which work to legitimate the social order—especially by the process of representing sectional or class interests as universal ones.[4] This process presupposes that there are others, subordinate classes, who far from sharing the interests of the dominant class are in fact being exploited by that class. This is one reason why the dominant tend not only to "speak for" subordinate classes but actively to repress them as well. This repression operates coercively but also ideologically (the two are in practice inseparable). So for example at the same time that the Elizabethan ruling fraction claimed to lead and speak for all, it persecuted those who did not fit in, even blaming them for the social instability which originated in its own policies. This is an instance of a process of displacement crucial then (and since) in the formation of dominant identities—class, cultural, racial and sexual.

Ideology is not just a set of ideas, it is material practice, woven into the fabric of everyday life. At the same time, the dominant ideology is realized specifically through the institutions of education, the family, the law, religion, journalism and culture. In the Elizabethan state all these institutions worked to achieve ideological unity—not always successfully, for conflicts and contradictions remained visible at all levels, even within the dominant class fraction and its institutions. The theatre was monitored closely by the state—both companies and plays had to be licensed—and yet its institutional position was complex. On the one hand, it was sometimes summoned to perform at Court and as such may seem a direct extension of royal power (see Orgel 1982); on the other hand, it was the mode of cultural production in which market forces were strongest, and as such it was especially exposed to the influence of subordinate and emergent classes. We should not, therefore, expect any straightforward relationship between plays and ideology: on the contrary, it is even likely that the topics which engaged writers and audiences alike were those where ideology was under strain. We will take as an instance for study *Henry V*, and it will appear that even in this play, which is often assumed to be the one where Shakespeare is closest to state propaganda, the construction of ideology is complex—even as it consolidates, it betrays inherent instability.

The principal strategy of ideology is to legitimate inequality and exploitation by representing the social order which perpetuates these things as immutable and unalterable—as decreed by God or simply natural. Since the Elizabethan period the ideological appeal to God has tended to give way to the equally powerful appeal to the natural. But in the earlier period both were crucial: the laws of degree and order inferred from nature were further construed as having been put there by God. One religious vision represented ultimate reality in terms of unity and stasis: human endeavour, governed by the laws of change and occupying the material domain, is ever thwarted in its aspiration, ever haunted by its loss of an absolute which can only be regained in transcendence, the move through death to eternal rest, to an ultimate unity inseparable from a full stasis, "when no more Change shall be" and "all shall rest eternally" (Spenser, *The Faerie Queene*, VII,ii). This metaphysical vision has its political uses, especially when aiding the process of subjection by encouraging renunciation of the material world and a disregard of its social aspects such that oppression is experienced as a fate rather than an alterable condition. Protestantism tended to encourage engagement in the world rather than withdrawal from it; most of the *The Faerie Queene* is about the urgent questing of knights and ladies. The theological underpinning of this activist religion was the doctrine of callings: "God bestows his gifts upon us . . . that they might be employed in his service and to his glory, and that in this life."[5] This doctrine legitimated the expansive assertiveness of a social order which was bringing much of Britain under centralized control, colonizing parts of the New World and trading vigorously with most of the Old, and which was to experience revolutionary changes. At the same time, acquiescence in an unjust social order (like that encouraged by a fatalistic metaphysic of stasis) seemed to be effected, though less securely, by an insistence that "whatsoever any man enterpriseth or doth, either in word or deed, he must do it by virtue of his calling, and he must keep himself within the compass, limits or precincts thereof" (Perkins 1970, p. 449). This ideology was none the less metaphysical.

Such an activist ideology is obviously appropriate for the legitimation of warfare, and so we find it offered by the Archbishop of Canterbury in *Henry V*—as the Earl of Essex set off for Ireland in 1599 Lancelot Andrewes assured the Queen in a sermon that it was "a war sanctified" (Andrewes 1841, I, p. 325). In the honeybees speech human endeavour is not denigrated but harnessed in an imaginary unity quite different from that afforded by stasis: "So may a thousand actions, once afoot, / End in one purpose" (1.2.211–12). Like so many political ideologies, this one shares something essential with the overtly religious metaphysic it appears to replace, namely a teleological explanation of its own image of legitimate power—that is, an explanation which is justified through the assertion that such power derives from an inherent natural and human order encoded by God. Thus the "one purpose" derives from an order rooted in "a rule in nature" (188), itself a manifestation of "heavenly" creation, God's regulative structuring of the universe. What this inherent structure guarantees above all is, predictably, obedience:

> Therefore doth heaven divide
> The state of man in divers functions,
> Setting endeavor in continual motion;
> To which is fixèd, as an aim or butt,
> Obedience;   (183–87)

And what in turn underpins obedience is the idea of one's job or calling—in effect one's bee-like *function*—as following naturally from a God-given identity: soldiers,

> armèd in their stings,
> Make boot upon the summer's velvet buds,
> Which pillage they with merry march bring home
> To the tent-royal of their emperor.   (193–96)

The activist ideology thus displaces the emphasis on stasis yet remains thoroughly metaphysical none the less. More generally: in this period, perhaps more than any since, we can see a secular appropriation of theological categories to the extent that it may be argued that Reformation theology actually contributed to secularization (see Sinfield 1983a, Chapter 7); nevertheless, it was an appropriation which depended upon continuities, the most important of which, in ideological legitimation, is this appeal to teleology.

Not only the justification of the war but, more specifically, the heroic representation of Henry, works in such terms. His is a power rooted in nature—blood, lineage and breeding: "The blood and courage that renowned them / Runs in your veins" (118–19)—but also deriving ultimately from God's law as it is encoded in nature and, by extension, society: France belongs to him "by gift of heaven, / By law of nature and of nations" (2.4.79–80). Conversely the French king's power is construed in terms of "borrow'd glories," "custom" and "mettle . . . bred out" (79,83; 3.5.29). With this theory of legitimate versus illegitimate power the responsibility for aggression is displaced onto its victims. Thus does war find its rationale, injustice its justification.

There are two levels of disturbance in the state and the ideology which legitimates it: contradiction and conflict.[6] Contradiction is the more fundamental, in the sense of being intrinsic to the social process as a whole—when for example the dominant order negates what it needs or, more generally, in perpetuating itself produces also its own negation. Thus, for example, in the seventeenth century monarchy legitimates itself in terms of religious attitudes which themselves come to afford a justification for opposition to monarchy. We shall be observing contradiction mainly as it manifests itself in the attempts of ideology to contain it. Conflict occurs between opposed interests, either as a state of disequilibrium or as active struggle; it occurs along the structural fault lines produced by contradictions. Ideology has

always been challenged, not least by the exploited themselves, who have resisted its oppressive construction of
them and its mystification of their disadvantaged social position. One concern of a materialist criticism is with the
history of such resistance, with the attempt to recover the
voices and cultures of the repressed and marginalized in history and writing. Moreover, ideology is destabilized not
only from below, but by antagonisms within and among the
dominant class or class fraction (high, as opposed to
popular, literature will often manifest this kind of destabi-
lization). Whereas idealist literary criticism has tended to
emphasize the transcendence of conflict and contradiction,
materialist criticism seeks to stay with them, wanting to
understand them better.

Ideologies which represent society as a spurious unity
must of necessity also efface conflict and contradiction.
How successful they are in achieving this depends on a
range of complex and interrelated factors, only a few of
which we have space to identify here. One such will be the
relative strength of emergent, subordinate and oppositional
elements within society (see Raymond Williams 1977,
pp. 121–27). The endless process of contest and negotiation
between these elements and the dominant culture is often
overlooked in the use of some structuralist perspectives
within cultural analysis.

One other factor which militates against the success of
ideological misrepresentation involves a contradiction fundamental to ideology itself (and this will prove specially
relevant to *Henry V*): the more ideology (necessarily) en-
gages with the conflict and contradiction which it is its
raison d'être to occlude, the more it becomes susceptible to
incorporating them within itself. It faces the contradictory
situation whereby to silence dissent one must first give it a
voice, to misrepresent it one must first present it.

These factors make for an inconsistency and indeterminacy in the representation of ideological harmony in writing:
the divergencies have to be included if the insistence on
unity is to have any purchase, yet at the same time their
inclusion invites sceptical interrogation of the ideological
appearance of unity, of the effacements of actual conflict.
There may be no way of resolving whether one, or which

one, of these tendencies (unity versus divergencies) over-rides the other in a particular play, but in a sense it does not matter: there is here an indeterminacy which alerts us to the complex but always significant process of theatrical representation and, although that, of political and social process.

Notes

1. See Derrida, Jacques, *Writing and Difference*, trans. Alan Bass; London: Routledge & Kegan Paul (1978), p. 19; and Derrida, *Of Grammatology*, trans. Gayatri Chakravorty Spivak; Baltimore, Md.: Johns Hopkins University Press (1976), p. 315.

2. See Sinfield, Alan, *Society and Literature 1945–1970*; London: Methuen (1983), pp. 94–105; and Dollimore, Jonathan, and Sinfield, Alan (eds.), *Political Shakespeare*; Manchester: Manchester University Press (1985).

3. Here we are primarily concerned to offer a critique of the ideology which falsely unifies history; for a similar and fuller critique of subjectivity see Dollimore, Jonathan, *Radical Tragedy: Religion, Ideology and Power in the Drama of Shakespeare and His Contemporaries*; Brighton, England: Harvester Press; Chicago: University of Chicago Press (1984), especially Chapters 1, 10, and 16.

4. A materialist criticism will be concerned with aspects of ideology additional to those dealt with here and our emphasis on ideology as legitimation, though crucial, should not be taken as an exhaustive definition of the concept. For a fuller discussion of ideology in the period, see Dollimore, *op. cit.*, especially Chapters 1 and 16; Dollimore and Sinfield, *op cit.*, and, more generally, Wolff, Janet, *The Social Production of Art*; London: Macmillan (1981), especially Chapter 3.

5. Perkins, William. *Works*, ed. Ian Breward; Abingdon, England: Sutton Country Press (1970), p. 150. See Sinfield, Alan, *Literature in Protestant England 1560–1660*; London: Croom Helm; Totowa, N.J.: Barnes & Noble (1983), pp. 37–38, 134–35.

6. This distinction derives (but also differs from) Giddens, Anthony, *A Contemporary Critique of Historical Materialism*, vol. I; London: Macmillan (1981), pp. 231–37.

Works Cited

Andrewes, Lancelot (1841) *Works*, 11 vols. Oxford: Clarendon Press.

Campbell, Lily B. (1964) *Shakespeare's Histories*. London: Methuen.

Hunter, G. K. (1978) *Dramatic Identities and Cultural Tradition*. Liverpool: Liverpool University Press.

Kott, Jan (1967) *Shakespeare Our Contemporary*, 2nd edn. London: Methuen.

Orgel, Stephen (1982) 'Making greatness familiar', in Greenblatt, Stephen (ed.) *The Power of Forms in the English Renaissance*. Oklahoma: Pilgrim Books.

Perkins, William (1970) *Works*, ed. Ian Breward. Abingdon: Sutton Country Press.

Sanders, Wilbur (1968) *The Dramatist and the Received Idea*. Cambridge: Cambridge University Press.

Sinfield, Alan (1983) *Literature in Protestant England 1560–1660*. London: Croom Helm; Totowa, N.J.: Barnes & Noble.

Tillyard, E.M.W. (1944) *Shakespeare's History Plays*. London: Chatto & Windus. Reprinted Harmondsworth: Penguin, 1962.

Williams, Raymond (1977) *Marxism and Literature*. London: Oxford University Press.

DIANA E. HENDERSON

"Enter Queen Isabel":
The Difference It Makes

The French Queen Consort does not appear until Act 5 of
Henry V, and then she speaks fewer than thirty lines. Why
include a character who arrives so late and says so little?
Some influential contemporary productions don't: Kenneth
Branagh's 1989 film, like the Royal Shakespeare Company's stage productions directed by Terry Hands and
Adrian Noble, cuts the queen and reassigns some of her lines
to the men onstage. Indeed, Branagh awards her final words,
a prayer for peace, to himself. He thereby reenacts the
English conquest of France and caps his film's systematic
presentation of Henry as a beneficent "star of England." Yet
this victory comes at a cost: putting Isabel back in the picture clarifies Shakespeare's delicate balancing act at the end
of *Henry V*.

Like her fellow latecomer Burgundy, Queen Isabel calls
attention to the negative consequences of Henry's victory
for conquered France, the nation associated with femininity.
The queen's first speech approaches an overt challenge; her
punning reference to Henry's "basilisk" eyes recalls the cannonballs that battered Harfleur and the deadliness of his
gaze. Along with Burgundy's lamentation for a feminized
French landscape, Isabel's lines expose the false dichotomy
in Henry's initial assertion: "France being ours we'll bend it
to our awe, / Or break it all to pieces." He has bent it precisely

by breaking it. Given the link between war and English virility throughout the play, it is especially appropriate and poignant that a French woman emphasize the cost of war and the urgent need for peace.

Moreover, this woman is a French mother—the only mother in the play. The war between France and England began with disputes over the Salic law, the bar to inheritance through the female line. Although the Archbishop of Canterbury does not name her, Henry's claim to the French throne derived from another French queen named Isabel, Edward III's mother. Beyond her name and presence, Shakespeare's queen recalls the importance of maternity and reproduction in her second speech, wishing for a fertile marriage to sustain an international alliance. But she also observes how often "ill office or fell jealousy" "make divorce" between couples and nations, anticipating the play's Epilogue and qualifying the comedic conclusion toward which Henry and the play otherwise aspire.

Isabel's very participation in the state negotiations ("Haply a woman's voice may do some good / When articles too nicely urged be stood on") challenges the men's politics of force and the marginalization of women within emergent nation-states. While Laurence Olivier's film makes this moment a visual joke (confirming Henry's control through the queen's willingness to leave so that he can get on with his wooing), the lines signal the political importance of the queen mother.

Indeed, the more one knows of the history Shakespeare represents, the more crucial becomes this mother's part. While the *Famous Victories of Henry the Fifth* provided some material for Shakespeare's concluding act, Isabel did not appear there. It was to the chronicle historians Hall and Holinshed that Shakespeare turned when deciding to reanimate this figure. And if ever there was a queen to incite controversy, it was Isabeau de Bavière.

Her most remarkable action at the Treaty of Troyes (1420) was to disinherit her own son, the Dauphin Charles (surviving brother of the Dauphin Louis, who sent Henry tennis balls). She proclaimed him to be her bastard by an unnamed lover. This scandalous renunciation of legitimate maternity provided the rationale for the treaty making Henry

V, as the new son of Charles and Isabeau, heir to France. The chroniclers' Isabeau, in fact, resembles those wanton women who haunted Shakespeare's imagination in the *Henry VI* tetralogy; by comparison, Shakespeare's Isabel appears tame. Omitting explicit reference to her unmaternal act and presenting her as both critic and collaborator with Henry of England, Shakespeare finesses the problem of Henry's needing endorsement from this unconventional woman. Yet she became Henry's mother-in-law through actions that challenged male prerogative in the public realm as well as a son's faith in the maternal bond.

Some recent performances have tried to capture Isabel's assertiveness. The English Shakespeare Company's production (dir. Michael Bogdanov) had June Watson double Mistress Quickly and Queen Isabel, calling greater attention to that actress and, thereby, to Isabel's role in the state negotiations. Having altered Shakespeare's text to include the Dauphin Louis in Act 5, Bogdanov had Isabel's willingness to leave princess Katherine with Henry anger this French prince; when he disrupts the proceedings a second time, Isabel repairs the awkwardness. This production partially undoes the logic behind Shakespeare's "domestication" of the historical Isabel: by replacing the dauphin with his mother in the final scene, he rendered public what Henry's wooing accomplishes in the more intimate scene with Katherine. The females are enlisted as Henry's allies, as if he were their champion in recognition of their reproductive power. When director Bogdanov brought back the dauphin, he more severely complicated the comedic conclusion.

Most unconventional was the Company of Women's 1994 all-female production, in which a physically dominating actress doubled the parts of two suffering survivors: Pistol and the queen. During the final scene, Diane Beckett appeared in an African-influenced robe, evoking the fate of other colonized peoples. This Isabel embodied a counter-image of noble lamentation challenging Henry's imperial triumph.

Nevertheless, in most productions that include the queen, the dominant effect is harmony and order, the mother's blessing providing an emotional and diplomatic endorsement for what the English have already achieved. Sometimes this role is simplified by cutting or relocating her more critical lines; such was the case in the nineteenth-century productions of William Macready, Charles Kean, and Charles Calvert. Along with the use of a female Chorus, these performance choices muted the gendered pattern associating England with masculinity conquering effeminate France.

Shakespeare's inclusion of Isabel as a political negotiator and commentator is structurally crucial to the formally comedic resolution of this history play, and she provides further opportunities for complexity in performance. Surely Isabel is worth keeping.

JOHN RUSSELL BROWN

Henry V on Stage and Screen

Laurence Olivier made a film of *Henry V* in wartime Britain while the allied forces were preparing for D-Day landings in France. First shown in 1944, it presents Shakespeare's play as a thrilling, popular, and patriotic saga.

The film takes every cue in the text to project a romantic picture of a courageous nation at odds with the world and led by a hero endowed with a fine physique, spirit, daring, and intelligence.

As director, Olivier's decision to start shooting the film in a reconstruction of Shakespeare's Globe Theatre establishes a theatrical bravura in performance that permeates and sustains the whole work. His willingness to modify this style as the story progressed encouraged a Shakespearean richness and variety: real ships at a quayside prepare to cross the Channel; settings based on medieval illuminated manuscripts lighten and clarify the wordy scenes that take place in the French court; battle shots indebted to the Russian film *Alexander Nevsky* by the master director Eisenstein bring the throb of drama and a sense of vastness to the encounter of two comparatively small armies; soft and intimate camera work heightens pathos for the death of Falstaff and helps an audience identify with the thoughtful King as he moves around his sleeping soldiers on the eve of battle. William Walton's score, varying from romantic symphonic sound to Elizabethan and medieval pastiche, simple ballads and a choral anthem, supports and sometimes leads the changes of mood with irresistible assurance.

This film was the first based on a Shakespeare play that

achieved both artistic and popular success. Time has shown its authority to be lasting: it continues to be shown throughout the world today, and it influences many readers who turn now to Shakespeare's text for the first time. Other Shakespearean films look as splendid, but few have brought the marvelous words so fully alive as well. One cause of this was Olivier's decision to reverse the usual technique of bringing the camera in for close shots whenever a single character is talking. For the Crispin Day speech before Agincourt (3.1), the camera moves progressively further away, to show the King jumping on a wagon surrounded by his soldiers; his delivery of the rousing words does not have to be curtailed within the limits of verisimilitude suitable for a large-scale image of an individual face, but has a strong dynamic, expressive color, and full-throated ease. Listeners in a movie house or sitting before a TV screen are as much moved by the thrilling words as those who are portrayed on the screen awaiting the crucial battle.

Moreover Olivier recruited a stellar cast for his film, seasoned actors able to respond to the text with strong personalities and practiced voices. Many of them had already been *the* star of stage play or film, or shortly would be so. Olivier also pushed almost every performance except his own toward caricature, stopping just short but having the effect of making his own King shine with a contrasting appearance of heartfelt simplicity and sincerity.

But the success of the film depended also on Olivier's excision of nearly half of Shakespeare's text and on a few additions to it. Comic business for two elderly prelates, while they talk about the Salic Law on which Henry based his claim to the throne of France, was added to Act 1, Scenes 1 and 2, so that the audience could get a slight hint of the political chicanery that underlies the churchmen's response to the King. The interpolation of a scene showing Falstaff dying in his bed—in the play his last moments are recounted only—emphasizes the young Henry's firm resolve to become a fully responsible monarch at whatever cost to his own personal friendships. Large-scale cuts prevented Henry from being seen in anything other than advantageous light: he does not threaten the citizens of Harfleur with "impious war" and "naked infants spitted upon pikes" (3.3.7–41); he does not sentence his old friend Bardolph to death; he is not tormented by guilt for his father's murder of Richard II, by which means he had inherited the crown of England; he does not order the French prisoners to be killed in violation of the agreed rights of war. Similarly, the concluding Chorus does not tell the audience that all Henry's efforts led, after his death, to the loss of France and the death of many more Englishmen; and Pistol does not go to France in order to suck blood, "the very blood to suck" (2.4.57). The film has been made to tell a glorious story and the audience is led to respond to Henry, in the words of the Chorus, as "the mirror of all Christian kings" and the "star of England" (2.Chor., 6 and Epilogue, 6).

Adapting Shakespeare's play so boldly was not innovative or particularly iconoclastic, because the stage had already led the way. Actor-managers, directors, and producers had always seen its potential as a celebratory and rousing entertainment, so that Olivier's alterations and elaborations for his film are in a theatrical tradition going back to the eighteenth century and perhaps earlier. It is quite likely that *Henry V* was first performed as a public celebration—that it was the play Shakespeare wrote for the opening of the new Globe Theatre on the South Bank in London in the autumn of 1599. (The Chorus in the Prologue speaking of "this wooden *O*" and aspiring to a "kingdom for a stage," starts the play off by drawing attention to the players' craft and to their building that imagination could turn into the "great globe" itself.) The first Quarto of the play, printed in 1600, is a version that has been prepared for a touring company of players, numbering only eleven or twelve, including two boys. This edition, appearing soon after the first performances at the Globe, is often plagued with errors caused by actors' imprecise memories as they dictated the printer's copy, but it shows us very clearly that Pistol's bloodthirsty call to arms and the Epilogue's warning of disasters to come, together with a number of other episodes casting Henry in a less than favorable light, had been cut for performance early in the play's stage history.

The title page of the Quarto tells us that *Henry V* was "sundry times played by the Right Honorable the Lord Chamberlain his players," and some degree of popularity may be deduced from the fact that this unofficial publication, despite its various and obvious imperfections, was reprinted in 1602 and 1619. Moreover the Revels Accounts at the court give evidence of a revival on January 7, 1605; and this, in turn, implies that the play was then in the current repertory of the King's Men, as the company of actors to which Shakespeare belonged had been renamed on the accession of James I. But beyond some few allusions in later plays, there is no evidence of further performances before the closing of the theaters for the Civil War of 1640. Its stirring evocation of royal and martial excellence and its culminating victory and negotiations for peace would not recommend themselves as James I and then Charles I were progressively at odds with half their realm and the threat of unrest became ever more apparent.

Nor did the play recommend itself for production during the Restoration. Perhaps the King's close ties with France, where he had found refuge in the years following his father's defeat and execution, rendered the entire subject unacceptable. Years later, in 1723, *Henry V* was produced at the Drury Lane Theatre, but this was such a radical reworking that the play can no longer be called Shakespeare's: Katherine of France becomes a romantic leading lady and a subplot has been introduced in which Harriet, who had been seduced by Henry when Prince Hal, confronts the King and commits suicide. The author of this piece, for all his stealing from Shakespeare's play, was Aaron Hill. It was in the next decade that *Henry V* itself was revived in a heavily cut version, and thereafter it made sporadic reappearances without ever becoming a regular favorite with eighteenth-century audiences.

The wars with France occasioned a number of performances. John Philip Kemble, the leading actor of his day, staged it in 1789, the year of the French Revolution. He billed it as "not acted these twenty years," when indeed it had not been seen at his own Drury Lane Theatre since 1748. It had been Covent Garden that had kept the play on the boards in the meantime, with Spranger Barry, Henry Smith, or Richard Wroughton in the title role; David Garrick, the actor-manager, had played the Chorus, a part that had usually been cut in this century. In 1803 a special performance was given for the benefit of the "Patriotic Fund."

Kemble's chief reason for reviving the play was probably that he needed a production without a strong female lead: Mrs. Siddons, with whom he had established his reputation, had to retire through ill health, and the repertoire needed strong reinforcement. Like Olivier and his own immediate predecessors, Kemble cut the text drastically: all the Choruses disappeared, the threats to Harfleur, Fluellen's dispute with Macmorris, the Boy's encounter with the French Soldier on behalf of Pistol and, more surprisingly, "Once more into the breach, dear friends. . . ." (3.1.1) was reduced to four lines only—which include one new line and another from *1, Henry IV*. The leading role was adapted to Kemble's special strengths, and although Henry was not regarded generally as highly as his Hamlet, Richard III or Coriolanus, John Boaden, his biographer, believed that Kemble's "royal Hal" exceeded all his other roles. He noted that "as a *coup de théâtre*, his starting up from prayer at the sound of the trumpet, in the passage where he states his attempted atonement to Richard the Second, formed one of the most spirited excitements that the stage has ever displayed." He added that "occasional reversions to the 'mad wag,' the 'sweet young prince,' had a singular charm, as the condescension of one who could be so terrible" (*Memoirs*, 1825, ii.7–8).

The opportunity to elaborate the scenic aspects of the play was recognized early, at first as an added pleasure on the occasion of the accession of King George III in 1761: a processional scene was then devised in which Katherine was seen coming from the Abbey crowned as queen. A further episode was grafted on in 1769, when the "Ceremony of the Champion" brought the challenger onstage mounted on a war horse. In 1839, for the last production of his management at Covent Garden, William Macready introduced a sensational new device, a "moving Diorama" for Act 3. A painted cloth was mounted on a pair of rollers at either side of the stage and was then seen moving from one to the other so that the audience viewed the English fleet crossing the channel and the soldiers marching to take part in the siege of Harfleur. Other painted panoramas displayed the Battle of Agincourt and the King's entry into London in triumph.

Pageantry and the reproduction of historical costumes, properties, and ceremonies were taken still further by the actor-manager Charles Kean at the Princess's Theatre in 1859. Mrs. Kean was the Chorus, speaking in the person of Clio, the Muse of History, and at her words scenic marvels unfolded: a tableau of Conspirators receiving bribes from the French during the second Chorus; a group of soldiers praying in the English camp during the fourth; and before the fifth act, the "Historical Episode" of "Old London Bridge from the Surrey Side of the river" showing the "Reception of King Henry the Fifth on Entering London" with details taken from a contemporary account and featuring the Lord Mayor, one Nicholas Wotton. Other embellishments took place during the scenes themselves: the bodies of the Duke of York and Earl of Suffolk were borne by soldiers across the stage at the beginning of 4.5 and just before the close of that act: "The curtains of the royal Pavilion are drawn aside, and discover an Altar and Priests." When Henry calls for *Non nobis* and *Te Deum* to be sung: "Organ music; all kneel, and join in Song of Thanksgiving."

J. W. Cole, in his *Life of Charles Kean* (1859), comments on the battle scenes, for example:

> The assault on Harfleur, which opens the third act; the desperate resistance of the French garrison; the close conflict on the ramparts; the practice of the rude artillery of the day, with the advance of other besieging engines; and the final entry of the victorious assailants through the breach,—formed altogether the most marvellous realisation of war, in its deadliest phase, that imitative art has ever attempted. The marvel is increased by the smallness of the space within which such numbers of men and so much complicated machinery are marshalled, together with the organization of the entire scene.   (ii.344)

Despite considerable cuts, the performance "occupied nearly four hours" (ii.346).

At the end of the nineteenth century, actors rather than scene painters and crowd scenes began to dominate the story once more. Samuel Phelps had staged the play with comparatively small resources at Sadlers Wells, London, choosing October 25, the anniversary of Agincourt, for his opening night. In 1872, Charles Calvert produced it in Manchester and subsequently in North America, where the handsome and manly George Rignold was the King and drew almost as much praise as the complications of staging, which included a white horse, called Crispin, for the hero to ride and hundreds of persons on stage in the last scene; there was incidental music from Verdi and other operatic sources. For Henry James, however, it was Rignold who caught the eye: "He was worth looking at and listening to." Later, in London at Drury Lane, Rignold again triumphed:

> As falchion in hand, clothed in complete steel, with a richly emblazoned tabard, he stands in that spot so prized by the histrionic mind, the exact centre of the stage, the limelight pouring upon him from the flies its most dazzling rays, and declaims speech after speech to his devoted followers, he presents as striking a stage figure as I think I ever saw.   (E. Dutton Cook)

In the year 1900, three rival performances could be seen: Lewis Waller ("handsome and dignified" in romantic roles—G. B. Shaw) and Frank Benson (in his own production from the Memorial Theatre at Stratford-upon-Avon) in London, and Richard Mansfield in New York. The star actor had chosen the play for the American production in

> consideration of its healthy and virile tone (so diametrically in contrast to many of the performances now current); the lesson it teaches of Godliness, honour, loyalty, courage, cheerfulness and perseverance; its beneficial influence upon young and old. . . . . [and] the opportunity it affords for a pictorial representation of the costumes and armour, manners and customs, of that interesting period.

These star actors were followed by many others, each projecting a strong individuality and presence through the starring role: Martin Harvey (1916), Balliol Holloway (1926), Lewis Casson (1928), Ralph Richardson (1931), Ivor Novello (1938).

By this time, fashion had turned against scenic elaboration and the reproduction of medieval sights. In 1901 at a special matinée in Stratford-upon-Avon, William Poel produced the play using no scenery beyond curtains and a small gallery at the back of the stage; the action flowed rapidly from scene to scene and a full text was spoken; costumes were Elizabethan rather than medieval. This experiment was followed by Bridges-Adams who directed an almost full text at Stratford in the main season of 1920, using little spectacle or scenery; and the following year Robert Atkins went still further in both tendencies at the Old Vic Theatre in London. Later, in 1937, Tyrone Guthrie mediated between the conventional elaborate staging and the new austere mode and, with the young Laurence Olivier as king, deployed a great number of banners carried on to a simple setting; the stage was filled with vibrant colors, alternately red, blue, and silver, as the director chose to accompany the action.

The play had become an established success, and productions in both North America and Britain became more frequent and more widespread. In the decades since the second World War, *Henry V* has never been absent from the stage for long. Most notably, it has become a company play, and directors have set their marks upon it even more clearly than leading actors or stage designers. The text has responded to the new crop of Shakespeare festivals, and the ambitions of established groups of actors and their directors. It is still chosen as a celebratory play, but not for such bellicose causes as formerly.

In 1951 it was produced at Stratford-upon-Avon in a cycle of Shakespeare's history plays on the occasion of the Festival of Britain, a nationwide event organized to demonstrate Britain's contribution to culture and industry. Beginning with a production of *Richard II*, the same company of actors under the same direction had proceeded through the two parts of *Henry IV* before concluding with *Henry V*. Now the King was shown emerging from a long educative process that had run throughout the earlier two "episodes" of the "series." Richard Burton was Henry and brought an inner stillness to the part which hinted at some secret quest or personal dissatisfaction with his role as monarch. After the broad strokes of Olivier's king, still fresh in the minds of audiences, this reading seemed puzzling, if not perverse:

> Burton's restrained performance, exploring the King's insecurity and self-doubt, did not provide what many critics still sought, an actor they could greet as "the Lewis Waller of the 1950's."
>
> (Sally Beauman)

But the interpretation was not entirely new, only its context in the cycle of plays: the serious-minded Samuel Phelps had been called "scholarlike" in the role, the athletic Benson had been judged "grave and thoughtful."

At the same theater in 1964, Peter Hall, assisted by John Barton and Clifford Williams, directed a much longer sequence of histories in celebration of the four-hundredth anniversary of Shakespeare's birth. The three parts of *Henry VI*, reduced to two plays, together with *Richard III*, had been produced the previous year and were now revived in the fuller cycle of seven plays starting with *Richard II*. The whole was as much a celebration of the Royal Shakespeare Company as it was a birthday offering to the author. But this King Henry and the whole production were, once more, contrary to their audience's expectation. The director had presented all the history plays as dramas about the use and abuse of power, legitimate and illegitimate:

> Over the years I became more and more fascinated by the contortions of politicians, and by the corrupting seductions experienced by anybody who wields power. I began to collect "sanctions"— those justifications which politicians use in the Press or on television to mask the dictates of their party politics or their personal ambitions. . . : I realised that Shakespeare's history plays were full of such sanctions: "God," "Fortune," "The Common Weal," "Duty," "St George," "England," "France." What had seemed conventional rhetoric was really, when spoken by Warwick or Richard III, an ironic revelation of the time-honoured practices of politicians. I realised that the mechanism of power had not changed in centuries. We also were in the middle of a blood-soaked century. I was convinced that a presentation of one of the bloodiest and most hypocritical periods in history would teach many lessons about the present.

Ian Holm, Peter Hall's Henry, did not have heroic stature or conventional good looks; his voice was keen and intense, rather than warm and ingratiating. His Henry was nervously watchful, calculating in mind and decisive in action:

> Ian Holm's performance grew with the play—an essentially democratic Henry, almost as tattered and mud-bespattered as the

"Old Contemptibles" with whom he marched; discovering his
kingship within himself and through his comradeship with other
men; a man still deeply thoughtful—still not seeing his way quite
clearly—but one who had achieved simplicity, and through resolution was acquiring strength; an anxious Henry, with something
of his father's calculation, busying giddy minds with foreign quarrels, but far from giddy himself. The inches were missing, but the
voice did not refuse the rhetoric when rhetoric was asked for, and
it took the colloquial in its stride.   (Robert Speaight)

Other critics saw only a manipulator of men, rather than a
leader or comrade. Never had warfare been portrayed so
unromantically: John Bury used a bare, open stage with
solid scenic units which were often clad in unpainted metal.
Most colors in setting and costumes were dark or muted,
while John Barton had devised brutal and prolonged stage
fights. Costumes were progressively distressed and tattered;
blood was often in evidence; men seemed thoroughly exhausted and bruised by the hardships of war and the costs of
individual survival. An earlier production of *Henry V* at the
Mermaid Theatre in London, in 1960, had dressed the soldiers in twentieth-century battle dress and used films of
actual battle, but that realism was not ingrained in the production as a whole as in Peter Hall's production.

Both Stratford productions of the fifties and sixties were
revived, and both influenced other theaters. In Stratford,
Ontario, Michael Langham directed the play twice: in 1956,
with Christopher Plummer as Henry, and in 1966 with
Douglas Rain. The former was appealing, but:

Although the character has drive and courage, he also has a certain
boyish modesty that disciplines the braggadocio. He accepts the
responsibilities of his office willingly but with underlying humility. He is not showy.

(Brooks Atkinson, *New York Times*)

In the second production however, the actor was not heroic
in stature or romantic in appeal, while the cruelties of war
were made everywhere apparent in the spilling of blood and
straining of physical resources. This unglamorous view was
that most commonly seen throughout the seventies and into

the eighties. The BBC/Time-Life television production of 1980 continued the brutal tradition, but without the acute political understanding of Peter Hall's innovatory history cycle.

By this time, however, another new-style production had been seen at Stratford in England—the overtly theatrical. In 1975 the Royal Shakespeare Company found itself in difficult circumstances, with reduced finance and the threatened closure of its London base, the Aldwych Theatre; and the central heating and air-conditioning at Stratford needed replacement. It was also the company's Centenary Season. A sequence of history plays seemed the best answer; economics could be made on a single set and a constant company, and three plays might be sufficient—the two parts of *Henry IV* and *Henry V*. The cycle had to be different from previous ones, and one decision was to start with *Henry V*, the play which came last chronologically. The director, Terry Hands, said this was a natural choice:

> First, it is a play of great vitality, with a surging up-beat text: potentially, it has all the impact necessary to herald such a crucial double season. Second, it is about improvisation, interdependence, and unity: three essential qualities if the company was to surmount its present difficulties.

So the production had a double face. The acting area was a bare rectangular ramp set within the theater stage, which had been stripped of all its usual illusionistic trimmings; the characters encountered each other in this showcase, the drama sustained and magnified by highly visible lighting changes and by strong musical accompaniment. (This was one of the earliest Shakespeare productions to utilize and develop modern technological devices commonly used in stage "musicals.") The production was at once austere and lavish, the stage bare and yet filled with a succession of striking images.

The King became a performer and the Stratford company grew together in unity. In his public statements, Terry Hands stressed the development of a community-consciousness in the play:

As human unity is more important than national unity and indeed transcends it, so Henry seeks redefinition as "common-man" before re-assuming his function as King. It is an agonising reappraisal on any level.

But in effect, his Henry, played by Alan Howard, was most remarkable for his attack and energy, his volatility and impassioned projection into every role; he was an exceptional, rather than a "common," man. And again the critics were divided, their amazement and occasional incredulity becoming apparent. Irving Wardle in *The Times* noted how:

Howard grapples on the floor with the treacherous Scroop, ... He practically vomits after hurling the barbarous threats at Harfleur; and again half way through reading the roll call of the French dead.

When the production reached New York, Maurice Charney in *Shakespeare Quarterly* was puzzled by Henry's "agitation and anger before the great victory at Agincourt" and judged that he "became fully kingly only in the final wooing scene with Katherine."

In the United States the play has been performed since World War II in many places and on frequent occasions, but no one production has mapped out an interpretation that was clearly new or discovered unforeseen themes in the play. At Stratford, Connecticut, in 1982, Christopher Plummer again played Henry, his voice now "glorious" and his performance "moving and sincere." He also played the Chorus and this innovative double-casting

called attention to the similarities between the Chorus, whose imperatives urge the audience to "follow," "grapple," and "work your thoughts," and the King himself, who urges his men to exert similar effort in their enterprise. . . . Both the Chorus and Henry demand assent to their vision.

(David Scott Kastan, *Shakespeare Quarterly*)

In 1984, Wilford Leach directed the play at the Delacorte Theatre in Central Park, New York, setting the action

against an unchanging background representing an Elizabethan theater in the manner of the opening sequences of
Olivier's film and the 1951 Stratford productions. There was
little spectacle, but smoke accompanied the battle scenes
and Kevin Kline as Henry emphasized the brutality in his
role. Unhesitatingly he ordered the slaughter of French prisoners and then

> whereas Olivier had ridden off to engage in manly single combat
> with the Constable of France, Kline personally slit the first French
> throat at hand, that of Pierre Epstein as the hapless soldier bullied
> by Pistol, to show his troops how this sort of thing is done.
> (Arthur Ganz, *Shakespeare Quarterly*)

Kline delivered the "grand rhetorical set pieces . . . in high
style, getting at the end of each a deserved round of applause."
   Also at the Delacorte, in 1996, Douglas Hughes's production emphasized the terrors and uncertainties of war. His
Henry was

> a repentant bad boy desperate to make good, impaled on the horns
> of a dilemma in which there is no decent choice. To make war is
> terrible, to avoid it dishonorable and humiliating . . . Shame,
> anger, fear, greed, doubt, and resentment are . . . what *Henry V* is
> about.   (Michael Feingold, *Village Voice*)

The absence of glamorous theatrical pageantry was not to
the taste of many reviewers, few pronouncing the production a success.
   During the same years in Britain, two Henries gained
comparable attention. At Stratford, a production by Adrian
Noble brought a realistic downpour of rain to bedraggle the
British troops in France—the greatest visual effect of the
evening. Kenneth Branagh, aged twenty-three, was cast as
the King, and his youthful innocence offset the horrors of
war surrounding him:

> he fainted from the top of a siege ladder. . . . , sank weeping to his
> knees for "Not today, O Lord" (4.1.297) and swooned away com-
> pletely after his victory in 4.8.
> (Nicholas Shrimpton, *Shakespeare Survey*)

In contrast Michael Pennington, for Michael Bogdanov's production for the English Shakespeare Company in 1987, was mature and deeply sensitive. He brought to the part the thoughtfulness of his Hamlet at Stratford some years previously: when he said "The day, my friends, and all things stay for me" at the end of Act 4, Scene 1, the audience sensed both weariness and resolution. The soldiers he commanded were hooligans in comparison; in the semimodern dress of the production, Pistol and his gang left for France brandishing the slogans and boorishness of a dangerously rowdy crowd of soccer supporters.

At the Royal Shakespeare Theatre, in 1995, Matthew Warchus put a new spin on the now common antiwar interpretation by mixing historical periods in the setting for the action and bringing on a crowd of English civilians dressed as in World War II. Like other directors, he emphasized the cost of war for the king who led it.

> His opening and closing image, with Henry's red regal gown with a gold collar placed on a dummy, roped off like an exhibit in the Imperial War Museum, established a sense of royal myth surrounded by tall red poppies, the strongest modern symbol of the cost of war. . . . Serious-minded, sincerely religious, this Henry took his share of the work of war, often seen shouldering a huge pack, like his troops.
>
> (Peter Holland, *Shakespeare Survey*)

However, it was Branagh's *Henry V*, when transferred from the stage to reappear in a film directed by himself, which was to set the strongest mark on the play's reputation in the nineteen-nineties. He has told how the experience of playing the king, while he himself was only twenty-three years old, had deepened his view of the character and especially of "the difference between the man and the king." The play had become "a profoundly moving debate about war." After trying numerous ways to manage the lengthy meeting with Katherine (5.2.98–293), he came to realize that the text would only work by playing it as two people "falling in love." These insights from the stage production, together with his director's emphasis on the hardships of war, were to feed into the transference of the play to cinema.

Like Olivier's, this film of 1989 has become many people's first introduction to Shakespeare's play in performance, showing how the words of the text can leap into vivid life in interplay between fully engaged persons, alike in many ways to those who watch its action. Branagh, like Olivier, his forerunner and pacemaker, placed his own performance at the center of the camera's attention and cut the text to suit its measure. (Some of these deletions are considered by Diana Henderson in the last of the Commentaries on the text reprinted in this edition.) While it shows the horrors of war, as many stage productions have done in recent years, the film offsets this by showing that, by facing those dangers, men achieve their finest and strongest hours: the highly questionable notion that through bloodshed can come greater manliness and irresistible charisma.

So Shakespeare's *Henry V* continues to change with the times and its audiences, but one aspect is unchanging: the relentless demands it makes in performance, which can be met only by a varied and experienced company of actors. Every role calls for a good actor—at least—and many scenes move toward climaxes which need coordinated responses from a large number of performers. The play shines when it is staged by a remarkable team at a theater with a strong record of Shakespearean performances. Then individual characters will often surprise and comparatively small roles leap into prominence. The title page of the first Quarto drew attention to Pistol: "The Chronicle History of Henry the Fifth, with his battle fought at Agincourt in France, together with Ancient Pistol." D. E. Baker's *Companion to the Playhouse* (1764) picked out Fluellen among other comedy roles:

> This play has also an intermixture of comedy, and is justly esteemed an admirable Piece, . . . and is constantly performed with universal applause. The character of Fluellen, the Welsh Captain, in particular is admirably drawn.

David Garrick, Michael Redgrave and John Woodvine have been admired greatly as the Chorus. In 1976, to the Henry of Paul Rudd, Meryl Streep excelled as Katherine.

The Duke of Burgundy, the Queen, King, and Dauphin of France, Montjoy the Herald, Mrs. Quickly, Lord Scroop, the Duke of Exeter, Michael Williams, Gower, Macmorris, Sir Thomas Erpingham, the anonymous Boy who follows Pistol to the wars—all are parts that respond to an actor's originality, vitality, and truth.

Bibliographic Note: A full documentation of the preceding stage history would be very lengthy and necessarily incomplete; the following books are listed as suitable for further reading and independent research.

One production has a book devoted entirely to it: Sally Beauman (ed.), *"Henry V" for the Centenary Season at the Royal Shakespeare Theatre* (1976). Productions also feature extensively in the following books: George C. D. Odell, *Shakespeare from Betterton to Irving*, 2 volumes (1920); A. C. Sprague, *Shakespeare's Histories: Plays for the Stage* (1964); Sally Beauman, *The Royal Shakespeare Company: A History of Ten Decades* (1982); Ralph Berry, *Changing Styles in Shakespeare* (1981); Richard David, *Shakespeare in the Theatre* (1978).

Olivier's film is considered in Roger Manvell, *Shakespeare and the Film* (1971) and Jack J. Jorgens, *Shakespeare on Film* (1977). Kenneth Branagh discusses the role of Henry in *Players of Shakespeare*, 2nd. ed. Russell Jackson *et al.* (1988); his film is considered by Peter S. Donaldson in *Shakespeare Quarterly* 42 (1991) and by Robert Lane in *English Literary History* 61 (1994).

The most comprehensive, but necessarily undetailed, stage history is that based on notes by Harold Child and printed in the *New Cambridge Edition* of the play edited by J. Dover Wilson (1947). For factual information about productions in Britain see J. C. Trewin, *Shakespeare on the English Stage, 1900–1964* (1964); for a personal and distinctive general account see Robert Speaight, *Shakespeare on the Stage* (1973).

Detailed and considered reviews of productions of this play, as of others, can be found in *Shakespeare Quarterly* and *Shakespeare Survey*, the former covering each year's productions worldwide, the latter confining itself, for the most part, to productions in London and Stratford-upon-Avon.

Suggested References

The number of possible references is vast and grows alarmingly. (The *Shakespeare Quarterly* devotes one issue each year to a list of the previous year's work, and *Shakespeare Survey*—an annual publication—includes a substantial review of biographical, critical, and textual studies, as well as a survey of performances.) The vast bibliography is best approached through James Harner, *The World Shakespeare Bibliography on CD-Rom: 1900–Present.* The first release, in 1996, included more than 12,000 annotated items from 1990–93, plus references to several thousand book reviews, productions, films, and audio recordings. The plan is to update the publication annually, moving forward one year and backward three years. Thus, the second issue (1997), with 24,700 entries, and another 35,000 or so references to reviews, newspaper pieces, and so on, covered 1987–94.

Though no works are indispensable, those listed below have been found especially helpful. The arrangement is as follows:

1. Shakespeare's Times
2. Shakespeare's Life
3. Shakespeare's Theater
4. Shakespeare on Stage and Screen
5. Miscellaneous Reference Works
6. Shakespeare's Plays: General Studies
7. The Comedies
8. The Romances
9. The Tragedies
10. The Histories
11. *The Life of Henry V*

The titles in the first five sections are accompanied by brief explanatory annotations.

1. Shakespeare's Times

Andrews, John F., ed. *William Shakespeare: His World, His Work, His Influence,* 3 vols. (1985). Sixty articles, dealing not only with such subjects as "The State," "The Church," "Law," "Science, Magic, and Folklore," but also with the plays and poems themselves and Shakespeare's influence (e.g., translations, films, reputation)

Byrne, Muriel St. Clare. *Elizabethan Life in Town and Country* (8th ed., 1970). Chapters on manners, beliefs, education, etc., with illustrations.

Dollimore, John, and Alan Sinfield, eds. *Political Shakespeare: New Essays in Cultural Materialism* (1985). Essays on such topics as the subordination of women and colonialism, presented in connection with some of Shakespeare's plays.

Greenblatt, Stephen. *Representing the English Renaissance* (1988). New Historicist essays, especially on connections between political and aesthetic matters, statecraft and stagecraft.

Joseph, B. L. *Shakespeare's Eden: the Commonwealth of England 1558–1629* (1971). An account of the social, political, economic, and cultural life of England.

Kernan, Alvin. *Shakespeare, the King's Playwright: Theater in the Stuart Court 1603–1613* (1995). The social setting and the politics of the court of James I, in relation to *Hamlet, Measure for Measure, Macbeth, King Lear, Antony and Cleopatra, Coriolanus,* and *The Tempest.*

Montrose, Louis. *The Purpose of Playing: Shakespeare and the Cultural Politics of the Elizabethan Theatre* (1996). A poststructuralist view, discussing the professional theater "within the ideological and material frameworks of Elizabethan culture and society," with an extended analysis of *A Midsummer Night's Dream.*

Mullaney, Steven. *The Place of the Stage: License, Play, and Power in Renaissance England* (1988). New Historicist analysis, arguing that popular drama became a cultural institution "only by . . . taking up a place on the margins of society."

Schoenbaum, S. *Shakespeare: The Globe and the World*

(1979). A readable, abundantly illustrated introductory book on the world of the Elizabethans.

Shakespeare's England, 2 vols. (1916). A large collection of scholarly essays on a wide variety of topics, e.g., astrology, costume, gardening, horsemanship, with special attention to Shakespeare's references to these topics.

2. Shakespeare's Life

Andrews, John F., ed. *William Shakespeare: His World, His Work, His Influence,* 3 vols. (1985). See the description above.

Bentley, Gerald E. *Shakespeare: A Biographical Handbook* (1961). The facts about Shakespeare, with virtually no conjecture intermingled.

Chambers, E. K. *William Shakespeare: A Study of Facts and Problems,* 2 vols. (1930). The fullest collection of data.

Fraser, Russell. *Young Shakespeare* (1988). A highly readable account that simultaneously considers Shakespeare's life and Shakespeare's art.

————. *Shakespeare: The Later Years* (1992).

Schoenbaum, S. *Shakespeare's Lives* (1970). A review of the evidence and an examination of many biographies, including those of Baconians and other heretics.

————. *William Shakespeare: A Compact Documentary Life* (1977). An abbreviated version, in a smaller format, of the next title. The compact version reproduces some fifty documents in reduced form. A readable presentation of all that the documents tell us about Shakespeare.

————. *William Shakespeare: A Documentary Life* (1975). A large-format book setting forth the biography with facsimiles of more than two hundred documents, and with transcriptions and commentaries.

3. Shakespeare's Theater

Astington, John H., ed. *The Development of Shakespeare's Theater* (1992). Eight specialized essays on theatrical companies, playing spaces, and performance.

Beckerman, Bernard. *Shakespeare at the Globe, 1599–1609* (1962). On the playhouse and on Elizabethan dramaturgy, acting, and staging.

Bentley, Gerald E. *The Profession of Dramatist in Shakespeare's Time* (1971). An account of the dramatist's status in the Elizabethan period.

———. *The Profession of Player in Shakespeare's Time, 1590–1642* (1984). An account of the status of members of London companies (sharers, hired men, apprentices, managers) and a discussion of conditions when they toured.

Berry, Herbert. *Shakespeare's Playhouses* (1987). Usefully emphasizes how little we know about the construction of Elizabethan theaters.

Brown, John Russell. *Shakespeare's Plays in Performance* (1966). A speculative and practical analysis relevant to all of the plays, but with emphasis on *The Merchant of Venice*, *Richard II*, *Hamlet*, *Romeo and Juliet*, and *Twelfth Night*.

———. *William Shakespeare: Writing for Performance* (1996). A discussion aimed at helping readers to develop theatrically conscious habits of reading.

Chambers, E. K. *The Elizabethan Stage*, 4 vols. (1945). A major reference work on theaters, theatrical companies, and staging at court.

Cook, Ann Jennalie. *The Privileged Playgoers of Shakespeare's London, 1576–1642* (1981). Sees Shakespeare's audience as wealthier, more middle-class, and more intellectual than Harbage (below) does.

Dessen, Alan C. *Elizabethan Drama and the Viewer's Eye* (1977). On how certain scenes may have looked to spectators in an Elizabethan theater.

Gurr, Andrew. *Playgoing in Shakespeare's London* (1987). Something of a middle ground between Cook (above) and Harbage (below).

———. *The Shakespearean Stage, 1579–1642* (2nd ed., 1980). On the acting companies, the actors, the playhouses, the stages, and the audiences.

Harbage, Alfred. *Shakespeare's Audience* (1941). A study of the size and nature of the theatrical public, emphasizing the representativeness of its working class and middle-class audience.

Hodges, C. Walter. *The Globe Restored* (1968). A conjectural restoration, with lucid drawings.

Hosley, Richard. "The Playhouses," in *The Revels History of Drama in English*, vol. 3, general editors Clifford Leech and T. W. Craik (1975). An essay of a hundred pages on the physical aspects of the playhouses.

Howard, Jane E. "Crossdressing, the Theatre, and Gender Struggle in Early Modern England," *Shakespeare Quarterly* 39 (1988): 418–40. Judicious comments on the effects of boys playing female roles.

Orrell, John. *The Human Stage: English Theatre Design, 1567–1640* (1988). Argues that the public, private, and court playhouses are less indebted to popular structures (e.g., innyards and bear-baiting pits) than to banqueting halls and to Renaissance conceptions of Roman amphitheaters.

Slater, Ann Pasternak. *Shakespeare the Director* (1982). An analysis of theatrical effects (e.g., kissing, kneeling) in stage directions and dialogue.

Styan, J. L. *Shakespeare's Stagecraft* (1967). An introduction to Shakespeare's visual and aural stagecraft, with chapters on such topics as acting conventions, stage groupings, and speech.

Thompson, Peter. *Shakespeare's Professional Career* (1992). An examination of patronage and related theatrical conditions.

———. *Shakespeare's Theatre* (1983). A discussion of how plays were staged in Shakespeare's time.

4. Shakespeare on Stage and Screen

Bate, Jonathan, and Russell Jackson, eds. *Shakespeare: An Illustrated Stage History* (1996). Highly readable essays on stage productions from the Renaissance to the present.

Berry, Ralph. *Changing Styles in Shakespeare* (1981). Discusses productions of six plays (*Coriolanus*, *Hamlet*, *Henry V*, *Measure for Measure*, *The Tempest*, and *Twelfth Night*) on the English stage, chiefly 1950–1980.

————. *On Directing Shakespeare: Interviews with Contemporary Directors* (1989). An enlarged edition of a book first published in 1977, this version includes the seven interviews from the early 1970s and adds five interviews conducted in 1988.

Brockbank, Philip, ed. *Players of Shakespeare: Essays in Shakespearean Performance* (1985). Comments by twelve actors, reporting their experiences with roles. See also the entry for Russell Jackson (below).

Bulman, J. C., and H. R. Coursen, eds. *Shakespeare on Television* (1988). An anthology of general and theoretical essays, essays on individual productions, and shorter reviews, with a bibliography and a videography listing cassettes that may be rented.

Coursen, H. P. *Watching Shakespeare on Television* (1993). Analyses not only of TV versions but also of films and videotapes of stage presentations that are shown on television.

Davies, Anthony, and Stanley Wells, eds. *Shakespeare and the Moving Image: The Plays on Film and Television* (1994). General essays (e.g., on the comedies) as well as essays devoted entirely to *Hamlet*, *King Lear*, and *Macbeth*.

Dawson, Anthony B. *Watching Shakespeare: A Playgoer's Guide* (1988). About half of the plays are discussed, chiefly in terms of decisions that actors and directors make in putting the works onto the stage.

Dessen, Alan. *Elizabethan Stage Conventions and Modern Interpretations* (1984). On interpreting conventions such as the representation of light and darkness and stage violence (duels, battles).

Donaldson, Peter. *Shakespearean Films/Shakespearean Directors* (1990). Postmodernist analyses, drawing on Freudianism, Feminism, Deconstruction, and Queer Theory.

Jackson, Russell, and Robert Smallwood, eds. *Players of Shakespeare 2: Further Essays in Shakespearean Performance by Players with the Royal Shakespeare Company* (1988). Fourteen actors discuss their roles in productions between 1982 and 1987.

————. *Players of Shakespeare 3: Further Essays in Shake-

spearean Performance by Players with the Royal Shakespeare Company (1993). Comments by thirteen performers.

Jorgens, Jack. *Shakespeare on Film* (1977). Fairly detailed studies of eighteen films, preceded by an introductory chapter addressing such issues as music, and whether to "open" the play by including scenes of landscape.

Kennedy, Dennis. *Looking at Shakespeare: A Visual History of Twentieth-Century Performance* (1993). Lucid descriptions (with 170 photographs) of European, British, and American performances.

Leiter, Samuel L. *Shakespeare Around the Globe: A Guide to Notable Postwar Revivals* (1986). For each play there are about two pages of introductory comments, then discussions (about five hundred words per production) of ten or so productions, and finally bibliographic references.

McMurty, Jo. *Shakespeare Films in the Classroom* (1994). Useful evaluations of the chief films most likely to be shown in undergraduate courses.

Rothwell, Kenneth, and Annabelle Henkin Melzer. *Shakespeare on Screen: An International Filmography and Videography* (1990). A reference guide to several hundred films and videos produced between 1899 and 1989, including spinoffs such as musicals and dance versions.

Sprague, Arthur Colby. *Shakespeare and the Actors* (1944). Detailed discussions of stage business (gestures, etc.) over the years.

Willis, Susan. *The BBC Shakespeare Plays: Making the Televised Canon* (1991). A history of the series, with interviews and production diaries for some plays.

5. Miscellaneous Reference Works

Abbott, E. A. *A Shakespearean Grammar* (new edition, 1877). An examination of differences between Elizabethan and modern grammar.

Allen, Michael J. B., and Kenneth Muir, eds. *Shakespeare's Plays in Quarto* (1981). One volume containing facsimiles of the plays issued in small format before they were collected in the First Folio of 1623.

Bevington, David. *Shakespeare* (1978). A short guide to hundreds of important writings on the subject.

Blake, Norman. *Shakespeare's Language: An Introduction* (1983). On vocabulary, parts of speech, and word order.

Bullough, Geoffrey. *Narrative and Dramatic Sources of Shakespeare*, 8 vols. (1957–75). A collection of many of the books Shakespeare drew on, with judicious comments.

Campbell, Oscar James, and Edward G. Quinn, eds. *The Reader's Encyclopedia of Shakespeare* (1966). Old, but still the most useful single reference work on Shakespeare.

Cercignani, Fausto. *Shakespeare's Works and Elizabethan Pronunciation* (1981). Considered the best work on the topic, but remains controversial.

Dent, R. W. *Shakespeare's Proverbial Language: An Index* (1981). An index of proverbs, with an introduction concerning a form Shakespeare frequently drew on.

Greg, W. W. *The Shakespeare First Folio* (1955). A detailed yet readable history of the first collection (1623) of Shakespeare's plays.

Harner, James. *The World Shakespeare Bibliography*. See headnote to Suggested References.

Hosley, Richard. *Shakespeare's Holinshed* (1968). Valuable presentation of one of Shakespeare's major sources.

Kökeritz, Helge. *Shakespeare's Names* (1959). A guide to pronouncing some 1,800 names appearing in Shakespeare.

———. *Shakespeare's Pronunciation* (1953). Contains much information about puns and rhymes, but see Cercignani (above).

Muir, Kenneth. *The Sources of Shakespeare's Plays* (1978). An account of Shakespeare's use of his reading. It covers all the plays, in chronological order.

Miriam Joseph, Sister. *Shakespeare's Use of the Arts of Language* (1947). A study of Shakespeare's use of rhetorical devices, reprinted in part as *Rhetoric in Shakespeare's Time* (1962).

The Norton Facsimile: The First Folio of Shakespeare's Plays (1968). A handsome and accurate facsimile of the first collection (1623) of Shakespeare's plays, with a valuable introduction by Charlton Hinman.

Onions, C. T. *A Shakespeare Glossary*, rev. and enlarged by ·

R. D. Eagleson (1986). Definitions of words (or senses of words) now obsolete.

Partridge, Eric. *Shakespeare's Bawdy*, rev. ed. (1955). Relatively brief dictionary of bawdy words; useful, but see Williams, below.

Shakespeare Quarterly. See headnote to Suggested References.

Shakespeare Survey. See headnote to Suggested References.

Spevack, Marvin. *The Harvard Concordance to Shakespeare* (1973). An index to Shakespeare's words.

Vickers, Brian. *Appropriating Shakespeare: Contemporary Critical Quarrels* (1993). A survey—chiefly hostile—of recent schools of criticism.

Wells, Stanley, ed. *Shakespeare: A Bibliographical Guide* (new edition, 1990). Nineteen chapters (some devoted to single plays, others devoted to groups of related plays) on recent scholarship on the life and all of the works.

Williams, Gordon. *A Dictionary of Sexual Language and Imagery in Shakespearean and Stuart Literature*, 3 vols. (1994). Extended discussions of words and passages; much fuller than Partridge, cited above.

6. Shakespeare's Plays: General Studies

Bamber, Linda. *Comic Women, Tragic Men: A Study of Gender and Genre in Shakespeare* (1982).

Barnet, Sylvan. *A Short Guide to Shakespeare* (1974).

Callaghan, Dympna, Lorraine Helms, and Jyotsna Singh. *The Weyward Sisters: Shakespeare and Feminist Politics* (1994).

Clemen, Wolfgang H. *The Development of Shakespeare's Imagery* (1951).

Cook, Ann Jennalie. *Making a Match: Courtship in Shakespeare and His Society* (1991).

Dollimore, Jonathan, and Alan Sinfield. *Political Shakespeare: New Essays in Cultural Materialism* (1985).

Dusinberre, Juliet. *Shakespeare and the Nature of Women* (1975).

Granville-Barker, Harley. *Prefaces to Shakespeare*, 2 vols. (1946–47; volume 1 contains essays on *Hamlet*, *King*

Lear, Merchant of Venice, Antony and Cleopatra, and *Cymbeline*; volume 2 contains essays on *Othello, Coriolanus, Julius Caesar, Romeo and Juliet, Love's Labor's Lost*).

————. *More Prefaces to Shakespeare* (1974; essays on *Twelfth Night, A Midsummer Night's Dream, The Winter's Tale, Macbeth*).

Harbage, Alfred. *William Shakespeare: A Reader's Guide* (1963).

Howard, Jean E. *Shakespeare's Art of Orchestration: Stage Technique and Audience Response* (1984).

Jones, Emrys. *Scenic Form in Shakespeare* (1971).

Lenz, Carolyn Ruth Swift, Gayle Greene, and Carol Thomas Neely, eds. *The Woman's Part: Feminist Criticism of Shakespeare* (1980).

Novy, Marianne. *Love's Argument: Gender Relations in Shakespeare* (1984).

Rose, Mark. *Shakespearean Design* (1972).

Scragg, Leah. *Discovering Shakespeare's Meaning* (1994).

————. *Shakespeare's "Mouldy Tales": Recurrent Plot Motifs in Shakespearean Drama* (1992).

Traub, Valerie. *Desire and Anxiety: Circulations of Sexuality in Shakespearean Drama* (1992).

Traversi, D. A. *An Approach to Shakespeare*, 2 vols. (3rd rev. ed, 1968–69).

Vickers, Brian. *The Artistry of Shakespeare's Prose* (1968).

Wells, Stanley. *Shakespeare: A Dramatic Life* (1994).

Wright, George T. *Shakespeare's Metrical Art* (1988).

7. The Comedies

Barber, C. L. *Shakespeare's Festive Comedy* (1959; discusses *Love's Labor's Lost, A Midsummer Night's Dream, The Merchant of Venice, As You Like It, Twelfth Night*).

Barton, Anne. *The Names of Comedy* (1990).

Berry, Ralph. *Shakespeare's Comedy: Explorations in Form* (1972).

Bradbury, Malcolm, and David Palmer, eds. *Shakespearean Comedy* (1972).

Bryant, J. A., Jr. *Shakespeare and the Uses of Comedy* (1986).

Carroll, William. *The Metamorphoses of Shakespearean Comedy* (1985).

Champion, Larry S. *The Evolution of Shakespeare's Comedy* (1970).

Evans, Bertrand. *Shakespeare's Comedies* (1960).

Frye, Northrop. *Shakespearean Comedy and Romance* (1965).

Leggatt, Alexander. *Shakespeare's Comedy of Love* (1974).

Miola, Robert S. *Shakespeare and Classical Comedy: The Influence of Plautus and Terence* (1994).

Nevo, Ruth. *Comic Transformations in Shakespeare* (1980).

Ornstein, Robert. *Shakespeare's Comedies: From Roman Farce to Romantic Mystery* (1986).

Richman, David. *Laughter, Pain, and Wonder: Shakespeare's Comedies and the Audience in the Theater* (1990).

Salingar, Leo. *Shakespeare and the Traditions of Comedy* (1974).

Slights, Camille Wells. *Shakespeare's Comic Commonwealths* (1993).

Waller, Gary, ed. *Shakespeare's Comedies* (1991).

Westlund, Joseph. *Shakespeare's Reparative Comedies: A Psychoanalytic View of the Middle Plays* (1984).

Williamson, Marilyn. *The Patriarchy of Shakespeare's Comedies* (1986).

8. The Romances (*Pericles, Cymbeline, The Winter's Tale, The Tempest, The Two Noble Kinsmen*)

Adams, Robert M. *Shakespeare: The Four Romances* (1989).

Felperin, Howard. *Shakespearean Romance* (1972).

Frye, Northrop. *A Natural Perspective: The Development of Shakespearean Comedy and Romance* (1965).

Mowat, Barbara. *The Dramaturgy of Shakespeare's Romances* (1976).

Warren, Roger. *Staging Shakespeare's Late Plays* (1990).

Young, David. *The Heart's Forest: A Study of Shakespeare's Pastoral Plays* (1972).

9. The Tragedies

Bradley, A. C. *Shakespearean Tragedy* (1904).

Brooke, Nicholas. *Shakespeare's Early Tragedies* (1968).

Champion, Larry. *Shakespeare's Tragic Perspective* (1976).

Drakakis, John, ed. *Shakespearean Tragedy* (1992).

Evans, Bertrand. *Shakespeare's Tragic Practice* (1979).

Everett, Barbara. *Young Hamlet: Essays on Shakespeare's Tragedies* (1989).

Foakes, R. A. *Hamlet versus Lear: Cultural Politics and Shakespeare's Art* (1993).

Frye, Northrop. *Fools of Time: Studies in Shakespearean Tragedy* (1967).

Harbage, Alfred, ed. *Shakespeare: The Tragedies* (1964).

Mack, Maynard. *Everybody's Shakespeare: Reflections Chiefly on the Tragedies* (1993).

McAlindon, T. *Shakespeare's Tragic Cosmos* (1991).

Miola, Robert S. *Shakespeare and Classical Tragedy: The Influence of Seneca* (1992).

———. *Shakespeare's Rome* (1983).

Nevo, Ruth. *Tragic Form in Shakespeare* (1972).

Rackin, Phyllis. *Shakespeare's Tragedies* (1978).

Rose, Mark, ed. *Shakespeare's Early Tragedies: A Collection of Critical Essays* (1995).

Rosen, William. *Shakespeare and the Craft of Tragedy* (1960).

Snyder, Susan. *The Comic Matrix of Shakespeare's Tragedies* (1979).

Wofford, Susanne. *Shakespeare's Late Tragedies: A Collection of Critical Essays* (1996).

Young, David. *The Action to the Word: Structure and Style in Shakespearean Tragedy* (1990).

———. *Shakespeare's Middle Tragedies: A Collection of Critical Essays* (1993).

10. The Histories

Blanpied, John W. *Time and the Artist in Shakespeare's English Histories* (1983).

Campbell, Lily B. *Shakespeare's "Histories": Mirrors of Elizabethan Policy* (1947).

Champion, Larry S. *Perspective in Shakespeare's English Histories* (1980).

Hodgdon, Barbara. *The End Crowns All: Closure and Contradiction in Shakespeare's History* (1991).

Holderness, Graham. *Shakespeare Recycled: The Making of Historical Drama* (1992).

———, ed. *Shakespeare's History Plays: "Richard II" to "Henry V"* (1992).

Leggatt, Alexander. *Shakespeare's Political Drama: The History Plays and the Roman Plays* (1988).

Ornstein, Robert. *A Kingdom for a Stage: The Achievement of Shakespeare's History Plays* (1972).

Rackin, Phyllis. *Stages of History: Shakespeare's English Chronicles* (1990).

Saccio, Peter. *Shakespeare's English Kings: History, Chronicle, and Drama* (1977).

Tillyard, E. M. W. *Shakespeare's History Plays* (1944).

Velz, John W., ed. *Shakespeare's English Histories: A Quest for Form and Genre* (1996).

11. *Henry V*

In addition to the suggested references concerning the stage history of the play (pages 225–26), and the references in Section 10, The Histories, the following are recommended.

Barton, Anne. "The King Disguised: Shakespeare's *Henry V* and the Comical History," in *The Triple Bond: Plays, Mainly Shakespearean, in Performance.* Ed. Joseph G. Price (1970).

Coursen, H. R. *The Leasing-Out of England: Shakespeare's Second Henriad* (1982).

Danson, Lawrence. "*Henry V*: King, Chorus, and Critics." *Shakespeare Quarterly* 34 (1983): 27–43.

Granville-Barker, Harley. "From *Henry V* to *Hamlet*," *The Annual Shakespeare Lecture, 1925* (1925); rptd., with revisions, in *Studies in Shakespeare*, ed. Peter Alexander (1964).

Howard, Jean E. *The Stage and Social Struggle in Early Modern England* (1994).

Jorgenson, Paul A. *Shakespeare's Military World* (1956).

Palmer, John. *Political Characters of Shakespeare* (1945).

Patterson, Annabel. *Shakespeare and the Popular Voice* (1989).

Reese, Max Meredith. *The Cease of Majesty: A Study of Shakespeare's History Plays* (1961).

Ribner, Irving. *The English History Play in the Age of Shakespeare* (1957).

Taylor, Gary, ed. *The Oxford Shakespeare: Henry V* (1982).

Walter, J. H., ed. *The Arden Edition of the Works of William Shakespeare: King Henry V* (1954).

Winney, James. *The Player King: A Theme of Shakespeare's Histories* (1968).

Prior, Moody E. *The Dream of Power: Studies in Shakespeare's History Plays* (1973).

Traversi, Derek. *Shakespeare from "Richard II" to "Henry V"* (1958).

READ THE TOP 20
SIGNET CLASSICS

ANIMAL FARM BY GEORGE ORWELL

1984 BY GEORGE ORWELL

NARRATIVE OF THE LIFE OF FREDERICK DOUGLASS
   BY FREDERICK DOUGLASS

BEOWULF (BURTON RAFFEL, TRANSLATOR)

FRANKENSTEIN BY MARY SHELLEY

ALICE'S ADVENTURES IN WONDERLAND &
   THROUGH THE LOOKING GLASS BY LEWIS CARROLL

THE INFERNO BY DANTE

COMMON SENSE, RIGHTS OF MAN, AND OTHER
   ESSENTIAL WRITINGS BY THOMAS PAINE

HAMLET BY WILLIAM SHAKESPEARE

A TALE OF TWO CITIES BY CHARLES DICKENS

THE HUNCHBACK OF NOTRE DAME BY VICTOR HUGO

THE FEDERALIST PAPERS BY ALEXANDER HAMILTON

THE SCARLET LETTER BY NATHANIEL HAWTHORNE

DRACULA BY BRAM STOKER

THE HOUND OF THE BASKERVILLES
   BY SIR ARTHUR CONAN DOYLE

WUTHERING HEIGHTS BY EMILY BRONTË

THE ODYSSEY BY HOMER

A MIDSUMMER NIGHT'S DREAM BY WILLIAM SHAKESPEARE

FRANKENSTEIN; DRACULA; DR. JEKYLL AND MR. HYDE
   BY MARY SHELLEY, BRAM STOKER, AND ROBERT LOUIS STEVENSON

THE CLASSIC SLAVE NARRATIVES
   EDITED BY

SIGNETCLASSICS.COM